Simon Mabon is Lecturer in International Relations at the University of Lancaster. He is the author of *Saudi Arabia and Iran: Power and Rivalry in the Middle East* (I.B.Tauris, 2016).

Stephen Royle is a research fellow at the Richardson Institute, Lancaster University. He holds a PhD from Lancaster University and is the author of *Islamic Development in Palestine: A Comparative Study* (2016).

'Using exclusive on-the-ground research, Mabon and Royle reveal the real root causes behind the emergence of Islamic State and shed new light on the situation in Iraq. This book should be required reading for the incoming Secretary of State.'

Hassan Hassan, author of *ISIS: Inside the Army of Terror*

'This is a timely and useful addition to the literature on the 2003 Iraq War, the subsequent dislocation of state-society relations, and security vacuum in which ISIS has risen to dominate national, regional and international security agendas. Simon Mabon and Stephen Royle chart the political organisation of Iraq and ISIS, sectarianism, and the rising human costs associated with the brutality of the militant group. They should be commended for tackling a difficult and complex subject with appropriate gusto.'

**Robert Mason, Middle East Studies Center,
American University in Cairo**

THE ORIGINS OF ISIS

OF ISIS

THE COLLAPSE OF NATIONS AND
REVOLUTION IN THE MIDDLE EAST

**SIMON MABON AND
STEPHEN ROYLE**

I.B. TAURIS
LONDON · NEW YORK

Published in 2017 by
I.B.Tauris & Co. Ltd
London • New York
Reprinted 2017
www.ibtauris.com

ISBN:	978 1 78453 696 1
eISBN:	978 1 78672 148 8
ePDF:	978 1 78673 148 7

A full CIP record for this book is available from the British Library
A full CIP record is available from the Library of Congress

Library of Congress Catalog Card Number: available

Typeset in Goudy by OKS Prepress Services, Chennai, India
Printed and bound by CPI Group (UK) Ltd, Croydon, CR0 4YY

MIX
Paper from
responsible sources
FSC® C020471

We dedicate this book to the people of Iraq
whose struggle is in our hearts.

Contents

List of Illustrations

Maps

Graphs

Figure

List of Abbreviations

AAH	Asaib al-Haq
AOG	armed opposition group
AQAP	Al Qaeda in the Arabian Peninsula
AQI	Al Qaeda in Iraq
CPA	Coalition Provisional Authority
FMC	Fallujah Military Council
GAF	government aligned forces
GCC	Gulf Co-operation Council
HG	hand-grenade
IAI	Islamic Army of Iraq
IDF	indirect fire
IDP	internally displaced persons
IED	improvised explosive device
INIS	Iraqi National Intelligence Service
IOM	International Organization for Migration
IRGC	Iranian Revolutionary Guards Corps
ISCI	Islamic Supreme Council of Iraq
ISF	Iraqi security forces
ISI	Islamic State of Iraq
ISIL	Islamic State of Iraq and Levant
ISIS	Islamic State of Iraq and al-Sham
JAM	Jaish al-Mahdi
JRTN	Jaysh Rijal al-Tariq al-Naqshabandi
KDP	Kurdistan Democratic Party
KH	Kataib Hezbollah
MA	Mujahideen Army
MCTR	Military Council of the Tribal Revolutionaries
MSNS	Ministry of State for National Security Affairs
NGO	non-governmental organisation

ORHA	Office of Reconstruction and Humanitarian Assistance
PKK	Kurdistan Workers Party
PUK	Patriotic Union of Kurdistan
QF	Quds Force
SAF	small arms fire
SVBIED	suicide vehicle attack
SVEST	suicide vest
UNAMI	United Nations Assistance Mission for Iraq
UNHCR	UN High Commissioner for Refugees
UNSCRUN	Security Resolution
UVIED	under vehicle improvised explosive device
VBIED	vehicle-borne improvised explosive devices
YBS	Sinjar Resistance Units
YPG	People's Protection Units

Acknowledgements

This book tells the story of the tragic struggle for survival in Iraq.

In attempting to tell this story we embarked on our own struggle and we would not have been able to complete it without the help of others. One of the most rewarding aspects of finishing work on a book is the ability to thank all those people who helped to make it possible. To this end, we would like to thank Major Saad Hamdani, General Kamil abu-Fahed al-Dulaymi, Major Basim Alwan, Colonel Saud Hamdani and Ahmed Asim Efan for facilitating our access to vital local knowledge and networks in Iraq. We are also grateful for the support received from Marcus d'Apice, Andreas Carleton-Smith, David Amos and John Harris. Nor can we forget Dragan Zivonjinovic from the University of Belgrade for providing a travelling researcher access to library resources.

At Lancaster, we must thank Ludovica Di Giorgi for her painstakingly thorough research assistance over the summer of 2015, which has proved invaluable. In addition, Grant Helm, Maria Louisa Engl Lopez and other Richardson Institute interns provided important assistance along the way; we are in your debt. We received helpful feedback from colleagues from a number of institutions across the UK but it would be invidious to list them all, for fear of missing anyone. Thank you to everyone who engaged in discussions with us about ideas in the book; you know who you are and we remain eternally grateful.

We would also like to thank all the staff at I.B.Tauris, especially Joanna Godfrey and Sophie Campbell whose patience made the process far more enjoyable. We must also thank Maria Marsh for helping to get the project off the ground. Finally, our families have provided us with unwavering support since embarking on this project and we could not have done it without you. Thank you!

Ultimately, the book is dedicated to those who continue their struggle to survive and take care of their families and friends, doing so in incredibly difficult circumstances, our thoughts remain with you.

Map 1　The Middle East

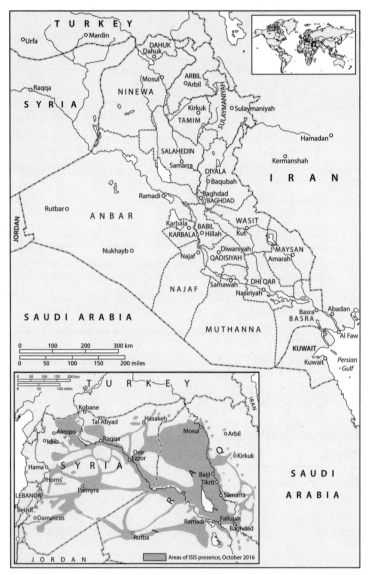

Map 2 Iraq and areas of ISIS presence

Introduction

On the first day of Ramadan 1435 – 28 June 2014 in the Gregorian calendar – Abu Bakr al-Baghdadi, the self-proclaimed Caliph Ibrahim, announced the establishment of a caliphate. Celebrating this event, the official spokesman of ISIS, Sheikh Abu Muhammad al-Adnani ash-Shami, proclaimed:

> O Muslims everywhere, glad tidings to you and expect good. Raise your head high, for today – by Allah's grace – you have a state and Khilafah, which will return your dignity, might, rights, and leadership. It is a state where the Arab and non-Arab, the white man and black man, the easterner and westerner are all brothers. It is a Khilafah that gathered the Caucasian, Indian, Chinese, Shami, Iraqi, Yemeni, Egyptian, Maghribi (North African), American, French, German, and Australian. Allah brought their hearts together, and thus, they became brothers by His grace, loving each other for the sake of Allah, standing in a single trench, defending and guarding each other, and sacrificing themselves for one another.[1]

The declaration of a caliphate provoked much consternation amongst Muslims, scholars and practitioners and dramatically altered the nature of Middle Eastern politics. In the next 18 months, the emergence of the Islamic State of Iraq and al-Sham (ISIS) in Syria and Iraq posed serious questions for regional and global security, fuelling sectarian tensions across the Muslim world and resulting in international actors once more becoming embroiled in military action in the Middle East.

ISIS has presented a strong image through a combination of ideology, ruthless violence, military force, financial astuteness and an innovative social media campaign, designed to spread its message and to appeal to disenfranchised, marginalised Sunnis across the world. In doing this, it identifies itself as the Sunni protector of Islam and a defence against colonialism. In an English-language video filmed at the Syrian border with Iraq, an ISIS spokesperson loyal to leader Abu Bakr al-Baghdadi highlighted a desire to remove the 'invisible' boundaries that emerged after the Sykes–Picot agreement in 1916–17.[2] He also declared ISIS's willingness to expand its influence across Iraq, Jordan and Lebanon until they reach 'al-Quds, inshallah' (Jerusalem, God willing).[3]

At the time of writing, there have been 15 issues of *Dabiq*, the English-language magazine that draws inspiration from Al Qaeda in the Arabian Peninsula (AQAP)'s *Inspire*. The magazine articulates the vision of the group, serving both as a propaganda and recruitment tool, and features issues with titles including 'The Return of Khalifah', 'The Failed Crusade', 'A Call to Hijrah' and 'Just Terror'. Within *Dabiq* are apocalyptic messages, articulating the forthcoming confrontation between *dar al-Islam* and the 'Army of Rome' at the Syrian town of Dabiq, which gives its name to the ISIS publication.[4] Although strategically insignificant and surrounded by farmland, according to one reading of the hadith (Islamic traditions) the defeat of the Army of Rome at Dabiq will precipitate the Apocalypse.

The magazine also seeks to articulate the messages of Abu Bakr al-Baghdadi. Born in Samarra, north of Baghdad, as Ibrahim Awad Ibrahim al-Badri, al-Baghdadi took up arms in response to the 2003 invasion and gained his reputation fighting with Al Qaeda in Iraq (AQI). He was arrested by American forces in 2006 and held at Camp Bucca, the American prison that was home to a number of AQI inmates. He was released in 2009 when it is thought that he became the leader of AQI, or its subordinate branch ISIS, in Anbar. In 2013, al-Baghdadi sensed the opportunity to take advantage of circumstances in Syria and Iraq and established what would become ISIS.

Posturing against Assad's regime and the government of al-Maliki, al-Baghdadi was able to utilise anti-government networks across Syria and Iraq to finance the development of ISIS through racketeering and oil smuggling.[5] He has also benefited from the sectarian schism by presenting his organisation as a Sunni vanguard against Iranian-sponsored Shiʻism, appealing to those residing in countries such as Qatar, the United Arab Emirates (UAE), Bahrain, Kuwait and Saudi Arabia. Saudi concerns regarding the expansion of Shiʻa Islam and Iran have been well documented,[6] and are partly a by-product of its societal demographics and a desire to maintain regime stability.[7] Despite Saudi efforts to quash links to ISIS,[8] Saudi involvement continues to be propagated. According to Sir Richard Dearlove, former head of Britain's MI6, the recently deposed head of Saudi intelligence, Prince Bandar bin Sultan, had warned him of the impending struggle, inferring that 'More than a billion Sunnis have simply had enough of them (Shiʻa)'.[9] While ISIS has targeted Saudi Arabia, and the al-Saud family have been vociferous in their condemnation of the group, some, such as Madawi al-Rasheed, have noted parallels between the Wahhabist ideology that is woven into the fabric of the Saudi state and the ideology at the heart of ISIS.[10] Indeed, the message of certainty, inherent within the Wahhabi ideology, appeals to a range of people who struggle to situate their identities within the complexity and fluidity of modern life.[11]

With financial support, a military strategy that has demonstrated its ability to be flexible and to evolve and the support provided by sectarian kin, ISIS has opted for an aggressive military approach, paying for the service of professional soldiers and aligning itself with a number of local factions seeking to remove state and governmental structures within the region. Its radical approach and military aggression has alienated a number of perceived allies, not least Al Qaeda and its affiliate Jabhat al-Nusra (now Jabhat Fatah al-Sham), and Jaish al-Islam, who have become increasingly threatened by ISIS's monopoly over the so-called 'Islamic' response to events in Iraq and Syria. Nevertheless, this has not affected its momentum or popularity as, according to Peter R. Neumann, it is estimated that 80 per cent of Western fighters who have travelled to Syria have joined ISIS,[12] predominantly because of its ability to project strict Islamic values and practice but also because of the manner in which it uses ultra-violence to present itself as a protector of Islam against the perceived threat of outside forces, notably the 'West' and Iran.

A number of violent groups across the Middle East and in Africa have since pledged allegiance to ISIS, demonstrating the resonance that the group's narrative found amongst like-minded individuals. The group conducted extreme acts of violence against those who opposed them, many of which were stylishly documented for consumption by a wider audience. The group also orchestrated attacks in Western nations, including marauding attacks like those seen in Paris and Brussels in November 2015 and March 2016 respectively. The Paris attacks raised questions about how best to respond to the group, serving also as a catalyst for increased airstrikes on ISIS targets across Iraq and Syria. While the UK had responded to a request from the Iraqi government to help in the fight against ISIS in Iraq, it was only in the aftermath of the attacks in Paris that the British Parliament voted to join the international coalition fighting the group in Syria. Even this decision, however, was mired in division about how best to fight the ISIS threat. Inertia as to how to respond is implicit in debates about how to refer to the group. The failure to agree on a name, be it ISIS, ISIL, Daesh, Islamic State, IS, so-called Islamic State, or variations on a theme, demonstrates the failure of counter-narratives and the lack of coherence of strategies designed to defeat the group.

As we will highlight in this book, defeating ISIS requires a greater understanding of the highly complex conditions in which groups such as ISIS gain support from local populations. The emergence of ISIS comes at a time when the Middle East has been engulfed in political turmoil, perhaps best characterised by the Arab Spring protests that erupted in Tunisia in late 2010 and spread across the region. Both Iraq and Syria have experienced political fragmentation, with individuals across the state often caught between a range of powerful actors. Amidst increasing chaos, people struggled to ensure that their basic needs – food, shelter and security – were met. As this became increasingly difficult, groups such as ISIS were able to draw support from people struggling to secure their basic needs.

Political turmoil also opened up long-standing cleavages across the region, creating a climate of suspicion towards the 'other'. Post-2003, rhetoric from political and religious leaders led to the deepening of cleavages across Iraq. Perhaps the most severe of these occurs along sectarian lines, with religious differences proving increasingly violent in the years following the US-led invasion. In those years, politics took on a sectarian dimension as Shi'a parties gained power in Iraq for the first time in the state's history. After decades of marginalisation, persecution and discrimination under a 'tyranny of the minority', Shi'a politicians sought to ensure that they would be able to retain power, yet the Shi'a of Iraq are not a coherent bloc and differences within Shi'a communities became increasingly fraught. These tensions rose to prominence with the reorganisation of Iraqi society that took place after the 2003 invasion. A growing number of people seek to reduce the emergence of ISIS – and indeed the ills of the Middle East – to sectarian differences between Sunni and Shi'a, yet to do so would be infelicitous. There is nothing inherently violent about the differences between the two sects; rather, one must consider how such differences are used politically, and one of the goals of this book is to trace the politicisation – and indeed securitisation – of sectarian identities across the history of modern Iraq, which has created long-standing grievances that shape contemporary Iraqi politics.

In an attempt to prevent the resurgence of Baathism – the ideology that had given rise to Saddam Hussein – following the 2003 invasion of Iraq, coalition forces removed all traces of the Saddam regime, leading to thousands of people becoming unemployed and facing serious challenges in trying to provide food and security for themselves and their families. Following this, military action in the years after the Coalition's victory was increasingly driven by counter-insurgency operations, responding to violence from a range of militias both Sunni and Shi'a. One of the most prominent of these groups was Al Qaeda in Iraq (AQI), led by a Jordanian, Abu Musab al-Zarqawi. Al-Zarqawi used extreme violence to strike fear into his enemies, a tactic that would later be adopted by ISIS.

The emergence of ISIS from the Syrian desert in the summer of 2014 and the group's seizure of the Iraqi city of Mosul caught the world's attention. Only six months earlier, President Barack Obama had dismissed the group as the 'Jayvee Team', suggesting that just because a junior varsity team plays in the LA Lakers uniforms, 'that doesn't make them Kobe Bryant'.[13] Yet the orchestration of attacks in

Paris, Beirut, Brussels, Istanbul and Orlando, and also across the various *wilayat*s – the Arabic term for a province – including the alleged bombing of a Russian plane over Egypt, demonstrated the reach and influence of the group, adding urgency to calls for a global response to combat the ISIS threat.

Of course, a number of reasons have prevented a unified global response, although a large number of states are engaged in airstrikes against ISIS targets in Syria. As mentioned, one of the most important issues that have still not been adequately addressed is how to refer to the group. Internationally, a range of names has been used to refer to it, including Islamic State of Iraq and Al Sham (ISIS); Islamic State of Iraq and Levant (ISIL); Islamic State; so-called Islamic State; Daesh; and CystISIS.[14] These names have come from different actors across different states, including political leaders and comedians. While some may argue that this is a trivial part of the fight against the group, having a commonly agreed-upon name helps in the battle against the group's ideas, and counter-narratives play an increasingly important role. It is here that humour can play an important role in challenging perceptions of the group, and the work of *The Last Leg* and a number of Arab comedians must be commended. Of course, it is imperative to avoid using terms that offer any kind of legitimisation to the group and it is for this reason that we refer to the group as ISIS.

ISIS has managed to generate a significant degree of fear through its actions and strict Salafist-inspired constitution, yet it has also provided a degree of support to people who have been marginalised by governments in Syria and Iraq. The slick propaganda campaign only serves to add to this fear, demonstrating the extent to which the group has been able to learn from earlier Al Qaeda franchises, notably Al Qaeda in the Arabian Peninsula. It also has an appeal to local militants and international jihadis who are attracted to rhetoric that claims to offer a practical 'Islamic' solution to the Middle East's woes. Despite a number of differences, the group has been able to draw support from the range of opposition groups fighting in Syria, whose members are united by their opposition to Bashar al-Assad. It has therefore, through a combination of these factors and lack of alternatives in the areas in which it operates, been able to present itself as a foundation of order amidst the surrounding chaos. It has also managed to build strategic alliances with local Islamists, tribes and former military persons, all of which has increased its influence, publicity and strength. Military successes leading to the acquisition of territory in Tikrit, Fallujah and Mosul (to name but a few) have incorporated the predominately Sunni anti-regime movement, many of whom are not ideological, who don't necessarily buy into the ISIS vision, but have local roots and a vested interest in the future of Iraq and their own survival. Military advancements through such 'marriages of convenience' have therefore projected ISIS onto a global scale, but the make-up of this movement should be understood within the context in which it exists.

Given how embedded the group is within the political, economic, social and religious landscapes of Syria and Iraq, defeating the group – and Sunni militancy generally – will be difficult, particularly as so many people rely upon it for security and stability; indeed, the Obama administration has recently acknowledged reluctance to conduct airstrikes against ISIS targets for fear of civilian casualties.[15] The closing sentence of Michael Weiss and Hassan Hassan's book *ISIS: Inside the Army of Terror* articulates the long-term nature of this struggle: 'The army of terror will be with us indefinitely.'[16]

Given the group's prominence within the zeitgeist, questions about its emergence should not be restricted to scholars or practitioners. While participating in a roundtable discussion on ISIS in Newcastle, UK, in early 2015, one of the authors was asked by a teenager, 'why don't we just leave them alone and let them have a state?'. Such a question has also found traction amongst a number of scholars, who have argued that, strategically, defeating the group is difficult and that violent extremism is a hydra-like beast and, as such, decapitation strategies will only result in the emergence of new groups. Despite this, normative concerns stemming from the treatment of Shi'a Muslims, Christians, Yazidis, homosexuals, women and children and dissenting voices mean that the international community should not embrace the group.

Despite many arguing that ISIS is a phenomenon unlike any seen before, this serves to fetishise the group and, ultimately, cultivates more fear. Instead, parallels can be drawn with the *Ikhwan* in Saudi Arabia, the Wahhabist tribal fighters who were instrumental in the creation of the Saudi state before rebelling against Ibn Saud and being crushed. Moreover, one can trace parallels with AQI and also Al Qaeda in the Arabian Peninsula (AQAP) in terms of strategies. It is imperative to challenge such fetishisation and to locate the group firmly within the environment in which it exists and operates. While many seek to boil the emergence of ISIS down to external factors – and clearly these must not be ignored – internal factors have been important in facilitating the group's growth. Indeed, to understand the emergence of the group it is imperative to look at the internal machinations of political organisation within a state.

The 2003 invasion played an integral role in reshaping the political organisation of Iraq, with previously marginalised communities gaining power and those who had been involved in a tyranny of the minority under Saddam losing power. The following 12 years witnessed a rise in sectarian violence, a large degree of which was conducted either by the state or with its tacit approval. In neighbouring Syria, protests that began as part of the Arab Uprisings in early 2011 called for greater democratic participation and an improvement in economic conditions across the state. Many expected that Bashar al-Assad, the young leader, would acquiesce and, in doing so, bring an end to the protests. Instead, Assad sought to crush the protestors, efforts that have resulted in over 400,000 deaths and the displacement of 11 million people from their homes, 4 million externally. In the autumn of 2015 this became a serious issue for many European states as they struggled to cope with the influx of refugees, yet this was a problem faced in much higher numbers – and for much longer – by neighbouring states in the region. It is worth stressing, of course, that one of the main reasons that people fled their homes was to avoid the regime's bombing campaigns. Lebanon, despite facing its own serious social challenges, is now home to close to 2 million Syrian refugees, putting further strain on the state.

In addition to the catastrophic human cost, the heritage of Syria and Iraq has been destroyed. In an effort to shape the future, ISIS has attempted to erase the past by destroying prominent archaeological sites. The international focus has been on Palmyra, a UN heritage site, yet across Iraq, mosques, shrines and tombs of prominent Shi'a figures have been destroyed. Such attacks have been met with widespread condemnation and calls for greater protection of sites of historical and religious importance.

In late December 2015, the UN Security Council passed resolution 2254, setting out a roadmap for peace, including a ceasefire and transition to elections within 18 months. Despite this agreement, the resolution failed to provide a solution to questions about the future role of Bashar al-Assad, with seemingly intractable differences between the USA, UK and Saudi Arabia, to name the most vocal, and Russia and Iran, over whether Assad should be allowed to stay in power. While international focus and attempts to foster a ceasefire are commendable, the notion of top-down approaches to both military intervention and peace-building is steeped in problems.

With the focus on resolving the conflict in Syria, too little attention is being paid to Iraq, which continues to fight against ISIS members. This book therefore seeks to offer a different approach to dealing with ISIS, looking at a bottom-up approach, rather than the top-down, international community response of military strikes. We focus on Iraq for a number of reasons, although the reader will no doubt identify similar patterns in Syria. First, the group was born out of the embers of AQI, one of the Sunni militant groups that fought in Iraq post-2003, and, as such, the work must engage with the conditions that helped AQI emerge. To do this responsibly, one must trace the history of political organisation in Iraq to the formation of the state. Second, the group controls large swathes of territory across Iraq, in part a legacy of the conditions that gave rise to AQI and the US-led intervention. Third, the group's leader, Abu Bakr al-Baghdadi, is an Iraqi citizen.

Across the burgeoning literature exploring ISIS, and the myriad opinion pieces that are dominating media, two main views of the group begin to emerge. The first suggests that, with the declaration of the caliphate, ISIS is attempting to build a state and attempting to populate it by calling on Muslims to make *hijrah* – migration – to ISIS-controlled territory, named after the prophet's journey from Mecca to Medina. This position is supported by the release of a number of documents detailing ISIS's governance strategies, including the implementation of regimes of taxation. From this, a number of commentators are beginning to suggest that to understand the emergence of ISIS it is imperative to look at the formation of the Iraqi state.

Patrick Cockburn, in what proved to be the first book on ISIS, draws the reader's attention to socio-economic conditions across Anbar – in the west of Iraq – which, he argues, gave rise to a new dawn of Sunni militancy. Cockburn's discussion of the economic conditions and marginalisation of Sunni communities by the Shi'a-led government in Baghdad feeds into the analysis that identity groups have been marginalised and securitised in the post-2003 Iraqi political landscape. Given this, resentment and grievances created fertile ground which ISIS could move onto, either garnering direct, active support from tribes, or capitalising on fear and receiving a more passive type of support. Where this failed, the group was able to take advantage of conditions on the ground to coerce people into following them. As Jason Burke argues in his latest exploration of Islamist terror, the need to explore the roots of the Iraqi state is paramount,[17] although Burke himself is unable to do this in an impressive volume, *The New Threat*, that traverses the post-9/11 global Islamist landscape. Most of this literature stresses the need to consider the conditions from which a group emerges, rather than to focus solely on its ideology.

The second view articulates a desire to facilitate a confrontation between *dar al-Islam* and what is referred to in *Dabiq* as the Army of Rome and, in doing so, to bring about the end of the world. This vision is explored in greater detail by William McCants[18] and ably supported by Graeme Wood's piece, 'What ISIS Really Wants', in *The Atlantic*,[19] both of which unpack the fundamentalist beliefs at the heart of the group. Such a focus on the group's ideology is important when looking at its appeal to those that have travelled to join it, yet our quest is to consider how the group gained traction across Iraq and Syria.

In order to defeat ISIS, it is essential to understand its origins, which we seek to do by considering the rise of ISIS in Iraq. It is important to stress at this point that this book is not an exploration or examination of ISIS, per se; rather, it is an exploration of the conditions across Iraq that allowed the group to emerge and through which it has been able to garner support. To this end, we explore the conditions that gave rise to it, with the hope of contributing to a range of different literatures and policy discussions. Identifying the key characteristics on the ground that have shaped the nature of the group and allowed it to emerge and make such territorial gains is important when engaging with questions about how to defeat it and how to prevent other groups from emerging from similar conditions. As Western governments queue up to launch airstrikes on ISIS-held territories across Iraq and Syria, we argue that it is more valuable to seek bottom-up approaches to defeating the group, akin to those that helped defeat Al Qaeda in the post-invasion period. Such an approach requires an exploration of conditions on the ground, along with a conceptual approach that helps to identify the longer-term patterns across Iraq. Indeed, to defeat violent extremism, it is paramount to erase the conditions that help it to thrive, which necessitates a more nuanced approach than airstrikes alone can offer.

To this end, our project explores the fragmentation of the Iraqi state since 2003, which has created the conditions necessary for violent extremism to thrive. Indeed, from this chaos, ISIS was able to present an image of strength and security, drawing support from people struggling to find this elsewhere. As a consequence, understanding these conditions will help to understand how best to defeat the group. While we do not claim to possess the magic formula to defeat ISIS, we hope that our analysis will aid people tasked with both fighting the group and ensuring that similar groups are not able to emerge in the future.

We seek to tease out the nature of this marginalisation and the essence of these interactions and, in doing so, to understand the conditions across Iraq that have led to the emergence of ISIS. We use complexity theory to do this, which allows us to assess the broader landscapes of history in Iraq through a more dynamic lens, meaning that current conditions should be viewed through the variety of interactions (local, regional and international)[20] that have brought us to this particular point. While we cannot account for all the factors that have driven the creation of groups such as ISIS, we can identify overlapping issues through the tenets of a complex adaptive process. In the case of ISIS in Iraq for example, while Sunni militancy did not exist in its current form prior to the 2003 invasion – although a number of radical groups existed in peripheral Sunni Arab and Kurdish areas – we have to question the policies of Saddam Hussein, UN sanctions, Iranian influence, the development of patronage networks and the influence of the Ottoman Empire and the British, who, along with France, divided the Middle East into separate countries through the Sykes–Picot agreement of 1916. Along with these physical factors we also have to contend with identity, religion, ethnicity and, beyond this, psychology. As Reed and Harvey note in reference to human systems, not only are historical and contextual factors likely to influence change but also 'values and actions of humans themselves'.[21] What we do know about the 2003 invasion is that it unleashed many of the issues behind these factors, introducing forces that created a chaotic situation where order and ultimately sovereignty has diminished.

For a system to survive in an evolving landscape (such as a community or state) it must adapt, and to adapt it needs to have diversity (in human terms this could include genetics, gender, food sources), flexibility (avoiding stringent laws or policies, for example) and the ability to self-organise (allowing the local parts of a system or community to interact and forge coherent patterns), which in turn will allow for healthy complexity to emerge. In Iraq's case again, the current volume of interactions and lack of order have pushed the country towards chaos. However, what order has emerged in Iraq (apart from the Kurdistan region) does not fulfil the criteria for adaptation, as can be seen in the predominately Shi'a Arab government's unwillingness to include Sunni Arabs in its long-term development. Likewise, the semblance of order – and safety – offered by ISIS to Sunni communities also falls short, as non-Sunnis, females and homosexuals are denied a role in establishing a community capable of adapting to ever-evolving global forces.

We seek to offer an understanding of how and why the group was able to gain prominence across the region through considering the nature of political organisation in Iraq. The following chapters explore the interaction of a number of different identities within the context of political organisation in Iraq. We draw on a range of material, both primary and secondary, with a number of interviews being conducted across Iraq with security officials, tribal leaders and Iraqis. We also draw upon material released by the Wikileaks organisation, in the form of US diplomatic cables from the time of the US occupation. Whilst we acknowledge ethical concerns about using such material, they provide valuable insight into the perceptions that shaped events across Iraq at that time and, as a consequence, are an invaluable resource.

To destroy or at least minimise ISIS as a movement, these conditions will need to be eradicated, allowing people the right to self-organise through greater freedom, not least by giving people a voice and political space. While the conditions we discuss in this book that led to the rise of ISIS are unique to Iraq, although not exceptional, the response can be universal: empower people and give them access to political systems. As such, in this book we set out to explore how those conditions emerged, and from this it is possible to address the problems. Ultimately, this is a story of a struggle for survival amidst the chaos of a collapsing state.

1

Sovereignty, Political Organisation and the Rise of ISIS

On 1 May 2016, the prime minister of Iraq, Haider al-Abadi, ordered the arrest of protestors who had stormed the Green Zone in Baghdad. The protestors, led by the Shi'a cleric Muqtada al-Sadr, had seized control of parliament in frustration at the political situation in Iraq. Al-Sadr and his followers were demanding reform of the political system imposed by the USA following the 2003 invasion, which relies on networks of patronage to function, allowing widespread corruption to flourish across the state. Since 2003, Iraq has been in the throes of an existential struggle. At stake is the very future of Iraq as a state. If it wishes to experience its centenary – in 2032 – it must resolve a number of problems that are pulling at the very fabric of the state. Ethnic, tribal and religious identities are clashing, and with these tensions the state of Iraq is fragmenting. As a number of these identities take on increasingly violent dimensions, Baghdad's position grows more precarious. Iraqi society has long been characterised by cleavages, along religious, ethnic and tribal lines. Across the history of Iraq, these identities have been mobilised for political ends, entrenching deep grievances that, when the fabric of the state was eviscerated in 2003, came to the fore. The story of the rise of ISIS in Iraq is best understood by exploring the creation and manipulation of these grievances, along with how they have manifested in violence.

Back in 2003, while standing on the deck of the USS *Abraham Lincoln*, President George W. Bush declared an end to major combat operations in Iraq. In his speech, Bush articulated how:

> our coalition is engaged in securing and reconstructing that country [. . .] Men and women in every culture need liberty like they need food, and water, and air. Everywhere that freedom arrives, humanity rejoices. And everywhere that freedom stirs, let tyrants fear [. . .] We are helping to rebuild Iraq, where the dictator built palaces for himself, instead of hospitals and schools. And we will stand with the new leaders of Iraq as they establish a government of, by, and for the Iraqi people. The transition from dictatorship to democracy will take time, but it is worth every effort. Our coalition will stay until our work is done. And then we will leave – and we will leave behind a free Iraq.[1]

Recalling these words highlights the complexity of political authority and the difficulty of rebuilding a sovereign state. The failure to address problems that Iraq has experienced since Bush's speech in 2003 ultimately led to the rise of ISIS, a sentiment echoed by UK Foreign Secretary Philip Hammond in the aftermath of the Chilcot Inquiry.

In this chapter we set out to do two things: first, to set out an understanding of sovereignty and political organisation that will help to understand the issues explored in greater detail later in the book, and second, to locate the group within the wider Middle East. Such an approach helps us to understand that a combination of deteriorating socio-economic conditions and increased sectarian violence made Iraq a breeding ground for the establishment of militant groups, sectarian militias and criminal enterprises.

Sovereignty and political organisation in the Middle East

In order to understand the emergence of ISIS it is necessary to explore the context from which the group emerged. Although the capital of the caliphate is Raqqa, in Syria, the group controls territory in both Syria and Iraq, cutting across the border between the two states. Control of land in Syria and Iraq demonstrates the erosion of both states' sovereignty. With the fragmentation of Syria and Iraq since 2003, peripheral groups gained power while the authority of Damascus and Baghdad diminished, raising questions about the extent to which these states can be considered sovereign. These questions can help us engage with political organisation on the ground and, ultimately, with the conditions that gave rise to ISIS.

Western understandings of sovereignty are typically grounded in the Peace of Westphalia of 1648,[2] which ended the Thirty Years' War and was based on the principle that states possess exclusive authority within clearly defined territorial borders. This was later built upon with the principle of non-interference, which remains the cornerstone of International Relations discourse.[3] International Relations scholars refer to a 'Westphalian states system', whereby a state is 'a system of political authority based on territory and autonomy'.[4] As such, one can derive equality between states, based upon the premise of non-interference, which is protected in Article 2(1) of the United Nations Charter. Article 2(1) stresses that '[t]he Organization is based on the principle of the sovereign equality of all its Members',[5] Members meaning member *states* of the UN.

Stephen Krasner distinguishes three component parts of sovereignty: international legal sovereignty, Westphalian sovereignty and domestic sovereignty.[6] The latter two are most important for this study, as the nature of internal and external understandings of sovereignty helps to determine how a state can operate. Historically, work on sovereignty is driven by the notion that it is 'a unity, in itself indivisible'.[7] This suggests that a zero-sum understanding of sovereignty operates, wherein a state is either sovereign or not. Yet, the rise of ISIS calls this into question. Conceptual work on understanding sovereignty broadens understandings of the term. For Max Weber, sovereignty can be found in 'human community that successfully claims the monopoly of the legitimate use of physical force within a given territory',[8] and thus a state is a 'compulsory political association with continuous organisation [whose] administrative staff successfully upholds a claim to the monopoly of legitimate use of force in the enforcement of its order [...] within a given territorial area'.[9]

This understanding of statehood contains three indicators: an administrative staff; a military that is able to legitimately monopolise violence; and the necessary structures to collect taxes.[10]

This understanding is problematic in the Middle Eastern context, given the existence of rentier economies in the Gulf, and the emergence of groups that challenge the state's monopoly of the use of violence. More contemporary understandings of sovereignty draw upon the interaction of authority, territoriality and citizenship in order to claim that an entity is sovereign.[11]

For Krasner, understandings of Westphalian sovereignty include 'an institutional arrangement for organising political life that is based on territoriality and autonomy. States exist in specific territories. Within these territories domestic political authorities are the only arbiters of legitimate behaviour.'[12] Yet, as Krasner notes, sovereignty is regularly 'violated', a process he refers to as 'organised hypocrisy'. Violations typically occur through interactions with external actors, with some stemming from an inability to control trans-border flows or aspects of domestic behaviour. This inability has given rise to contractual arrangements that correspond to international legal understandings of sovereignty, but which violate the Westphalian model by compromising domestic autonomy or establishing new institutional arrangements that transcend territoriality. Thus it is important to note that violations can occur with the consent of rulers in addition to being imposed.

It is when sovereignty is unwillingly violated – against the wishes of rulers – that many of the conditions are created for the emergence of groups such as ISIS. The reduction of authority, coupled with violations of territorial integrity, has presented space and opportunities for groups to challenge the state. Many of the conditions integral to these violations are due to the nature of the state-building process in the region, leading to an artificial construction that comprises different tribal, ethnic and religious groups. In many cases, authority resides in the periphery of these states, rather than in the core. A number of states are home to ethnic groups who possess either irredentist or secessionist aspirations, which challenge both the territorial integrity of the state and the authority of the rulers.[13] Further complicating this relationship is the religious dimension, whereby authority is often challenged by Islam.

In a more nuanced approach to the issue, James Caporaso[14] suggests that four themes interact in sovereignty: autonomy, authority, territoriality and citizenship. In the Middle East, many of these component parts are problematic, given the legacy of colonialism, a lack of territorial clarity and competing sources of authority, be they tribal or religious. An awareness of these component parts of sovereignty can help elucidate tensions within a state, and the fragmentation of sovereignty can also raise awareness of the nature of power relations within a state.

State-building projects across the region have sought to bring together disparate identity groups within the context of a singular national identity, formed neatly within the confines of territorial boundaries. Within this, ideas of citizenship are clearly defined, and systems of governance have been developed to help states function. Yet when tensions between different identity groups begin to emerge and competition between different groups erodes the concept of a national identity, the consequences for ideas of citizenship – but also the sovereign state – are potentially serious.

When the interaction between identity groups begins to take on a violent form then the centralised authority is weakened and power is often diffused from the core – where the regime resides – to the periphery. This is rarely endorsed by ruling elites; rather, peripheral groups are able to increase their autonomy within particular areas on the periphery of the state. Given the perceived artificial nature of many states across the region, the clarity of borders is often lacking. This can result in increased insecurity and instability between as well as within states. Thus, when a group emerges that is able to lay greater claim to the loyalty of many of these identity groups than the state, claims to sovereignty appear infelicitous.

The Western-centric nature of much of the literature engaging with these questions is worth stressing at this point.[15] Despite sovereignty being widely accepted as a norm of the international system, it is grounded in the Western philosophical tradition, which potentially poses problems when applied to non-Western domestic affairs, particularly when engaging with questions of territorial governance and citizenship. To provide a non-Western voice into political organisation, the remainder of the book draws upon the work of Ibn Khaldun, notably his concept of *asabiyya*, which expresses solidarity and kinship. However, the concept of sovereignty remains integral to understanding the rise of ISIS across the Middle East and provides innovative insight into exploring power relations within the state.

Syria and Iraq: fragmenting sovereignty and political disorder

From this initial exploration of the idea of fragmenting sovereignty, the emergence of ISIS in Syria and Iraq can be traced back to the nature of political organisation within both states. Both have experienced fragmentation of the state in recent years: Iraq following the US-led invasion in 2003 and Syria in the aftermath of the Arab Uprisings in 2011. When the sovereignty of a state is eroded, chaotic spaces emerge, wherein powerful groups are able to exercise autonomy over particular areas. Through various tactics (discussed in greater detail below), ISIS has been able to cultivate a fiercely loyal support base and also to lay claim to control over a much wider territory by creating a climate of fear. However, in order to reach a stage where this is possible, domestic conditions must be such that the group can emerge.

Syria has a population of approximately 18 million, of whom over 90 per cent are Arab and the rest a melange of other ethnicities including Kurds and Armenians. An estimated 74 per cent of the population are Sunni Muslim while 13 per cent are Shi'a, Alawi and Ismaili. Christian denominations make up 10 per cent of the population and Druze 3 per cent.[16] Despite its religious diversity, Syria, up until the 2011 uprisings, had been a bastion of stability in the region, with Alawi-aligned President Bashar al-Assad, like his father Hafez before him, having a relative degree of popularity. The upheaval began as part of a series of protests across the region, facilitating the expression of long-standing grievances against the regime, which had failed to deliver political and economic reform while simultaneously maintaining a securitised structure over society through the imposition of a 'state of emergency'. While initially driven by local social, economic and political demands, like many others across the region, the protests soon took on sectarian overtones. In the beginning, Assad sought to appease some local political demands, even removing the 'state of emergency'; however, this was done alongside brutal crackdowns on protests in Derra, Homs and Banias, which led to international condemnation and further escalation of the unrest.

External actors, seeing in the opposition's momentum and the worsening humanitarian situation an opportunity to destabilise and remove Assad's regime, cultivated links with members of rebel forces and used the situation to lobby for international intervention. Rebel groups rallied, placing Damascus under threat while cities such as Aleppo were left in a state of destruction. The conflict became increasingly internationalised, drawing in a range of regional and international actors, notably Saudi Arabia, Iran, Hizballah, the UK, the USA, Russia and Turkey. At this time, Syria became an arena of proxy competition between Saudi Arabia and Iran[17] and between the USA and Russia. The humanitarian impact of the conflict is undeniable, with an estimated 300,000 deaths, 4 million people becoming refugees and a further 7 million displaced internally.

With regime control waning and borders becoming increasingly porous, international fighters filtered across the border from Turkey, strengthening radical Islamist groups such as Al Qaeda, Jabhat Al-Nusra and Jaish al-Islam who were quick to fill the power vacuum left in predominately Sunni areas to the east of Assad's control. Saudi Arabia, guided by former head of intelligence Prince Bandar, provided financial and logistical support to Jaish al-Islam, a group led by the Syrian Salafi Zahran Alloush, son of a Saudi-based cleric. While their operations gained increased publicity during 2012 and 2013, it is the emergence of ISIS that has commanded the most fear. Syria became the platform from which ISIS launched its operations, embedding itself in towns and villages spanning from Aleppo to the border with Iraq. As the conflict in Syria moves into its fifth year, the Assad regime has regained control over large parts of Syria, in no small part due to the influence of Hizballah fighters and Iranian military commanders.

Iraq has a population of around 32 million, ethnically divided amongst Arab (75–80 per cent), Kurdish (15–20 per cent) and smaller denominations such as Turkmen (5 per cent).[18] Iraq's Sunni population accounts for approximately 35 per cent of the overall population (predominately Arab and Kurd) and Shi'a 65 per cent. Amongst this ethnic and religious mix, there are also 150 recognised tribes, themselves made up from an estimated 2,000 smaller clans.[19] The north of Iraq is predominately populated by Sunni Arabs and Sunni Kurds, and while the latter have largely benefited from the removal of Saddam Hussein in 2003, the former have struggled to contend with a Shi'a-controlled government. Indeed, numerous long-standing grievances have come to the fore and altered power relations over land, finances and resources, resulting in disharmony and open revolt.

The prevalence of organisations such as AQI during the aftermath of the 2003 invasion was typical of the chaotic circumstances in a country further burdened by the disbanding of its military and the process of de-Baathification. The creation of militias in predominately Sunni areas, notably in Anbar, in coordination with American security forces, gaining the title 'Sons of Iraq' or Sahwa, was designed to balance this threat and, in the long term, integrate Sunni members into the national army. However, despite its relative success in defeating AQI, al-Maliki's concern not to empower figures loyal to the former leader meant that this never happened and, instead, resulted in the slow evaporation of a programme that left 90,000 fighters without pay or position.[20] This lack of trust and further blocking of Sunni access to the public infrastructure hastened the divide within Iraq and in doing so weakened national security. The vacuum created in northern cities such as Tikrit, Mosul and Fallujah, coupled with frustration at the Shi'a-led government, has thus left it open to new influences, such as ISIS.

The political marginalisation of Sunnis also created an environment within which the Sunni identity was securitised and persecuted by a range of actors across Iraq, creating a climate of fear. This persecution was largely undertaken by Shi'a militias with implicit support – at times – from the state, furthering the notion of deep sectarian divisions within the fabric of the state. ISIS has benefited from this situation, bolstering its ranks and establishing alliances with aggrieved tribes. For instance, the Iraqi Tribal Revolutionaries Coalition has been able to gain considerable ground through its alignment with ISIS, enabling the capture of Mosul, Fallujah and Tikrit. Indeed, reports have indicated increased involvement of tribal groups and factions such as the 1920 Revolutionary Brigades, the Islamic Army, the Mujahideen Army, the Rashidin Army, Ansar al-Islam (or Ansar al-Sunna) and the Army of the Men of the Naqshbandi Order. The latter in particular provides us with a useful example of how this current arrangement exists.

The Naqshbandi are predominately Sufi and secular, loyal to the former ruler and Baathist cause. Its so-called leader is Izzat Ibrahim al-Douri, a former high-ranking commander in the Iraqi army and vice-president within Saddam's government, and now the self-declared leader of the Baathist movement. Al-Douri escaped capture following the 2003 invasion and is said to have fled to Syria, where, in possession of a considerable amount of financial resources gained from illegal oil trade with Syria, he began to mobilise networks against the occupation of Iraq and the Shi'a-led government. In 2013 he was recorded addressing protestors via video, saying, 'The people of Iraq and all its nationalist and Islamic forces support you until the realization of your just demands for the fall of the Safavid–Persian alliance'. In reference to the capture of Tikrit, a senior Baathist leader echoed these sentiments, saying, 'These groups were unified by the same goal, which is getting rid of this sectarian government, ending this corrupt army and negotiating to form the Sunni Region'.[21]

The Naqshbandi and many Baathists are not Islamist, but their goals increasingly tend to the establishment of a Sunni region in Iraq, which, due to their secular aims, in turn contradicts the ISIS aim of creating an Islamic caliphate. This Iraqi regional agenda is also supported by the leader of the Islamic Army of Iraq, Sheikh Ahmed Hussein Dabash al-Batawi. Like al-Baghdadi, al-Batawi was imprisoned by American forces in Iraq during 2006 for sponsoring acts of terror, notably a bomb attack in the Shi'a holy city of Karbala in 2004. However, he was subsequently released and it is thought that he then went to Jordan to orchestrate militant operations.[22] In a recent interview, al-Batawi reasoned the goals of the ISIS alignment by saying, 'We are here to fight any occupation, whether American or Iranian. We have a common enemy with ISIS now, and for this we are fighting together.' However, he was also keen to point out that 'We are not extreme like ISIS [...] we oppose the distorted version of Sharia that they endorse.'[23] Instead, al-Batawi advocates for an Iraq of three autonomous regions representing separate Sunni, Kurd and Shi'a entities.

The inability of leaders in both states to maintain authority over a given territory challenges a zero-sum reading of sovereignty; as a consequence, the erosion of state sovereignty has presented opportunities for other actors to exercise autonomy. What can then be seen in the case of both Syria and Iraq is that the fracturing of the state has created a vacuum in which a number of different groups are able to flourish. As such, peripheral areas have fallen under the control of ISIS. Furthermore, the use of sectarian narratives has aided the ISIS cause, in both cases being able to refer to the state's Shi'a focus, engendering support from regional and global audiences.

ISIS and regional dynamics

The spread of identities across the region, be they tribal, ethnic or religious, poses several challenges to the idea of a coherent nation state, where loyalty to the nation corresponds neatly to loyalty to the state. This complexity is increased when identity groups face persecution at the hands of the state, which fails to assimilate them adequately, or where people experience marginalisation, persecution or violence, seemingly with impunity. This is especially the case in the Middle East, where identity groups often endure difficult relationships with ruling elites in their states. When these tensions are furthered by socio-economic conditions, the challenges facing identity groups can increase.

In these difficult conditions, militant groups that can galvanise people around a common cause are able to thrive. As seen across the Middle East, internal socio-economic issues and persisting regional violence can combine, leaving communities – and often the state – vulnerable to circumstances beyond their control. While sometimes this can lead to dissatisfaction with the government, resulting in protests and a surge in crime, it also has the potential to serve more radical purposes, inviting external elements or encouraging local people to participate in acts of violence or terror, especially if such protests are met with violence. When coupled with the melange of identities across the Middle East, these interactions can create internal–external dynamics that spill over and threaten the stability of surrounding governments.

In the fight against ISIS, a range of factors have come to the fore, with the Syrian conflict opening up a range of schisms that have shaped the nature of the response to the group. In understanding the engagement with ISIS, it is important to take a brief survey of regional responses to ISIS. In responding to ISIS on the northern borders of Syria and Iraq, Turkey has approached the situation carefully, not only aware of the effects that such a movement could have on its southern border but also because of ISIS's kidnapping of Turkish nationals in Mosul.[24] Moreover, Turkey has to engage with strategic calculations with regard to the Kurds, whose irredentist agenda is a cause for concern for Ankara. Western governments, particularly the US government, have watched with concern as recent conquests in Fallujah and Mosul have altered the regional dynamics once more. In recent months, following attacks across Europe and the bombing of a Russian plane over Egypt, international actors have increased strikes on ISIS targets across Syria and Iraq in an attempt to destroy the group.

Regional states have faced serious challenges emanating from the conflicts in Syria and Iraq, notably from the flow of refugees into their states, placing serious economic and social strains upon the fabric of states that rarely have the capacity to handle such an influx of people. Jordan is no stranger to heightened levels of insecurity considering its western border with Palestine and Israel, and its northern border with Syria. It has therefore sought to respond to threats and current levels of instability by reinforcing its eastern front with Iraq. Jordan's situation is precarious, despite its relative stability within the region. Internally it is struggling to address poverty, unemployment and a lack of natural resources such as water, a situation that has been exacerbated by regional conflict, the continued influx of external persons and the settlement of refugees within its borders. As a result, it is estimated that 2,000 Jordanian nationals have already crossed into

Syria to fight for radical Islamist groups,[25] while its heavily populated refugee camps also remain a source for recruitment amongst similar organisations.

In recent years, comparable circumstances were prevalent in Lebanon, where, in the aftermath of the Iraq War, Palestinian refugee camps such as Nahr Al-Bared became hosts for external fighters and a source for local enrolment, leading to the emergence of radical organisations such as Fatah Al-Islam.[26] According to Franklin Lamb, this is happening again in camps such as Ein al-Helwe near Sidon where 'new arrivals, plus young, unemployed, discouraged and increasingly disenchanted and angry youth are reportedly secretly holding meetings with DAASH [ISIS], Al Nusra and other recruiters' with promises of material rewards and rights to work.[27] Like Lebanon, Jordan is aware of its socio-economic conditions and the potential problems they present, a prime example being the now deceased leader of al-Tawhid Wal-Jihad or Al Qaeda in Iraq, Abu Musab al-Zarqawi who was born in Zarqa, Jordan.

There is no denying that the situation in Jordan is precarious, especially given the tribal construction of Jordanian society, yet the strength of the regime in Amman is preventing the fragmentation of the state and, as a consequence, denying ISIS the ability to gain a foothold. In Gaza, the return of ISIS fighters, including a former spokesperson for ISIS, has been accompanied by social media and posters supporting ISIS objectives. In a film dated 11 February 2014, militants apparently based in Gaza stated, 'Your armies in Syria and Iraq, are joined by this army of the environs of Jerusalem, which shall champion you undeterred by its fight against the Jews'.[28] However, while a general sympathy amongst some Palestinian youth exists, much of which is related to social media and the sectarian struggle, Islamist expert Mohammad Hijazi believes the prevalence and size of ISIS in Gaza is overstated and it is therefore unlikely that they would be willing to challenge the 'power and influence' of Hamas.[29] Nevertheless, any removal of Hamas's order could present a vacuum that may be filled by radical organisations. Following events in Gaza in 2014, ISIS announced it is 'only a matter of time' before they reach Palestine to fight against the 'barbaric Jews'.[30] ISIS is aware of its own limits and its current objectives considering its modest size in numbers.[31] As reported by an ISIS spokesperson on 8 July 2014, 'Jerusalem will not be freed until we get rid of the idolaters, such as the wealthy families and the players appointed by the colonial government and who control the fate of the Islamic world'.[32] ISIS is therefore focused on its role in Syria and particularly Iraq where at present it has the networks to make a significant impact.

Other regional actors became involved in the fight against ISIS, notably Saudi Arabia and Iran, whose proxy rivalry in the aftermath of the 2003 invasion helped to cultivate the conditions from which the group would emerge. While a mutual concern at the rise of ISIS is one of only a small number of points of resonance between Riyadh and Tehran, efforts to combat the group, either through the use of proxy actors or through a regional anti-terror coalition, have thus far proved futile. The situation is further complicated by the burgeoning rivalry between the USA and a resurgent Russia, which has stymied diplomatic efforts to bring about peace in Syria. Indeed, the failure to find traction on a diplomatic solution to end the conflict in Syria is as much to do with wider geopolitical self-interest as the intractability of the conflict itself.

***

Since the 2003 invasion, Iraq has been blighted by deteriorating socio-economic conditions, which have fuelled sectarian violence and political uncertainty. As a consequence, it has become a breeding ground for criminal activity, acts of terror and the formation of militant groups, many of which have taken on sectarian allegiances. For ISIS, Iraq has become the front line in its protection of Islam against 'colonial governments', the threat of Shi'ism and anything it deems as apostasy, which has resulted in the group undertaking the destruction of archaeological sites important to both Christian and Muslim faiths. While this is, in part, an attempt to remove sites that support apostasy, it can also be seen as an attempt to erase the past to shape the future.

The chaotic conditions that emerged in the aftermath of the fragmentation of sovereignty in Iraq, following the 2003 invasion, and Syria, following the Arab Uprisings, allowed for the emergence and strengthening of ISIS. In Iraq, the subsequent failure to provide any political balance or order contributed to the internal–external dynamics within the region, and the escalation of sectarian violence. Syria, on the other hand, became a safe haven for those fleeing Iraq, but while its collapse into civil war is partly due to its mismanagement of internal political and socio-economic conditions, the uncertainty that reigned created a vacuum for opportunists to fill. In sum, ISIS thrives on the destabilised conditions in Syria and Iraq and also relies on the support of local actors to survive.

There are no immediate solutions to this problem, but what can be asserted is an immediate need for stability and a semblance of order in the region. Empowering identities and providing access to political space and economic resources is equally important. From then, long-term plans can be made that encourage self-organisation and greater societal involvement in political processes. To understand the origins of ISIS, it is necessary to explore the conditions that have facilitated its rise. To this end, we suggest that it is important to consider the various factors that have shaped the group, notably the conditions across Iraq, but also the sectarian dynamics that have shaped the Iraqi state post-2003. The next chapter provides an account of the history of the Iraqi state, including the long-standing grievances that have shaped the nature of political organisation in Iraq. The rest of the book attempts to articulate the conditions from which ISIS has emerged. It is the story of people operating and existing within political communities and, ultimately, their struggle for survival.

2
Political Organisation and the State in Iraq

Introduction: just a line in the sand?

In June 2014, a video of a Chilean–Norwegian man, Bastián Vásquez, standing on the border between Syria and Iraq was uploaded to the internet. Vásquez had travelled to Syria to join ISIS and fight in the civil war;[1] however, his words in the video entitled 'The End of Sykes–Picot' outlined a much grander intention:

> Bismillah ir-Rahman ir-Rahim. As you can see right now, I'm on the border of Iraq and al Sham. Right now I'm inside of As sham. As you can see this is the so-called border of Sykes–Picot. Alhamdulillah, we don't recognise it and we will never recognise it. Inshallah this is not the first border that we will break and inshallah, we shall break all the borders, but we shall start with this, inshallah. So inshallah we walk and inshallah we cross the border and we see that Alhamdulillah, there used to be the stuff and they used to stand here. This is the so called border where the police and the people used to pass. Alhamdullilah there is nobody now except the soldiers of dar al Islam. So alhamdulillah inshallah we cross the border. Bismillah [...] As you can see, this is under our feet right now [...] As Abu Bakr Al Baghdadi used to say 'He is the breaker of barriers'. Inshallah we will break the barrier of Iraq, Jordan, Lebanon, all the county [sic] inshallah. Until we reach Quds. This is the first of many barriers we shall break inshallah.[2]

Such comments about ancient borders and the Sykes–Picot agreement were also made in the first edition of the ISIS publication *Dabiq*.[3] In recent years, many have referred to the Sykes–Picot agreement of 1916–17 as a means of explaining crises in the Middle East along with the apparent failure of the state as a coherent, unitary form of political organisation across the region.[4]

The agreement reached between the British diplomat Sir Mark Sykes and his French counterpart François-Georges Picot never came to fruition because of a number of global events. Yet the narrative and connotations of the agreement have a much stronger resonance. As Sykes himself stressed, with the impact of the Russian Revolution and America's entry into the Great War, 'imperialism, annexation, military triumph, prestige, White man's burdens, have been expunged from the popular political vocabulary, consequently Protectorates, spheres of interest or influence, annexations, bases, etc. have to be consigned to the Diplomatic lumber-room.'[5] The power of the Sykes–Picot narrative is paramount across the region, feeding into – and highlighting – what Toby Dodge has referred to as the 'perfidious interference' of colonial powers.[6]

Dodge sagaciously unpacks the pitfalls of buying into the Sykes–Picot narrative, with which, he suggests there are two main problems. The first suggests that states created in the aftermath of World War I were bound to fail because of regional dynamics and identity politics. These artificial states have no loyalty from those living within the borders of the state and, as such, should be replaced by organisations that better reflect the dynamics on the ground. The second pitfall and, for Dodge, even more damning than the first, follows this initial premise and seeks to find an alternative means of organisation, which is often religion. This view stresses the homogeneity of the region, rejecting the complex interaction of identities operating within and between states.[7]

What 'The End of Sykes–Picot' appears to be suggesting is a desire to tear up the current states system based upon the premise that states are sovereign states, driven by Westphalian understandings of sovereignty. This Westphalian understanding of sovereignty has been developed in recent times to include the interaction of a number of principles. For the purposes of this book, the concepts of autonomy, authority, territoriality and citizenship help to facilitate under-standing of the mechanisms of a state and the interactions of identities operating within. When these concepts are not upheld by the ruling regime, the penetration of territorial borders and the manipulation of identities leads to the exclusion of individuals from political life, forcing them to turn elsewhere for their security. In the work of Georgio Agamben, this exclusion from political life is referred to as *bare life*, wherein individuals can be killed with impunity.[8]

In understanding the emergence of the sovereign state, it is essential to explore the interaction of the various identities located across Iraq. The interaction of these identities, be they religious, ethnic, tribal, economic or colonial, played a key role within the state-building process, and the ensuing inability to facilitate a coherent, inclusive national identity within the confines of a sovereign state, free from discrimination or persecution, demon-strates the failure of state-building processes. Furthermore, building on this, transitions from the rural to the urban, along with the socio-economic repercussions of such changes can help explain much of the latent structural violence that manifested in the aftermath of the 2003 invasion.

Much has been written on the history of Iraq, with sagacious work from the likes of Charles Tripp and Toby Dodge shaping much of the understanding of contemporary Iraqi politics within the English-language literature.[9] This literature provides a solid groundwork for those approaching the study of the country. This chapter, in a slight departure from many of these accounts, offers a genealogical account of Iraqi sovereignty, drawing upon the conceptual approach located in Chapter 1. It explores the interaction between the component parts of authority, autonomy, territoriality and citizenship to explore power relations across the state. In doing so, it allows for a different form of analysis of Iraqi politics that will offer a novel way of understanding the emergence of ISIS through looking at the marginalisation of actors and groups across the history of the state. The chapter offers an account of the ebbs and flows of state-building and the processes of consolidation that led to the emergence of grievances. Across these periods, the interaction of territory, authority, citizenship and autonomy helps interrogate notions of sovereignty and statehood.

The end of Ottoman rule and the formation of the state

To comprehend the nature of identity politics across twentieth- and twenty-first-century Iraq it is important to begin the exploration with the legacy of the Ottoman Empire. In the embers of Ottoman rule across Iraq, a great deal of socio-economic change occurred, resulting in the reform of education and land tenure, which had far-reaching social and ideological consequences.[10] At the time, Ottoman rule was most clearly seen in the *wilayat*s (provinces) of Mosul, Baghdad and Basra, while outside of these the power of the state oscillated, between absence and occasional token attempts to collect taxes. This failure to exert control over rural areas reflects the dominance of tribal organisation, facilitated by the ownership of land. During the 40 years leading up to the revolt of 1920, Ottoman leaders sought to reduce the power of the tribal leaders. As part of this attempt, they instituted registration of land, facilitating large-scale ownership of private property at the expense of collective ownership.[11] This brought with it a period of great change, pitting tribes against one another in an attempt to acquire land. Accelerating this transition was the onset of industrialisation, with increased demand for Iraqi grain and wool.

While the following years were characterised by increasingly energised calls for Iraqi autonomy, World War I ended the immediate dreams of many involved. After the war, however, those dreams resurfaced, culminating in the revolt of 1920.[12] This event is hugely significant as it demonstrated the coalescence of tribal, nationalist and religious leaders around the common goal of a united, independent Iraq. At this time, Sunni and Shi'a were without significant disagreement over the future leadership of Iraq, with both agreeing upon the need for a Muslim, Arab leader. The agreement between Sunni tribal shaykhs and Shi'a leaders was expressed in the drafting of a number of letters, sent to the Sharif of Mecca, stressing desires for an Arab government headed by a Muslim king.

Yet, before the installation of a Muslim, Arab leader and at the same time as this fermenting Iraqi nationalism, British forces landed at Fao in early November 1914. The British force was quick to stress that this was not a campaign against Arab inhabitants; rather, the British intended to be liberators. Of course, the Arab population quickly mobilised against the British forces, with both Sunni and Shi'a *ulemma* issuing fatwas calling for jihad against the infidels. On 21 November, two brigades from the Indian Expeditionary Force D captured Basra, securing a strategic position for British and Indian armies, and secured the Anglo-Persian Oil Company installations in Abadan.[13] The British sought control over Mesopotamia in an attempt to ensure that both their strategic goals were met within the conflict, but also with a longer-term vision in mind.

The process of colonial penetration undertaken by the British, akin to the Indian experience, brought Britain into direct confrontation with local actors, shaped by a legacy of Ottoman reform – and retreat – and the coalescence of a quest for autonomy and religion. British policy towards Mesopotamia only served to exacerbate these issues. As Kristian Coates-Ulrichsen argues, the British sought to expand their influence into Mesopotamia, provoking a nationalist backlash, particularly as the demands on manpower and agricultural resources continued into 1920.[14] While the demographic organisation of Iraq meant that tribes in the south had largely avoided Ottoman rule, the arrival and imposition of British rule across these areas only served to fuel unrest, particularly when rulers misunderstood the nature of tribal dynamics in Iraq.

By 1918, a number of societies were founded across the south of the state. In Najaf, Jim'yat al-Nahda al-Islamiya (the League of the Islamic Awakening) was formed, in Karbala this was followed by al-Jim'ya al-Wataniya al-Islamiya (The Muslim National League), but, most importantly, Haras al-Istiqal (The Guardians of Independence) was formed in Baghdad. While the first two had varied memberships, drawing on religious figures and youthful political activists, Haras al-Istiqal was able to draw support from a base that included Sunnis and Shi'a. As Gertrude Bell noted, 'the nationalists had picked up their tempo in continual meetings at the mosques. Extremists are calling for independence and refuse moderation and these have dominated the mob in the name of Islamic unity and the rights of the Arabs.'[15]

The nature of the revolt that followed is explored in several competing narratives, as outlined by Amal Vinogradov.[16] Some, such as Sir Arnold Wilson, denied the agency of tribes, suggesting that they were manipulated by Hashemite agents,[17] while, in contrast, Elie

Kedouri argued that the revolt was a Shi'a-inspired and -dominated movement, seeking to secure power from Sunnis and Ottomans.[18] Others, such as Fariq al-Fir'aun, suggested that the insurrection was driven by a desire to rebel against heavy taxes and foreign rule.[19] Vinogradov's own view was that this was a response to 'fundamental dislocations' in the socio-economic and political organisation of tribally organised areas in Iraq.[20]

On 2 July 1920, the revolt began in Rumaytha and lasted until October, resulting in the deaths of 312 British and Indian soldiers, with a further 1,228 wounded.[21] The revolt had serious repercussions across the Iraqi state, but also for the British, with its total cost to the British exchequer totalling £40,000,000. As a reward for not participating in the revolt, the British administration rewarded powerful Sunnis in Baghdad with positions of dominance in the Iraqi state that was born in 1922, institutionalising the sectarian balance that would shape the nature of Iraq until 2003.

Faisal, independence and the Hashemite monarchy

The British mandate of Iraq was established in 1921 and enacted the following year, in the aftermath of the Cairo conference, with the installation of Faisal ibn Husayn as king. Following the revolt, the British realised that the current method of political administration was not sustainable and began to secure conditions on the ground for the installation of a king, where it was hoped that he would reign, not rule. Ultimately, the British underestimated Faisal, who was all too aware of his reliance upon the colonial overlords and sought to strengthen his position by cultivating popular sentiment and eroding the power of pro-British tribes.[22] Faisal, the third son of the sharif of Mecca, was seen by the British to be a popular Arab leader who could rally burgeoning nationalist sentiment.

Despite lacking Iraqi credentials, Faisal's activities in the war, coupled with his prominence at the Versailles conference, meant that he embodied the post-Ottoman, pan-Arab vision of Iraq. Faisal, whose father had engaged with the Ottomans to gain control over Mecca, was well aware of what a colonial power could provide, and – after his expulsion from Damascus, despite British patronage – was also all too aware of the ephemeral nature of the sponsor's whim. Given his military escapades during World War I, Faisal was aware of his leadership abilities, but also of his limitations: he was conscious that very few across Iraq would be aware of him, which was potentially problematic. Despite this, a few weeks after his installation, in a bogus referendum designed as a barometer to test his rule, 96 per cent of the Iraqi population supposedly viewed him positively.[23] The situation facing Faisal was precarious, perhaps best articulated by Charles Tripp, who suggests that Faisal was 'sovereign of a state that was itself not sovereign'.[24]

During this time, Faisal was assisted by Sir Percy Cox, the British high commissioner in Baghdad, who helped to fill key Iraqi positions with British advisors. While many Iraqis were pleased by the removal of their Ottoman occupiers, equally they were resistant to the prospect of one external ruling power being replaced by another. However, opposition to Faisal's rule was limited, in part, because of a lack of viable alternatives who were able to unite the disparate groups within Iraq, but this did not mean that Faisal's project would be easy.

T.E. Lawrence, in a report to Colonel Wilson, reported Faisal's observations about the Iraqi people:

> There is still – and I say this with a heart full of sorrow – no Iraqi people but unimaginable masses of human beings, devoid of any patriotic idea, imbued with religious traditions and absurdities, connected by no common tie, giving ear to evil, prone to anarchy, and perpetually ready to rise against any government whatsoever.[25]

Faisal's observations highlight the extent of the challenges facing him. In the formative years of his rule, none was bigger than the challenge of moulding a number of disparate communities into a viable, nationalist project, in particular, bringing together Sunni and Shi'a.[26] In the early days of Faisal's rule, under British guidance, it appeared that the old Ottoman social order of Sunnis dominating Shi'a was being reproduced. The legacy of Ottoman and British rule had marginalised Shi'a communities and governance strategies across the state. As Kamel al-Chaderji, a prominent Sunni Iraqi politician, noted,

> no Shi'ite was accepted in the military college or in the bureaucracy, except on very rare occasions. There were all kinds of hurdles preventing Shi'ites from even entering high schools. The State did not think of the Shi'ite community as part of it, and the Shi'ites did not consider themselves to be part of the state.[27]

Yet in the early 1920s, an apparent rapprochement between Sunnis and Shi'a was achieved in the face of a common enemy – the fervent *Ikhwan*, the nomadic group across the border who would prove instrumental in the formation of the third Saudi Arabian state in 1932.[28]

In the next few years, a competition for power in the state, where all seemed up for grabs, drew people to Baghdad, where, shortly after, the new constitution and Electoral Law cemented the allocation of power. The new government began to mobilise networks of patronage that drew in actors on the periphery, transforming local interests and aligning them alongside the burgeoning national interest.[29] One such method of mobilising patronage networks was through distribution of land, which, as in the previous decade, had serious repercussions.

During the following decade, land reforms and a move towards developing irrigated, arable land placed further strain on the socio-cultural organisation of the state. There were also questions about the autonomy and independence of particular regions of Iraq, in particular, across the north of the country. In the south, Shi'a groups, feeling marginalised by successive rulers, sought to mobilise popular opinion. The implementation of conscription caused serious resentment amongst the Kurdish and Shi'a populations, who feared that this was a strategy designed to promote centralised penetration of peripheral communities. These concerns were furthered by the publication of a book by a Sunni government official that was critical of the Shi'a, questioning their loyalty to both the Iraqi and pan-Arab cause,[30] which triggered a spate of protests.[31]

Faced with these pressures, together with the onset of the Great Depression and a change in government in London, a decision was taken in 1929 to end the British mandate over Iraq and welcome Iraq into the League of Nations. On 3 October 1932, Iraq was granted independence, yet remained under the leadership of Faisal. While little would change immediately, with British forces and administrators remaining in key positions, Iraq became an internationally recognised sovereign state, led by a constitutional monarchy.

Despite this newly found sovereign status, questions about the nature of the new state dominated the political landscape, resulting in rivalries for patronage and fierce competition between networks of patronage. As Charles Tripp argues,

> These processes drew in different political worlds and histories, obliging their protagonists to cohabit a world of Iraqi state politics, defined by those who controlled the centre, sometimes creating commonalities, but also exacerbating differences. It was a world that was increasingly secular in nature, revolving around questions of economic privilege and around calls for redistribution of wealth and the assertion of fundamental rights, as well as around varying interpretations of national identity and duty. Sectarian and communal identities were often important in shaping people's responses to these various issues and could surface at moments of crisis, but they by no means determined those responses.[32]

Divisions characterised the state, and the process of state-building appeared to be in disarray, as there was very little agreement as to what the state should look like and how it should be viewed. Faisal immediately enacted a land settlement law, designed to safeguard tribal influence, and allowed all tribesmen who had been cultivating land, without legal title, for at least 15 years, to claim ownership, for the tribe. Despite the intent behind the policy, it was wealthy tribal leaders and city dwellers who were able to capitalise on it, often at the expense of the Shi'a of the south. On Faisal's death in 1933 he was succeeded by his 21-year-old son, Ghazi, who was largely sympathetic to the pan-Arab cause and resentful of the British legacy.[33]

Domestic unrest continued under Ghazi, who lacked his father's sensitivities and ability to draw forces hostile to the monarchy into royal patronage networks. A Shi'a-led tribal rebellion developed, born out of frustration at Baghdad's policies, notably, the implementation of mechanisms of conscription, and land disputes. Shi'a grievances were expressed throughout Ghazi's rule, especially in rural areas.[34] Ghazi was succeeded by his son, Faisal, who was three at the time of his father's death, so his uncle, Abd al-Ilah ruled as regent until 1953 when Faisal came of age.

Nuri al-Sa'id, a prominent nationalist politician who served as prime minister under Faisal I, Ghazi and Faisal II, sought to maintain the balance between Iraqi nationalism and positive relations with Britain.[35] Despite his efforts, the reign of Faisal II was characterised by tensions within the nascent state. These were coupled with a rise in pan-Arab nationalism, facilitated by the development of the Iraqi education system. Groups associated with these two nationalist identities constituted the main sources of opposition to the Hashemite rule, driven by the socio-economic reforms across Iraq. British forces returned to Iraq in World War II, which only served to fuel growing anti-British sentiment. While Faisal was able to develop systems of governance that facilitated the survival of the territorial state, the Hashemite dynasty was unable to resolve questions of national identity. The failure of the state-building process to draw the various identities existing within the territorial borders of Iraq into a coherent, inclusive state during this period cemented sectarian power relations within Iraq, resulting in structural grievances that would straddle generations.

Republics, coups, Baathism and Saddam Hussein

The 14 July Revolution, or 1958 *coup d'état*, ended the Hashemite dynasty in Iraq and ushered in a decade of instability that witnessed four changes of regime, a number of *coups d'état* and unrest across the state. The political climate in both Iraq and across the wider

Middle East provided fertile ground for the emergence of the Baath party, an Arab socialist ideological movement, which was able to traverse the Iraqi political terrain and seize power. The discovery of oil changed the economic capability of Iraq, so that, by 1959, oil revenues accounted for 60 per cent of the budget.[36] The shifting socio-economic conditions brought about by increasing oil reserves – in part facilitated by the 1973 oil embargo – resulted in the increased urbanisation of the Iraqi population, further adding to sectarian and economic tensions across Iraq.

The revolution also had serious consequences for tribal groups across Iraq, as the new regime abolished the 1924 Tribal Disputes Regulations, reducing the power of the tribal sheikh over his tribe. The 1933 Law Governing the Rights and Duties of Cultivators was also abolished, providing tribes-folk with the freedom to move from rural to urban areas, facilitating the urbanisation of Iraq.[37] Nevertheless, by 1965, 50 per cent of the population still lived in rural areas, with most of the rural population belonging to a tribe and espousing tribal values.[38] The Baath party was conscious of the power of the tribe, particularly when attempting to facilitate the process of urbanisation, and sought to erode its power.

As Amatazia Baram highlights, the Baath party sought to frame the tribe as 'the epitome of backwardness and social reaction'.[39] It also positioned itself against 'religious sectarianism (al-ta'ifiyya), racism, and tribalism (al-qabaliyya)'.[40] Yet under the rule of Saddam Hussein, the tribe occupied a somewhat incongruent role within Iraqi politics, at once serving as a source of legitimacy for the ruler and presenting a threat to the coherence of the Iraqi state. The tribe served as a source of legitimacy for Saddam, especially in the later stages of his rule, when sanctions across the state began to bite. In his role in the Baath party prior to coming to power, tribalism was an important facet of Saddam's personal identity, yet he viewed it as 'deleterious to his political power and survival' and by 1976 it was an offence to use names with tribal or regional affiliations.[41]

The second serious threat to the Iraqi state in its current, Sunni-dominated form arose from the power of the Shi'a groups across southern Iraq and was furthered by the tribal nature of the Shi'a communities. In the late 1960s, two prominent Shi'a groups emerged in Iraq, al-Da'awa al-Islamiyah and al-Mujahidin.[42] While the two drew membership from different groups, the former from Shi'a clerics across the south and the latter from religious graduates of Iraqi schools, both were inspired by the work of Muhammad Baqir al-Sadr, an Iraqi cleric born in Najaf in 1930. Al-Sadr's influence across Shi'a opposition groups at this time cannot be overstated, although his influence far transcends the Baath era.

Al-Da'awa, translated as 'the Call', was founded in the late 1950s in response to the modernisation and marginalisation of communities across the Iraqi state and drew its membership largely from those excluded from mainstream politics.[43] While considered a Shi'a organisation, it initially drew support from Sunnis, having also drawn upon the ideological work of Sayyid Qutb and Abu al-A'la Mawdud.[44] The group was spiritually led initially by Ayatollah Mohsen al-Hakim, but in the 1960s Ayatollah Muhammad Baqir al-Sadr played a prominent role, establishing the al-Sadr as one of the most influential Shi'a families in Iraq. Over subsequent decades, the al-Sadr-led organisations provided social welfare for the poor of the Shi'a communities and, in doing so, challenged the 'quietist ayatollahs'[45] within the Shi'a clerical tradition. The tensions thus created were to erupt across post-2003 Iraq.

The year of 1979 was one of great change across the Middle East. Revolution in Iran, the seizure of the Grand Mosque in Mecca, and a *coup d'état* in Iraq dramatically altered the dynamics between states and within states. The next year, the consequences of these events coalesced and an eight-year war broke out between Iran and Iraq that cost the lives of a generation of Iranians. This was in part facilitated by Saddam Hussein becoming the leader of Iraq following a *coup d'état* in summer 1979. After taking power, Saddam, a staunch Baathist and Pan-Arabist, sought to consolidate his rule and, given the recent history of political turmoil in Iraq, which, in the period 1958–68 witnessed four successful coups and a dozen that failed,[46] began a programme of coup-proofing. Acknowledging the impact of Edward Luttwak's book, *Coup d'Etat: A Practical Handbook*,[47] which essentially serves as a 'how to' guide for conducting a *coup d'état*, coupled with the large number of *coups d'état* in the Middle East, James Quinlivan defines coup-proofing as 'the set of actions a regime takes to prevent a military coup'.[48] In seeking to ensure regime security and prevent a *coup d'état*, Quinlivan suggests, rulers historically embarked on a five-stage process: (1) the exploitation of family, ethnic and religious loyalties; (2) the creation of parallel militaries that counterbalance the regular military forces; (3) the establishment of security agencies that watch everyone, including other security agencies; (4) the encouragement of expertness in the regular military; and (5) funding.[49]

Interestingly, as in Saudi Arabia,[50] the tribe both serves as a source of legitimacy and represents a threat to the regime. While, as a member of the previous Iraqi regime, Saddam sought to remove tribal identities from the public domain in 1976, reflecting the power of the tribe and its potential threat to national identity, he maintained contacts with prominent members of Tikriti tribes and even married two of his daughters in an attempt to cultivate tribal networks.[51] These tribal loyalties, however clandestine, played a prominent role within the concentric circles employed by Saddam as a key part of his coup-proofing strategy. Saddam sought to strengthen the centralisation of power, resulting in increased discrimination and marginalisation of Shi'a groups, Kurdish groups and opposition groups across the state. The extent to which he sought to crush opposition is perhaps most clearly seen in the use of chemical weapons against the Kurdish population at Halabja.[52]

In addition to concerns that Saddam had about the survival of his regime, regional shifts also furthered divisions across the Iraqi state, fuelling the perception that the Shi'a of Iraq were an Iranian fifth column. In 1980, Saddam attempted to crush the Shi'a movements by firstly having al-Sadr executed and then beginning a crackdown on al-Da'awa, yet only succeeded in driving many Shi'a opposition groups into Iran. Following this, the Supreme Council for the Islamic Revolution (SCIRI)[53] was established in Iran in the 1980s, bringing together a number of Shi'a opposition groups. SCIRI was established as part of Ayatollah Khomeini's attempts to export revolutionary goals across the Muslim world[54] and to provide support to the downtrodden of the Muslim world, an obligation that was enshrined within article 3.16 of the Iranian constitution. The establishment of SCIRI was facilitated by the presence of a number of al-Da'awa party members in

Iran, who had fled from Iraq to avoid persecution under Saddam, where even membership of the party was a capital crime.[55] Al Da'awa's opposition to Saddam Hussein would provide it with the legitimacy to play a prominent role in the post-2003 political landscape. SCIRI was led by Muhammad Baqir al-Hakim, the son of Grand Ayatollah al-Hakim and a pupil of Muhammad Baqir.

Unsurprisingly, while there are several parallels between al-Da'awa and SCIRI, including their proximity with Iran, the two differ ideologically, particularly over the role of clerics within politics, reflected in the tensions between Khomeini and al-Sadr. Despite this, both SCIRI and al-Da'awa would play a prominent role in shaping the post-2003 political landscape. Despite the power and influence of Shi'a clerics at this time, many of the prominent figures within this movement sought to remove the sectarian dimensions that had characterised Iraqi politics since the formation of the state. Indeed, in a letter written from his cell in Bagdhad, Muhammad Baqir al-Sadr was passionate in his pleas for Iraqi unity:

> Oh my dear people, I turn to you all, Sunnites and Shi'ites, Arabs and Kurds, in this crucial moment of crisis and jihad [...] since the crisis is that of the whole Iraqi people, the brave response and struggle must also become the reality of the whole Iraqi people. Thus I am with you, my Sunni brother and son, just as much as I am with you, my Shi'i brother and son [...] Oh my sons and brothers, the sons of Mosul and Basra, the sons of Baghdad, Karbala and Najaf [...] [unite in order to] build a free, glorious Iraq [...] where citizens of all nationalities and schools of thought would feel that they are brothers and would all contribute to the leadership of their country.[56]

Al-Sadr's language challenged both Pan-Arabism and Pan-Islamism and reflected a position on Iraqi nationalism that transcended sectarian divisions, which had been the quest undertaken by various Iraqi rulers, albeit with self-interest as a driving force. Yet somewhat surprisingly, this pan-Arab – and indeed Iraqi – unity was mobilised by Saddam Hussein in the Iran–Iraq War, given concerns about the Shiʻa fifth column:

> The ruling clique in Iran persists in using the face of religion to foment sedition and division among the ranks of the Arab nation despite the difficult circumstances through which the Arab nation is passing. The invocation of religion is only a mask to cover Persian racism and a buried resentment of the Arabs.[57]

While the Iran–Iraq War focused international attention on the Gulf, the conflict largely occurred without the involvement of external powers.[58] However, Iraq's invasion and annexation of Kuwait in 1990 led to the Gulf War,[59] where a coalition of forces from across the Middle East supported US military efforts.

The imposition of sanctions after the Gulf War further challenged Saddam's ability to provide for the Iraqi population, highlighting the failure of state infrastructure to meet the needs of the Iraqi population. Those communities that had previously been marginalised bore the brunt, distancing them further from the state and adding to deep-seated grievances. Two prominent uprisings took place, led by Kurdish groups in the north and Shiʻa groups in the south. Across early March, unrest that began in Basra spread from city to city, in part organised by SCIRI but also involving disaffected soldiers and deserters. By mid-March, a number of towns were held by the rebels, and extreme acts of violence began to be carried out by both regime and rebel forces, resulting in huge numbers of internally displaced people and refugees.[60] Saddam responded with force and, as a Human Rights Watch report states, with 'atrocities on a predictably massive scale'.[61]

The report noted the strategies employed by loyalist forces to retake cities, a process that involved killing thousands of civilians by firing indiscriminately at residential areas, public executions, mass arrests, and using helicopters to attack fleeing civilians.[62] These actions were not limited to Shiʻa areas, similar strategies being used in the north to suppress Kurdish opposition movements, and unrest within the peripheral areas continued throughout the decade. In 1999, Baathist agents triggered more unrest amongst the Shiʻa population of southern Iraq by assassinating Mohammad Sadeq al-Sadr. Following the overthrow of Saddam, the Saddam City suburb of Baghdad was renamed Sadr City in his honour.

The 2003 Iraq War and the fragmentation of the state

On 19 March 2003, after years of speculation about weapons of mass destruction programmes, and a number of breaches of UN Security Council Resolutions, Operation Iraqi Freedom – a US-led military coalition – launched airstrikes on targets across Iraq as part of the broader 'War on Terror'. Ever since the 9/11 attacks, Iraq had featured prominently within the War on Terror discourse and, once President Bush named Iraq alongside Iran and North Korea in an 'Axis of Evil',[63] military action against Iraq had appeared inevitable.

Unsurprisingly, in the face of overwhelming military force, resistance was scarce and on 10 April, a mere 21 days after the beginning of the conflict, Baghdad fell. Bush was quick to declare victory on the deck of the USS *Abraham Lincoln*, stating, 'In the Battle of Iraq, the United States and our allies have prevailed'.[64] The backdrop for this speech was a banner, reading 'Mission Accomplished'. Six years later, Bush would admit that this declaration was a mistake.[65] On 13 December 2003, Saddam Hussein was captured, and three years later the new Iraqi government executed him.

International action to restore stability and security across Iraq was secured in UN Security Resolution (UNSCR) 1511, although the resolution stressed the need for the Iraqi people to govern themselves quickly. The resolution reads as follows:

> Underscoring that the sovereignty of Iraq resides in the State of Iraq, reaffirming the right of the Iraqi people freely to determine their own political future and control their own natural resources, reiterating its resolve that the day when Iraqis govern themselves must come quickly, and recognizing the importance of international support, particularly that of countries in the region, Iraq's neighbours, and regional organizations, in taking forward this process expeditiously.

Recognizing that international support for restoration of conditions of stability and security is essential to the well-being of the people of Iraq as well as to the ability of all concerned to carry out their work on behalf of the people of Iraq, and welcoming Member State contributions in this regard under resolution 1483 (2003).

Welcoming the decision of the Governing Council of Iraq to form a preparatory constitutional committee to prepare for a constitutional conference that will draft a constitution to embody the aspirations of the Iraqi people, and urging it to complete this process quickly.[66]

What UNSCR 1511 failed to appreciate was the extent to which the Iraqi people had been decimated, divided and marginalised under Saddam Hussein. Moreover, coalition actions removed all recent traces of the state of Iraq. Opposition groups had been eviscerated under Saddam Hussein, leaving behind a political vacuum. As Charles Tripp notes, it 'would be mistaken to suppose that "politics" returned to Iraq with the ingathering of the exiles'.[67] The re-emergence of exiled figures fostered tensions with those who had taken to the street who perceived themselves to be more legitimate sources of political authority than those who had left the country. Further complicating the melange was the emergence of groups who sought to protect community interests from outsiders. Unsurprisingly, in the context of an increasingly sensitive and complex time, these tensions began to turn violent, resulting, perhaps most prominently, in the death of Sayyid Abdul Majid al-Khoei, a prominent Shi'a cleric and the son of Grand Ayatollah Sayyid Abul Qassim al-Khoei, in April 2003.[68] In the aftermath of this crisis and the apparent failure of the Office of Reconstruction and Humanitarian Assistance (ORHA) to negotiate the difficult terrain of post-Saddam Iraqi politics, Washington disbanded the ORHA and established the Coalition Provisional Authority (CPA), which, under the leadership of Paul Bremer, controlled

Iraq until sovereignty was transferred to an Iraqi government in June 2004.

In an attempt to achieve these goals, coalition forces embarked on a two-pronged approach, first, beginning a process of de-Baathification, removing all traces of the *ancien régime*, then creating the institutions needed to facilitate the development of a new political system. These two prongs were achieved through the creation of the CPA, which was born out of UNSCR 1483 and ran from 21 April 2003 to 28 June 2004. Decisions to include four tiers of Iraqi society were made by the CPA, without real input from the British and, increased the number of people affected by the order from 5,000 to 30,000. As the Chilcot Inquiry report notes, this 'made the task of reconstructing Iraq more difficult, both by reducing the pool of Iraqi administrators and by adding to the pool of the unemployed and disaffected, which in turn fed insurgent activity'.[69] Moreover, Chilcot documents a discussion between David Manning and Bremer in Baghdad, where it was acknowledged that 'De-Ba'athification and the dissolution of security ministries would create a new reservoir of angry men. So there was a need to step up patrols and tighten up security'.[70] The British Foreign and Commonwealth Office perceived the de-Baathification process as essential in order to achieve long-term goals of a stable and secure Iraq yet it was all too aware of the potential pitfalls of getting it wrong.

Coalition Provisional Authority Number 1 read:

> On April 16, 2003 the Coalition Provisional Authority disestablished the Baàth Party of Iraq. This order implements the declaration by eliminating the party's structures and removing its leadership from positions of authority and responsibility in Iraqi society. By this means, the Coalition Provisional Authority will ensure that representative government in Iraq is not threatened by Baàthist elements returning to power and that those in positions of authority in the future are acceptable to the people of Iraq.[71]

In doing this, the USA addressed Iraqi concerns about a renaissance of the Baath party and allowed Paul Bremer to assume power with a strong message. It also facilitated the diffusion of power from the core to the periphery, presenting groups operating outside of the formal institutions of the state with the opportunity to increase their power and influence across Iraqi society. Ultimately, the failure of the state to reclaim this territorial governance helped create the ground for the rise of ISIS.

In 2003, the CPA claimed authority over the executive, legislature and judiciary and also built on Coalition Provisional Order Number 1 to remove all traces of the Baath party. Ultimately, it sought to rebuild the political system and institutions of Iraq. Coalition Provisional Authority Order Number 2 began the process and read as follows:

(1) Any military or other rank, title, or status granted to a former employee or functionary of a Dissolved Entity by the former Regime is hereby cancelled.
(2) All conscripts are released from their service obligations. Conscription is suspended indefinitely, subject to decisions by future Iraq governments concerning whether a free Iraq should have conscription.
(3) Any person employed by a Dissolved Entity in any form or capacity, is dismissed effective as of April 16, 2003. Any person employed by a Dissolved Entity, in any form or capacity remains accountable for acts committed during such employment.[72]

The order was explicit in its intent to remove all traces of the Baath party. Indeed, as an appendix to the order, the following institutions were listed as 'dissolved entities':

– The Ministry of Defence
– The Ministry of Information
– The Ministry of State for Military Affairs
– The Iraqi Intelligence Service
– The National Security Bureau
– The Directorate of National Security (Amn al-'Am) The Special Security Organization

All entities affiliated with or comprising Saddam Hussein's body-guards to include:

– Murafaqin (Companions) -Himaya al Khasa (Special Guard)

The following military organizations:

– The Army, Air Force, Navy, the Air Defence Force, and other regular military services
– The Republican Guard
– The Special Republican Guard
– The Directorate of Military Intelligence – The Al Quds Force
– Emergency Forces (Quwat al Tawari)

The following paramilitaries:

– Saddam Fedayeen
– Baàth Party Militia
– Friends of Saddam
– Saddam's Lion Cubs (Ashbal Saddam)

Other Organizations:

– The Presidential Diwan
– The Presidential Secretariat
– The Revolutionary Command Council.[73]

Clearly, the ramifications of such a process were huge, and included large-scale unemployment – although the CPA attempted to mollify those fired with compensation – and the eradication of large swathes of state infrastructure. In addition to the 30,000 'Baathists' made redundant by the CPA, Tripp notes how the order 'put some 300,000 armed young men out of work at a stroke, stopped the pensions of tens of thousands of ex-officers and purged the slowly recovering government ministries of roughly 30,000 people, including their most experienced administrators'.[74] Driving such decisions was the perception that Baath party members should not be allowed to shape the future of the country and that to allow this would be tantamount to letting the Nazis help shape postwar Germany.[75] There was pushback against the idea of widespread de-Baathification, with some in the British establishment urging caution and a flexible approach, although this was countered by the Iraqi Governing Council which sought a harder line in the process. Of course, it was important to distinguish between those who were ideological supporters of the party and those who were coerced into joining, a distinction that was not made during this process.

Coupled with this was the legacy of sanctions, which had decimated the Iraqi economy over the previous decade, with catastrophic implications for communities that had increasingly been marginalised under Saddam. In the chaos, the state was left powerless, the ability to maintain autonomy and territoriality over the Iraqi state was lost and the country was in crisis, with power increasingly eviscerated from the core.

This erosion of Iraqi sovereignty and the ensuing destruction of the institutions of state restricted the new regime's ability to maintain its monopoly over the use of force. Although there was a great deal of jubilation at the removal of Saddam Hussein from power, the exorcising of the Baath party left a vacuum across political and social governance. As a result, people began to coalesce around new forms of political organisations as a means of ensuring that life could continue, often retreating back into the tribe or the sect as a way of achieving this.

In the aftermath of the 9/11 attacks, some in Washington sought to draw parallels between Al Qaeda and the regime of Saddam Hussein. While these claims were infelicitous, the invasion of Iraq did quickly bring Al Qaeda to the fore. As coalition forces remained in Iraq, groups across the state began to take up arms to fight against what was seen as an occupying force. Militant groups were established, both Sunni and Shi'a, which, in addition to fighting coalition forces, also took up arms against each other in what became a conflict along increasingly sectarian lines. In time, a derivative group established a foothold in western Iraq that, 11 years later, became a prominent part of the ISIS-declared caliphate. The evolution of Al Qaeda-affiliated actors in Iraq can be broken down into three main periods: Al Qaeda in Iraq; the Islamic State in Iraq; and ISIS.

Realising the potential to draw the US and coalition forces into an increasingly intractable conflict, Osama bin Laden saw Iraq as 'a golden and unique opportunity' and 'a point of attraction and recruitment of qualified resources'.[76] Leading Al Qaeda in Iraq (AQI) was a Jordanian, Abu Musab al-Zarqawi, whose sectarian violence and brutal modus operandi would have serious implications for the stability of Iraq and inspire ISIS. Indeed, it was from the very embers of AQI and the Sunni insurgency broadly that, in the Camp Bucca prison, Abu Bakr al-Baghdadi was able to develop the network of contacts that ultimately became ISIS.[77]

Much like the aforementioned Sunni insurgents, Shi'a groups were galvanised by the removal of Saddam. Across Sadr City, then known as Saddam City, associates of the late Shi'a cleric Grand Ayatollah Sayyid Mohammad Mohammad Sadiq al-Sadr attempted to fulfil social needs by distributing food, collecting refuse and monitoring traffic.[78] Leading the group at this time was Muqtada al-Sadr, the late Grand Ayatollah's grandson, who in the early months of the invasion was able to revive much of his grandfather's network. The Sadrists, as they became known, were vocal in their opposition to a range of actors and played a prominent role in opposition to the US-led invasion and also in the sectarian violence that shaped Iraqi politics thereafter. In the chaos of the fragmentation of the Iraqi state, many looked to Najaf for guidance and, in particular, to Grand Ayatollah Ali Sistani. Although Sistani's views on the role of clerics within politics differed greatly from those of the Iranian-backed groups of al-Da'awa and SCIRI, who had been influenced by Khomeini's move into politics in the 1970s, Sistani played an important legitimising role for many in Shi'a politics.

The vacuum created in the aftermath of Order Number 2 provided opportunities for actors to pursue their own agendas, ultimately leading to the establishment of a number of militias. While the invasion ended any concept of Iraq as a functioning, legitimate, sovereign state, Order Number 2 also provided scope for external actors to become increasingly involved in Iraqi politics, discussed in greater detail in Chapter 5. This left Iraq as a state that failed to maintain control over its borders, failing in its responsibilities in terms of territoriality, lacking a monopoly over the legitimate use of force and with a government that would soon embark on a programme of exclusionary policies. In December 2005, the United Iraqi Alliance won a majority in elections that followed the ratification of the new constitution. Ibrahim al-Jaafari, the leader of the alliance, was nominated to be prime minister, but ultimately proved ineffective. By April 2006, confidence in the al-Jaafari government had plummeted and he resigned, to be succeeded, the following month, by Nouri al-Maliki.

Al-Maliki was the obvious candidate to replace al-Jaafari, having long been a member of al-Da'awa and having opposed the regime of Saddam Hussein since the 1970s, incurring a death sentence along the way. Al-Maliki served two terms as prime minister of Iraq, but both were defined by rising sectarianism and rampant corruption. The al-Maliki regime was also characterised by growing distrust of the extent of Iranian involvement in Iraq. In a diplomatic cable from 2009 released by Wikileaks, a meeting between King Abdullah of Saudi Arabia and John Brennan, a US counter-terrorism advisor, detailed the extent of this suspicion:

> The King said he had 'no confidence whatsoever in (Iraqi PM) Maliki, and the Ambassador (Fraker) is well aware of my views.' The King affirmed that he had refused former President Bush's entreaties that he meet with Maliki. The King said he had met Maliki early in Maliki's term of office, and the Iraqi had given him a written list of commitments for reconciliation in Iraq, but had failed to follow through on any of them. For this reason, the King said, Maliki had no credibility. 'I don't trust this man,' the King stated, 'He's an Iranian agent.' The King said he had told both Bush and former Vice President Cheney 'how can I meet with someone I don't trust?' Maliki has 'opened the door for Iranian influence in Iraq' since taking power, the King said, and he was 'not hopeful at all' for Maliki, 'or I would have met with him.'[79]

These comments are hardly surprising in light of the growing regional sectarianism across al-Maliki's first term, although the situation across the region would deteriorate dramatically in the aftermath of the Arab Uprisings.[80] The establishment of a representative democracy in Iraq that remained faithful to the fundamental tenets of democracy resulted in a Shi'a majority state and Anderson and Stansfield are correct to stress that, unlike the Kurds, whose drive for autonomy went hand in hand with claims for independence and thus brought them into conflict with the state, the Shi'a are Iraqi nationals and this vision of Iraq is vastly different to what came before.[81]

In the summer of 2014, Haider al-Abadi, a senior al-Da'awa party official, became the new prime minister of Iraq. Trust in al-Maliki had been deteriorating across his second term and, despite al-Maliki's best efforts to retain power, al-Abadi offered hope for change. While coming to power at the same time as ISIS had seized vast swathes of Iraq, further undermining al-Maliki, al-Abadi set out to address the underlying socio-economic concerns that were at the heart of much of the instability across Iraq and, in a piece for the *Wall Street Journal* one year after coming to power, spoke of the need for reform. For al-Abadi it is only through addressing these issues, many of which impact upon daily life, such as access to electricity and corruption, that ISIS can be defeated. As al-Abadi argues, 'By strengthening the national, regional and local connections within our country, including the security forces, these reforms will create a more unified Iraq that can and will defeat Daesh'.[82] Phrased differently, by creating a political community within which other forms of political organisation can exist, without being mutually exclusive, free from corruption, then different identities can thrive together, without the need to resort to violence.

***

In understanding the interaction of the constituent parts of sovereignty articulated in Chapter 1, power relations between core and periphery and between the various identity groups across the state can be explored in greater detail. The marginalisation of particular groups from political systems across different periods of time can explain the contemporary construction of power relations, which, in turn, can marginalise other groups. In other words, to understand the contemporary nature of Iraqi society, it is imperative to look at, and trace, its political history.

Tracing the evolution of socio-economic and political conditions since the establishment of the British mandate can help explain the nature of modern-day Iraq, resulting in the retreat back into particular identities, which, ultimately, led to the rise of ISIS. Furthermore, these evolutions were undertaken in an attempt to ensure the survival of a group or regime, in the face of a range of other actors. As Toby Dodge argues, this often has serious repercussions across the state, including in the political realm. Dodge notes, 'it is the deliberate development or reinvention of sectarian identities by a ruling elite that judges this the best method for rallying an alienated electorate'.[83] Historically, across the state-building process, successive regimes sought to draw power from the periphery to the core, yet in the 12 years following the invasion of Iraq, this power was decentralised, reflecting the failure of the regime to develop a coherent state. The removal of key infrastructure meant that actors had to turn elsewhere to ensure that their basic needs were met, with the state regularly failing in its responsibility to protect.

The diffusion of power from the core to the periphery has also eroded the state's autonomy and its ability to retain control over its borders, leaving it porous and unable to withstand the influence of more powerful neighbours. These issues, particularly the mobilisation of sectarian identities, are discussed in much greater detail in the next chapter. In 2011, on the US withdrawal from Iraq, President Obama spoke of how US forces were 'leaving behind a sovereign, stable and self-reliant Iraq, with a representative government that was elected by its people'.[84] In reality, however, the Iraqi state was far from sovereign and its failure to engage fully with its population would lead to the increased power of sub-state groups and the marginalisation of one group who had been in power since the formation of the Iraqi state. One of the consequences of this marginalisation would be the creation of ISIS.

3

The Sectarian House of Cards?

Introduction

On 10 October AD 680, a small group of people led by Hussain, a grandson of the prophet Muhammad, was ambushed by a much larger force under the command of the Ummayad caliph Yazid I. During the battle which took place at the Iraqi city of Karbala, Hussain was killed, along with his infant son and other male followers. The story of the Battle of Karbala remains central to Shi'a thought and is remembered at the festival of Ashura. In tracing the roots of this battle, one also traces the roots of the schism at the heart of Islam, between Sunni and Shi'a, which at its inception was political in nature. Over time, the caliphate accrued a great deal of wealth, veering away from the path envisaged by Muhammad. During the course of his life, Hussain gained much credence for challenging the Ummayad court for its impropriety and corruption, and this ultimately led to his death. Many believe that Hussain sought martyrdom at Karbala, in an attempt to galvanise the *umma* while also restoring the caliphate to its righteous path. As such, the legacy of the Battle of Karbala remains essential when understanding the actions of Shi'a Muslims, many of whom feel a sense of guilt at not helping Hussain during the battle. This guilt often manifests itself in a requirement to help those who are oppressed, or less fortunate than themselves. Given the legacy of Karbala, and Iraq's large Shi'a population,[1] the importance of Shi'a thought in Iraq should not be downplayed. Moreover, the city of Najaf, in the south of the country, is perhaps the most influential seat of Shi'a thought in the world, with its *marja'iyya* (religious establishment) possessing greater legitimacy to most Shi'a Muslims than those in Qom, Iran.

Despite the increasingly prominent narrative that suggests that sectarianism is inherently violent, this need not be the case. Indeed, in the case of Iraq, different sects have coexisted since the creation of the modern Iraqi state, only becoming violent after their politicisation. Indeed, the emergence, politicisation and securitisation of these identities resulted in the emergence of particular groups that offered a degree of protection that the state was either unable or unwilling to provide. In understanding the emergence of ISIS, it is important to explore the construction of violent sectarian identities within Iraq, but also to locate these identities within much broader regional themes. As such, this chapter begins by focusing upon conceptual understandings of sectarianism and *asabiyyah*, in an effort to better understand the construction of identities within Iraq and across the Middle East. Understanding these concepts facilitates a greater awareness of the mobilisation and actions of particular identities across the region. The chapter then discusses the impact of the 1979 Revolution in Iran upon the geopolitics of the Middle East, with a particular focus upon the emerging rivalry between Iran and Saudi Arabia. It then discusses how, within the context of rising regional sectarian tensions, notions of *asabiyya* (group feeling) are constructed along with their impact upon regional dynamics. The chapter then explores sectarian dynamics within Iraq, focusing upon the politicisation and securitisation of sectarian identities in the aftermath of the 2003 Iraq War and how these dynamics have shaped the nature of Iraqi politics.

The imagined vs the imaginary: the illusory concept of the sectarian

In recent years, there has been a great deal of academic discussion of sectarianism in the Middle East. Given the rise in intra-religious violence, be it within Islam, Judaism or Christianity, many scholars have sought to explore the nature of this sectarian violence. While debates about sectarianism reflect much of the academic zeitgeist, the roots of the discussion can be traced much earlier. While there are numerous points of tension within this discussion, there appears to be a rough consensus on what it is to be part of a sect, namely, being a member of a group that has a shared identity, belief or ideology that defines them from the rest of society.[2] Although initially conceived of as difference within a religious group, often seen to be diverging from the norm and thus possessing a negative connotation,[3] in recent years, this has been expanded to include ethnic and political minorities.[4] As Ismael and Ismael articulate, the negative connotations within sectarianism stem from the 'generation of animus and feelings of exclusion between individuals and groups on the basis of attaching negative meaning to group traits'.[5] This suggests that notions of othering and suspicion are part of the baggage that comes along with the use of the term.[6]

Along with questions about this baggage, there is a fundamental question about the very nature of identity that also needs to be engaged with in order to understand contemporary debates around sectarianism, namely over whether identities are primordial or constructed. For the primordialist, identities exist and are fixed because of biological factors and territorial locations, which are then reinforced through traditions. In contrast, for the constructivist, collective identities are imagined and constructed rather than given. This builds upon the ideas of Benedict Anderson, who suggests that a nation – or political community – is an 'imagined' concept. The idea of an imagined community was a product of modernity, as a consequence of the rise of print capitalism, which allowed for the construction of a collective identity around a common vernacular. For Anderson, a nation 'is imagined because the members of even the smallest nation will never know most of their fellow-members, meet them, or even hear of them, yet in the minds of each lives the image of their communion'.[7]

Supporting this construction of an imagined community across the Middle East is the idea of *asabiyya*, or group feeling. Initially conceptualised in the work of Ibn Khaldun, *asabiyya* is the process in which group ties within a community are developed and, for Khaldun, is essential when understanding the strength of a community. For Khaldun, *asabiyya* is a 'zealous partisanship [. . .] party spirit, team spirit, *espirit de corps* [. . .] tribal solidarity, racialism, clannishness, tribalism'.[8] The construction of this sense of *asabiyya* can cut across state borders, mobilising supra-state identities that can challenge state (or national) identities. This idea of *asabiyya* becomes increasingly important when considering the regional nature of sectarian dynamics.

How one engages with the primordialist–constructivist debate about identities is key to understanding the behaviour of groups towards one another but also within the wider socio-political context. As Khalil Osman notes, if sectarianism is held to be primordial then there must be other factors that come into play when considering the move from a difference of identity to the outbreak of violence.[9] Indeed, difference within society is as old as the idea of a society itself, be it along socio-economic, religious, tribal or ethnic lines. Yet not all societies have been defined by conflict, so other factors are required.

Increasingly, scholars are interested more in the political manifestation of sectarian differences, or as Ismael and Ismael suggest, the recruitment of sectarian identities for political purposes.[10] As Justin Gengler notes, the manifestation of violence from difference is also a consequence of socio-economic discrepancies, along with perceptions of the other.[11] The manifestation of this difference within the political sphere has clear ramifications for power relations between groups and, consequently, for perceptions between groups. Some, such as Saouli and Bruce,[12] have suggested that schisms within societies are a consequence of the failure of state-building projects, which have been unable to construct identities that are stronger than those existing at either a sub-state or supra-state level. Furthermore, by pursuing policies that favour a particular group, often at the expense of another, the state is seen to be advocating a sectarian agenda, as has been the case in Iraq.

However, locating these identities within a regional context increases the complexity of the sectarian question. While nationalist sentiments are often mobilised as a means of transcending sectarian divisions, internally, nationalist tropes create divisions externally and given the ethno-religious complexity of the Middle East, what happens internally can have implications externally and vice versa. Questions can then emerge as to the loyalty of particular identities, amidst allegations that minorities are fifth columns.[13] As a consequence of this, to understand sectarian dynamics in Iraq, it is important to explore both the politicisation and securitisation of particular identities, along with their socio-economic contexts. In doing so, one must consider the ways in which both internal and external dynamics have an impact on identities within and across state borders. In doing this, the chapter now considers the changing regional dynamics in the aftermath of revolution in Iran in 1979.

A changing regional context: *asabiyya* and security

In understanding the rise of sectarian tensions across the region, it is imperative to explore the emergence of Pan-Islamist movements in the 1970s, along with the 1979 revolution in Iran. The emergence of Pan-Islamist movements in the 1970s can be seen as a response to the burgeoning Pan-Arab movement and Egypt's increasing influence across the region.[14] The failure of Pan-Arab movements to defeat Israel or to unite the Arab peoples in one state provided opportunities for other ideologies to take root, in part facilitated by oil wealth across the Gulf. Perhaps the zenith of the burgeoning prominence of Islamic politics across the region was the revolution in Iran in 1979. The revolution added a sectarian dimension to regional competition as both Iran (predominantly Shi'a) and Saudi Arabia (predominantly Sunni) sought to secure their Islamic legitimacy in relation to the other, also changing the nature of regional politics.[15] In the aftermath of the revolution, Iraq, fearing the proselytising agenda of Iran's leader Khomeini, embarked on military action against the newly declared Islamic Republic, which, as Sharam Chubin and Charles Tripp note, 'left a trail of devastation in its regional relations, littered with spontaneous utterances and unfettered intervention in neighbouring states'.[16]

Following the US-led intervention in Iraq in 2003, increasingly vitriolic sectarian tensions have begun to shape the region, disguising national interest but subsuming the region. In the aftermath of the invasion, Middle East regional politics became increasingly shaped by bipolar competition between Iran and Saudi Arabia,[17] and between the Shi'a and Sunni branches of Islam, which became increasingly fractious. The removal of Saddam Hussein from power created space for the two countries to engage in a regional competition which was, in part, driven by a desire for hegemony over the Muslim world.

Both Tehran and Riyadh derived legitimacy from their claims to be the leader of the *umma* (the Muslim world), highlighted in the immediate aftermath of the revolution in Iran in 1979. In seeking to portray the image of protectors of the *umma*, both Tehran and Riyadh had to be seen to be offering protection to their co-religious kin. For Iran, the legacy of Karbala and its prominence within Shi'a thought means that offering protection to fellow Shi'a Muslims was paramount. Indeed, this responsibility was reflected in the constitution of the newly formed Islamic Republic, with Article 3.16 'framing the foreign policy of the country on the basis of Islamic criteria, fraternal commitment to all Muslims, and unsparing support to the *mustad'afiin* of the world'.

In the immediate aftermath of the revolution, the two countries became embroiled in an increasingly vitriolic spiral of rhetoric[18] that saw the al-Saud dynasty referred to as 'corrupt and unworthy to be the guardians of Mecca and Medina'.[19] As such, Islamic legitimacy began to be seen in zero-sum terms, with both Tehran and Riyadh believing that the prominence of religion within the state meant having a responsibility to protect their co-religious kin in an effort to ensure their position within the Muslim world. In an impassioned speech in the aftermath of the revolution, Khomeini stressed the importance of providing support to the *mustad'afiin*, stating that:

> We will export our experiences to the whole world and present the outcome of our struggles against tyrants to those who are struggling along the path of God, without expecting the slightest reward. The result of this exportation will certainly result in the blooming of the buds of victory and independence and in the implementation of Islamic teachings among the enslaved nations.[20]

This speech was shaped by the legacy of the Battle of Karbala, wherein Khomeini spoke of the importance of the struggle against tyrants, with clear parallels with the struggles of Hussain.

The aftermath of the Arab Uprisings beginning in December 2010 – triggered by the self-immolation of Mohammed Bouazzizi, a

Tunisian street vendor – opened up schisms in society when rulers and ruled follow different sects of Islam. The ethno-religious spread of identities across the region meant that tensions between rulers and ruled emerged and quickly descended into violence. Given this, alongside the fraternal commitment to co-religious kin, Iran and Saudi Arabia embarked on a series of proxy conflicts, notably in Syria, Lebanon, Bahrain, Yemen and Iraq, which possess the greatest religious mix of Sunni and Shi'a in the region.[21] This presence of different sects allowed for a degree of proxy competition to emerge between the two, ranging from economic rivalry in Lebanon, to violent conflict in Syria and Iraq.

Following the 2006 war with Israel, much of southern Beirut, the Hizballah heartland, was destroyed by Israeli forces in the first instance of what would become known as the Dahiya Doctrine, wherein Israel would apply 'disproportionate force' on any area from which Israel was fired upon.[22] While Tehran had gained much from Hizballah's actions in the war with Israel, Riyadh sought to regain credibility by providing US$1.5 billion for postwar reconstruction of Dahiya, eclipsing Tehran's $120 million.[23] The provision of financial aid to Lebanon continued, with a further $3 billion given to the Lebanese army, in an effort to counter the prominence of Hizballah and thus Iran.[24]

In contrast to Lebanon, the proxy conflict in Bahrain has been as much shaped by perception as by evidence of external interference. The Bahraini population is predominantly Shi'a yet the ruling family is Sunni and has close ties with the al-Saud. Following the outbreak of protests against the al-Khalifa royal house in early 2011, a Saudi-led Gulf Co-operation Council (GCC) force crossed the King Fahd causeway to offer support to the beleaguered regime.[25] While sources differ over the role of the GCC force across the archipelago, suspicion of Iranian actions and intentions in Bahrain was strong,[26] reflected in the comments of former British ambassador to Bahrain, Iain Lindsay, who suggested that there was increasing evidence that Iran was 'providing support to people here who are bent on violence'.[27]

It is in Syria and Iraq, however, that the violent nature of the proxy conflict becomes most apparent. Both Iran and Saudi Arabia view the arenas in zero-sum terms, as noted in a discussion between the then-Saudi Minister of Interior Prince Naif bin Abdul Aziz and US Senator Bill Nelson, where Naif stressed that there was 'no justification to leave Iraq as a playground for Iran'.[28] Naif stressed that the USA:

> should not leave Iraq until its sovereignty has been restored, otherwise it will be vulnerable to the Iranians. He said the Saudis will not support one Iraqi group over the others and that the Kingdom is working for a united Iraq. However, he warned that, if the U.S. leaves precipitously, the Saudis will stand with the Sunnis.[29]

However, despite the increasing Iranian influence in Iraq, explored in detail below, two issues are worth noting. First, Najaf and not Qom is the most influential Shi'a site; and second, the legacy of Arab–Persian tensions continues to shape regional perceptions. While Iran is seen as the vanguard of the Shi'a world, nevertheless Grand Ayatollah Ali Sistani in Najaf possesses greater legitimacy across the Shi'a world than Ayatollah Ali Khamenei in Iran. The second point stems from the legacy of military action and distrust across the Persian Gulf,[30] coupled with a distrust of the 'other'. From this, it becomes clear that the failure to rebuild a sovereign state that transcended the construction of increasingly politicised and securitised sectarian identities resulted in both Saudi Arabia and Iran becoming involved in protecting their co-religious kin, further securitising these identities. As a consequence, while Naif was speaking hypothetically about supporting the Sunnis in Iraq, the increasingly sectarian nature of politics under the al-Maliki regime caused an increase in Saudi support for progressively marginalised Sunnis.

Sectarianism in Iraq: Saddam, 2003 and the struggle for security

The lack of congruence between 'nation' and 'state' in Iraq[31] means that the state is often referred to as an example of an artificial state, created by colonial powers, with little attention paid to political organisation 'on the ground'.[32] The power of sub-state identities in Iraq is a prominent aspect of literature on the topic, yet as Fanar Haddad argues, one should not frame them as 'the mutually antagonistic other of national identity'.[33] Of course, sectarian divisions in Iraq aren't just limited to schisms within Islam, rather, they include minorities of Christians, Kurds, Yazidis, Shabaks and Turkmen; however, it is within Islam that the divisions have become most violent.

Over the course of Iraq's turbulent history, sectarian identities have been securitised in an attempt to allow particular actors to pursue their agendas, and therefore the manifestation of sectarian divisions within Iraq needs to be understood through both structural and agential factors. In understanding the emergence of strong sectarian identities, coupled with the decentralising of power across the Iraqi state, one must consider the three Gulf Wars (1980–8, 1991 and 2003), which crippled societal dynamics in different ways. The crippling sanctions placed on the state during the 1990s and early 2000s meant social structures, including but not limited to welfare structures, were unable to achieve what they were designed to do. This further contributes to the fragmentation of the state, the diffusion of power away from the core and the marginalisation of particular identity groups.

In contrast, the memory of sectarian persecution, stemming from the securitisation and politicisation of sectarian identities, has long shaped Iraq. As noted in Chapter 2, the British policy of divide and rule took place along sectarian lines, imposing a Sunni monarch at the expense of the larger Shi'a population.[34] Under Saddam Hussein, sectarian differences flared up predominantly as tensions between a secular regime and an increasingly religious population. While Saddam sought to gain loyalty from his support bases,[35] the removal of the infrastructure and institutions that had characterised his rule provided space for many of the latent divisions within Iraqi society to come to the fore. In the face of growing sectarian divisions, the secular centre has 'largely vanished, sucked into the maelstrom of identity politics',[36] forcing individuals and groups to retreat back into long-held identities.

Following this, in the years 2003–5, violence occurred predominantly along sectarian lines, driven by the words and deeds of Abu Musab al-Zarqawi, who led the Al Qaeda franchise in Iraq.[37] Perhaps the starting point for the escalation of sectarian violence was a car bombing at the Imam Ali mosque on 29 August 2003, which killed over 85 Shi'as who had been worshipping there, including the leader of SCIRI, Ayatollah Muhammad Baqir al-Hakim. Over the next 18 months, a number of attacks followed, predominantly designed to cause fear amongst the Shi'a population, who responded with anger and calls for revenge, but few reciprocal attacks. However, with the establishment and success of the United Iraqi Alliance in the January 2005 elections, which allowed SCIRI access to the Interior Ministry, and thus the Badr Corps into the police, reciprocity became a defining factor of Iraqi politics. A series of brutal incidents followed,[38] which prompted Ouf Rahoumi, a Sunni deputy governor of Diyala, to refer to 'the beginning of a sectarian war'.[39] Fuelling this fire were Iraqi media outlets with political and religious affiliations, which propagated narratives of victimhood and blame, further supported by literature produced by political parties.[40]

The Sunnis are a heterogeneous community, yet have suffered greatly since 2003 from being homogenised as either Baathists or terrorists. The International Crisis Group report 'Make or Break: Iraq's Sunnis and the State' powerfully recounts much of this resentment:

> Young Sunnis share the concerns of all young Iraqis, as they see the government operating in slow motion only. But, beyond that, they also feel that they do not enjoy the same opportunities as others. They have yet to feel accepted by society and resent being suspected of affiliation with al-Qaeda.[41]

Another young Sunni spoke of how Sunnis were treated differently, with checkpoints used to intimidate. The interviewee spoke of ready accusations: 'Are you a terrorist or are you a Baathist?'[42] The legacy of the Coalition Provisional Authority, which framed Sunnis along these lines, coupled with the increase in sectarian violence, meant that Sunnis increasingly retreated from frontline politics.

An International Crisis Group report from August 2013 documents the rising sectarianism across Iraq, suggesting that the marginalisation by an ethno-sectarian apportionment has resulted in Sunnis being a minority in Iraq's political system, which was dominated by the Shi'a and the Kurds.[43] The extent of the discrimination facing Sunnis under al-Maliki was perhaps best documented in an International Crisis Group report from August 2013, which suggests that across his tenure:

> Prime Minister Nouri al-Maliki has implemented a divide-and-conquer strategy that has neutered any credible Sunni Arab leadership. The authorities also have taken steps that reinforce perceptions of a sectarian agenda. Prominent officials – predominantly Sunni – have been cast aside pursuant to the Justice and Accountability Law on the basis of alleged senior-level affiliation to the former Baath party. Federal security forces have disproportionately deployed in Baghdad's Sunni neighbourhoods as well as Sunni-populated governorates (Anbar, Salah al-Din, Ninew, Kirkuk and Diyala). Al-Iraqiya, the political movement to which Sunni Arabs most readily related, slowly came apart due to internal rivalries even as Maliki resorted to both legal and extra-judicial means to consolidate power.[44]

The report notes how the conflict is acquiring increasingly sectarian overtones that are also framed within the context of shifting regional politics. Furthermore, during the Sunni insurgency, Shi'a forces became integral parts of the coalition's counter-insurgency campaign, in particular a group called the Wolf Brigade, who systematically used extreme measures to gain information.[45] While coalition forces were forbidden to use violence, Iraqi-on-Iraqi violence was condoned, in part by Frago 242, a fragmentary order, which stated that: 'Provided the initial report confirms US forces were not involved in the detainee abuse, no further investigation will be conducted unless directed by HHQ.'[46] Furthermore, coalition forces regularly used the threat of the Wolf Brigade to extract information from detainees, often passing prisoners on to the Wolf Brigade. The Wolf Brigade was a Shi'a militia, under the leadership of Abu Waleed,[47] whose practices included the 'use of stun guns, hanging suspects from their wrists with arms behind back, holding detainees in basements with human waste, and beatings'.[48] When taken together with the empowerment and increased violence of Shi'a militias such as JAM and the Badr Corps discussed in more detail below, these divisions became more violent and increasingly intractable.

Securing the state or securing the sect?

The manifestation of sectarian difference can clearly be seen in the political and security institutions of the Iraqi state. Historically, the Iraqi military had been dominated by Sunnis, and, in the years after the 1958 *coup d'état*, Sunnis comprised 70 per cent of all officers in the army, with a further 20 per cent Shi'a and 10 per cent, Kurds and other minorities.[49] This process continued under Saddam Hussein, who sought to surround himself with people who were loyal, in a process of coup-proofing that was designed to ensure the survival of his regime.[50] After the invasion of Iraq in 2003, the Iraqi army was disbanded by Order #2, Dissolution of Entities,[51] in an attempt to prevent the re-emergence of Baath- and Sunni-dominated institutions. Clearly, the need to rebuild Iraq after the process of de-Baa'thification was paramount and required a strategy that would provide scope for those groups who had been marginalised and persecuted under Saddam Hussein. The creation of a new Iraqi army that gave key positions to historically marginalised groups was an integral part of this process, yet, ultimately, key positions would be filled by similarly disproportionate demographics.

Despite this, many held high hopes for what the army could do for Iraq. As Lieutenant General Martin E. Dempsey, the head of Multi-National Security Training Command – Iraq, speaking in 2006, stated, 'The Iraqi Army has the opportunity to be the single institution that can elevate the narrative beyond regional, local, religious interests [...] And in most cases they are succeeding in doing so, in other words becoming that institution of national unity.'[52] Clearly, this was the ideal; however, only one year later, a 2006 Iraq Study Group Report documented how 'significant questions remain about the ethnic composition and loyalties of some Iraqi units – specifically, whether they will carry out missions on behalf of national goals instead of a sectarian agenda'.[53] The report also suggests that certain units have refused to carry out missions. Major General Joseph Peterson, the US officer who was overseeing police and army training, stressed that no questions were asked as to the religion of the recruits. 'When we stood them up, we didn't ask, "Are you Sunni or are you Shia?" [...] They ended up being 99 percent Shia. Now, when we look at that, we say, "They do not reflect the population of Iraq."'[54]

One of the problems facing Iraq and, moreover, going some way to undermining the Iraqi army at this time was the presence of militias. While initially declared illegal under CPA Order #91,[55] the continued existence of the Badr Brigade, Mahdi Army and Peshmerga, amongst others, would help coalition forces as the situation on the ground worsened. However, Shi'a militias used the threat of the Sunni insurgency to extend their reach and influence and this paralysed 'any attempt to forge a non-sectarian Iraqi military',[56] ultimately, undermining attempts to use the institution to reimagine a post-Saddam Iraqi identity.

This effort was further undermined by the presence of numerous militias operating across Iraq's parallel security infrastructure, often condoned by prominent figures within the government and religious establishments. Indeed, the rise of al-Maliki to the office of prime minister, coupled with his close proximity to Muqtada al-Sadr, resulted in several allegations that the Iraqi army was circumvented and under-utilised in the period 2006–7. This was in addition to suggestions that both the Badr Brigade and the Mahdi Army had penetrated various security agencies, including police brigades and the Facilities Protection Service.[57] In the aftermath of the Sunni Insurgency, many Sunnis were afraid of joining the Iraqi security forces' (ISF) stabilisation efforts, including by joining the Iraqi army, with severe punishments given out to those viewed as 'collaborators'. The ISF were viewed as 'a hostile force loyal to a Shi'ite-dominated government in Baghdad, installed by the American invaders, and closely aligned with a traditional enemy, Iran'.[58]

Yet it was not just the Iraqi army that was suffering from sectarian divisions. The Iraqi police also suffered from serious divisions, along with the political–security dynamics of Iraq, which impinged on its ability to fulfil its obligations. As a 2006 Iraq Study Group report notes:

> It has neither the training nor legal authority to conduct criminal investigations, nor the firepower to take on organized crime, insurgents, or militias [...] Iraqi police cannot control crime, and they routinely engage in sectarian violence, including the unnecessary detention, torture, and targeted execution of Sunni Arab civilians. The police are organized under the Ministry of the Interior, which is confronted by corruption and militia infiltration and lacks control over police in the provinces.[59]

The importance of the militias in Iraq is essential when seeking to understand contemporary Iraqi politics, having posed serious challenges to the stability of the state post-2003.

Badr, JAM, the state and Iran

While not ostensibly divided along sectarian lines, the historical securitisation of sectarian identities left a legacy of distrust towards the sectarian 'other', which became increasingly violent as the fragmentation of the Iraqi state continued. Following the fragmentation of the Iraqi state, militias emerged that sought to protect particular identity groups. Over time, these militias became hugely important in shaping Iraqi politics. Two groups, in particular, gained prominence and vied for influence across Shi'a areas, namely, the Badr Corps and the Jaish al-Mahdi (JAM). The two groups, although both Shi'a, were rivals, in part as a consequence of Iranian support for the Badr Corps.

JAM, also referred to as the Mahdi Army, was formed in 2003 by the Shi'a cleric Seeyyed Muqtada al-Sadr,[60] in an effort to protect Sadrist (and Shi'a) interests across Iraq after the invasion. JAM featured prominently in the fight against coalition forces in the aftermath of the invasion, leading American forces to target al-Sadr. The followers of al-Sadr were also vocal in their condemnation of

Sunni Muslims, and during the civil war these condemnations turned increasingly violent. In contrast, the Badr Corps[61] was established in the immediate aftermath of the 1979 Revolution in Iran, both as part of Khomeini's strategy to export the Islamic Revolution across the region, but also to provide support to the downtrodden of the Muslim world, with the legacy of Karbala prominent once more. An International Crisis Group Report suggests that aside from personal differences between al-Sadr and al-Hakim, much of the support for the militias is grounded in economic factors, with al-Sadr representing the 'Shiite underclass' and al-Hakim representing the wealthier Shi'a of Baghdad and the holy cities.[62]

In 2005, despite the growth of democratic cooperation between the Shi'a parties (and apparent rapprochement between the militias), concern at Iranian influence in Iraq was on the rise. As a US official noted, 'Iran's vanguard political and unconventional warfare organization, are waging a multi-dimensional campaign to shape the geopolitical dynamic in central and southern Iraq.'[63] This was predominantly achieved through the provision of financial support, by consolidating the authority of the Badr militia over the security forces, with the Badr Corps often used for political ends by officials in the south of Iraq. The Badr militia was seen by Tehran as an adjunct of the Iranian Revolutionary Guards Corps (IRGC) Quds Force (QF), sanctioned by SCIRI to set up security infrastructure across Baghdad to provide security in Shi'a areas, including militia patrols and checkpoints.

Indeed, the same year, 'Iranian sources, including the IRGC-QF, reportedly supported SCIRI and its affiliates with approximately US $100 million; $45 million was specifically allocated to its militia arm, the Badr Corps.'[64] Support was also provided to groups such as Tha'rallah, who were 'implicated in the intimidation and assassination of Sunni Arabs in the southern provinces and in ongoing attempts to penetrate and control the Basra police forces'.[65]

One consequence of this economic investment was the marginalisation of alternative and indeed moderate Shi'a voices, who were left with little choice other than to participate in the SCIRI or to watch from the sidelines. Despite the provision of Iranian aid, however, SCIRI politicians 'openly disavowed the Iranian model of the Islamic jurisprudent, "veleyat-e faqih"',[66] as a model for Iraq, supporting the Najaf position that clerics should remain removed from politics.

Over time, financial incentives proved integral in order to recruit new members and pursue group interests. The Sadrist deputy governor of Karbala, Jawad al-Hasnawi, suggested that a stagnant Iraqi economy was enabling Iran to use financial incentives to recruit Sadrists, who were then paid a monthly salary of US$300 to fight coalition forces and Government of Iraq security forces. As a consequence, 'Sadrists face a powerful, well-armed, and well-financed enemy in ISCI/Badr, who act on Iran's behalf.'[67]

As a consequence, many Sadrists saw 'an Iranian hand behind recent events, accusing Tehran of pushing al-Maliki into a confrontation with the Sadrist movement to ensure the political dominance of its Iraqi allies and the spiritual dominance of the Persian marja'iyya',[68] once more acknowledging the tensions between Qom and Najaf. The Sadrist view was articulated by Ibrahim al-Sumaydi, an Iraqi with close ties to the Sadrists and JAM, who suggested that Iran had:

> sacrificed the Sadr movement to further its own agenda: to prevent Iraq's Shia from aligning with Arab rather than Persian marja'iyya; to guarantee that its true allies – ISCI and the Dawa Party – would win the upcoming elections; and foster the creation of a nine-government Shia regime in southern Iraq, which the Iranians would control.[69]

Jawad al-Hasnawi, in conversation with US officials, acknowledged the power of popular sentiment – and thus the militias – by stressing that 'the street is stronger than the Council of Representatives';[70] conversely, in doing this, al-Hasnawi also articulated the weakness of the GoI. Al-Maliki was all too aware of the power of the militias and the potential consequences for his nascent regime if their power remained unchecked. Efforts to quash the militias were documented by US officials following discussions with Haider al-Abadi. Then a senior Dawa party official, al-Abadi said that al-Maliki had support from a variety of sources for Operation Charge of the Horseman, his effort to quash the power of the Iraqi militias, including from the 'street', but also from the Najaf *marja'iyya*.[71] Al-Abadi claimed to play a prominent role in facilitating dialogue between al-Maliki and Grand Ayatollah Ali Sistani, who 'reportedly blessed the goal of the operation and directed his top preacher, Sheikh al-Karbalai, to express words of support for the operation in his March 28 sermon from Shia Islam's holiest shrine in Karbala'.[72]

Within the context of the erosion of the Iraqi state, the ability of Baghdad to exert its sovereign control over Iraqi territory was dramatically reduced, providing opportunities for other actors to exert influence over events in the state. The increased involvement of Iranian actors, as noted previously, was predominantly an attempt to increase Iran's standing within the region, but was facilitated through shared religious ties. Iran predominantly sought to increase its influence across the south and the key Shi'a holy cities of Karbala and Najaf and across the centre-south of Iraq as a whole. According to US contacts, Tehran's campaign to increase influence in Karbala was divided into two phases:

> The first, beginning with the liberation and lasting until 2006, featured the ham-fisted backing of militias such as the Jaysh al-Mahdi (JAM) and the Badr Corps. As it became clear that Karbala residents were fed up with violence and blamed Iran, Tehran shifted to the more subtle tactic of using its funds to build relationships with local government officials in order to solidify the central role of Iranian businesses in the province – especially businesses servicing the estimated one million religious visitors per year traveling to Karbala from Iran [...] By stressing its religious duty to help maintain the shrines of Imam Husayn and Imam Abbas, and its obligation to look after Iranian citizens here, Tehran is able to dress its Karbala operations in the cloak of legitimacy.[73]

The main vehicle through which Tehran sought to exert its influence across Karbala was Shamsah Travel and Tourism, an umbrella organisation, comprising some 2,500 Iranian companies, closely linked to the Iranian government [...] identifiable with the Kosar Organization. Described by the National Council of Resistance of Iran as the soft arm of the Qods force, Kosar is designed to set up logistics support for Iranian agents through business and charitable activities.

The cable names Kareem al-Musawi and Mohammad al-Yukabi as prominent agents within Shamsah, along with allegations of brutality and intimidation of local political figures. The cable concludes by suggesting that al-Musawi and his confreres 'are hard at work lining the pockets of likely candidates in the provincial elections.'[74]

A senior advisor to the Ministry of Interior, who referred to 'the Iranian city of Basrah', perhaps best documents the success of this operation to increase Iranian influence in Iraq.[75] According to a senior advisor to the GoI Minister of Interior, 'Police brigades are controlled not by the MOI but by ISCI/Badr, particularly in Karbala, Diwaniyah, and Nasiriyah,'[76] further demonstrating Iranian influence, albeit by proxy.

Despite their shared religious bonds, the relationship between the Shi'a of Iraq and Iran was not always positive. This friction stems from a number of factors, including the history of relations between Iran and Iraq, but perhaps also from the importance of the *marja'iyya* in Najaf. Grand Ayatollah Ali Sistani is held to be the most senior figure within the Shi'a world, but there are theological differences between Sistani's position and Khamenei's position over the role of clerics within politics.

The marja'iyah in Najaf also generally refrain from public comment on Iranian influence in Iraq's political arena. Privately, however, their disapproval of the Iranian government's theocratic ideology is clear, and they remain opposed to the propagation of that ideology in Iraq.[77]

The Najaf *marja'iyah*'s silence on Iranian actions has had an impact on Iran's attempts to both penetrate Iraq and win over the hearts and minds of the population, by not providing the blessing that Iranian actors had perhaps desired from Sistani. Yet at the same time:

A growing anti-Iran sentiment among the Iraqi populace is compelling Shia parties to distance themselves publicly from Iran, as evidenced by Islamic Supreme Council of Iraq (ISCI) leader Ammar al-Hakim's recent friendship tour to regional Arab capitals. Even in Shi'a strongholds in Iraq, such as the southern province of Basrah, public sentiment about Iran is often characterised by suspicion and resentment.[78]

This suspicion towards the Iranians was not restricted just to the general population, but also manifested itself amongst the political elite.[79] As early as 2006, Adnan al-Zurfi, a former governor of Najaf, is reported to have told the US State Department that 'Najaf belongs to the Iranians',[80] reflecting the growing Iranian influence across the centre-south of Iraq.

However, al-Zurfi also suggested that the Iranians struggled to win the hearts and minds of the Iraqi people, in part because of 'the blatant exercise of power by local intelligence personnel [which] cuts too close to the excesses of the Saddam era for most local residents', but also because of 'Ayatollah Sistani's disinclination to interact either with the governor or the Iranians'. Zurfi also alleged that despite the attempts of Iranians to invest in Iraq, many businesses in Najaf 'would prefer dealing with the Americans who at least bring aid dollars to the table'.[81]

Iranian attempts to increase their influence in Iraq had an undeniable impact upon the Sunni population of Iraq. The city of Samarra, which is home to a mix of Sunnis and Shi'as, provides a good example of how sectarian difference – and tensions – need not necessarily result in violence – but often did. In the aftermath of the 2003 invasion and the rising Iranian influence, tensions in Samarra were stoked. The city suffered during the fighting, sustaining serious damage to its infrastructure but also to the Golden Mosque. The Golden Mosque is a site of great importance for Shi'ites, as the burial place of the 10th and 11th Imams, but also as the site where the 12th Imam went into occultation and where he will return as the Mahdi. Of concern to many residents was that during the rebuilding process, basic infrastructure took a back seat to the reconstruction of the Golden Mosque.[82] The city was largely Sunni, and in recent memory also secular, but residents became increasingly concerned that the growing Iranian influence was designed to 'fundamentally alter the city's character', filling the largely secular Sunni city with observant Shi'a.[83] The case of Samarra also highlights the perceived tensions between Qom and Najaf, where suspicion exists that efforts to increase the Shi'a presence in Samarra, under the guidance of leaders from Qom and Tehran, may be an attempt 'to establish their influence in Samarra in order to compete with the spiritual leadership of Grand Ayatollah Sistani'.[84]

The perception of Iranian meddling in domestic Iraqi affairs was understandably prominent in the run-up to elections in 2008. US contacts reported that:

> South-central contacts tend to see an Iranian hand behind almost any significant political or security development in Iraq. However, contacts are often unable to provide concrete examples of Iranian intervention [...] This perception of a ubiquitous Iranian presence coexists with deep-seated antipathy and distrust towards Iran [...] Many Iraqis see Iranians as racists who look down on their Arab neighbours.[85]

Much of this suspicion stems from the memory of the Iran–Iraq War, when many Iraqi Shi'a were enlisted in the Iraqi army and fought against Iranian troops. Moreover, suspicion about the links between ISCI or Badr politicians and Iran can be traced back to time spent in Iran during the Saddam era, or to family ties. Interestingly, the Americans seemed to view Iran's actions at this time as an effort to 'solidify its influence and increase the security of its western border', acknowledging the serious challenges that Tehran was facing in seeking to ensure its territorial integrity.[86]

Analysis of events contained in the same cable suggested that allegations of Iranian interference within Iraq were probably exaggerated by Iraqis for three main reasons: first, a desire to maintain good relations with the USA; secondly, a tendency to 'favour conspiracy over self-critical analysis'; and thirdly, a 'particular form of

Iraqi-identity politics in which each side portrays itself as nationalist and its opponents as backed by foreign agents'. Despite this, people act on the basis of their perceptions and even though caveats were acknowledged, the perception of Iranian interference would cause many to act as if it were true.

Yet despite these caveats, amidst 'the high-level diplomacy, the GoI [Government of Iraq] continues to restrict the activities of Islamic Revolutionary Guards Corps Quds Force (IRGC-QF) officers operating under diplomatic cover in Iraq'.[87] To this end, the GoI collaborated with US actors in an attempt to restrict this, by passing:

> Iran watchers copies of the passport pages of 35 Iranian diplomats currently posted to Iraq to seek USG assistance in vetting them for IRGC and MOIS ties. (Note: The namechecks are still pending, but we believe a significant percentage are intelligence officers. End note.)[88]

Tensions between the GoI and Iran became increasingly apparent over the issue of pilgrims, with the Dawa party seemingly willing to challenge Iran 'in defence of Iraqi interests', particularly on economic grounds. This can be seen on the pilgrimage to Karbala and Najaf, where:

> Shamsah Travel and Tourism – negotiated a per-person price of 136 USD for seven days (four nights' lodging and three meals daily in Karbala, three nights' lodging and three meals daily in Najaf), minus a 25 USD per person commission for Shamsah's primary representative here, Kareem al-Musawi.[89]

New lodging prices were suggested to allow hoteliers to turn a profit and also to help the Iraqi economy.

A national response?

The impact of regional dynamics upon Iraq can clearly be seen in the months following the emergence of ISIS. The very nature of the conflict is international, seen in the number of foreign fighters travelling to Iraq and Syria, coupled with the number of regional powers being drawn into the conflict. One ISIS leader spoke of the 'need to settle our differences with you [...] These differences go back a long way. We will settle our differences not in Samarra or Baghdad, but in Karbala, the filth-ridden city, and in Najaf, the city of polytheism',[90] making clear reference to Shi'a Muslims across the region.[91] While Baghdad had sought to restrict the power and influence of militias, the emergence of a new threat provided scope for prominent figures to reassert their influence, not least Qais Khazali, a former JAM member and current leader of Asaib al-Haq (AAH) and Abu Mehdi Muhendis, the leader of Kataib Hezbollah, both of whom have benefited from their links to Iran. Al Sadr, who remained suspicious of the pro-Iranian alliance, reasserted his influence through a more centrist-national agenda, using this his remodelled militia, Saraya Salam (Peace Brigades), to protect Shia shrines. Since then, al Sadr has been reluctant to commit resources to joint militia (PMU) operations against ISIS. Logistic reasons may be at the heart of this decision, but al Sadr is also careful not to alienate Sunni Arab communities who he sees as vital to maintaining Iraq's identity and stability. A Sunni Arab travelling from Baghdad to his home village near Samarra also acknowledged that "there are numerous checkpoints on the road close to Samarra, many of which are controlled by Saraya Salam. When my vehicle was stopped at one of these checkpoints recently, al Sadr's men showed us (a driver and two more Sunni Arab passengers) respect. We would not expect this from the other militias in the area". Such behaviour has left al Sadr well regarded by many Sunnis across Iraq.

Despite ISIS's vociferously anti-Shi'a rhetoric, Sistani sought to frame the fight against the group as a national struggle. Al Karbalai, a prominent Sistani spokesperson, stressed the collective nature of the threat posed by ISIS:

> Iraq and the Iraqi people are facing great danger. The terrorists are not aiming to control just a few provinces. They are targeting all other provinces, including Baghdad, Karbala and Najaf. So the responsibility to face them and fight them is the responsibility of all Iraqis, not one sect or

one party. Our responsibility now is saving Iraq and saving our holy places.[92]

Given Iraq's history of division, and the growth in sectarian violence across the previous decade, attempts to stress national unity appear nothing more than an attempt to rebuild the sectarian house of cards in a different guise.

***

While *prima facie* considerations of the terrain of sectarian divisions suggest that these divisions are located within the theological realm, the politicisation and securitisation of these divisions has ramifications for Iraqi sovereignty. As identities become securitised and actors search elsewhere for security amidst rising violence, the sovereignty of the state is increasingly challenged along several lines. Firstly, the manipulation of sectarian identities has called into question the loyalty of Iraqi citizens to a national body. The policies pursued by the governments of al-Maliki and al-Abadi have explicitly favoured Shi'a Muslims, leaving Sunnis marginalised and often subjected to violence without legal recourse. The need to ensure that a state has a clearly defined notion of citizenship that transcends sectarian difference appears problematic across Iraq, given the challenges to the state-building project explored in Chapter 2.

The trans-state appeal of religious identities clearly poses challenges to several key aspects of the sovereign state. This is furthered by the increasingly sectarian nature of regional politics, driven by the Saudi–Iranian rivalry. External interference, predominantly by Iranian actors but also by the Wahhabi-influenced ideology of ISIS, coupled with the prominence of militias across the state also erodes the ability of the Iraqi government to exercise authority and its monopoly of the use of violence. As a consequence of the increased politicisation and securitisation of sectarian identities across Iraq and, given the regime's culpability within this process, actors turned elsewhere in an effort to find security.

4
Tribalism and the State

On 3 June 2015, in the city of Fallujah in Anbar province, a number of tribal figures from the revered Dulaymi confederation of tribes congregated to pay homage to ISIS's leader, Abu Bakr al-Baghdadi. In what appeared to be a pledge of allegiance to ISIS, questions immediately emerged regarding the legitimacy of this posturing and, if genuine, its significance relevant to the long-term pro-government goal (including the international coalition) of using local tribes to fight ISIS. In questioning the suggested influence of these supposed tribal leaders, a senior Dulaymi member from the al-Fahad tribe declared that the majority of the men were unknown within tribal circles, with Ahmed Dara'a al-Jumaili being the only recognisable figure. He added that he was 'not the main man for the al-Jumaili, but important within Dulaymi circles'. One week prior to this, on 30 May 2015, following the fall of Anbar's capital Ramadi to ISIS, a conference of tribal elders and notables was also held in Ramadi. During the event, Sheikh Ibrahim Rashid Abu Zay'an of the Albu Aitha tribe, also a member of the Dulaymi confederation, drew on sectarian rhetoric in reference to there being 'one ship' for Sunnis. He also asked displaced people to return to Ramadi and thanked al-Baghdadi for his support.

Such gestures highlight the prevailing importance of tribes and their leaders in Iraq, evidenced by the willingness of ISIS or anti-ISIS forces to use traditional networks to legitimise their own quest for control. However, the actions of the two tribal notables also emphasises the dynamic way in which tribes have evolved, and still do so, in Iraq. For instance, in the uncertainty that emerged after 2003, support for Sunni insurgent groups amongst the tribes was well known. Despite this, as momentum shifted with increased US focus, tribal members moved with the tide and were eventually at the forefront of successful operations against AQI – through the Sahwa, also known as the Awakening movement. Shi'a political groups have not looked favourably upon the empowering of local Sunni Arab tribes, and under Prime Minister Nouri al-Maliki (2006–14) these tensions increased. The Sahwa was never incorporated into the national security framework, and, after 2011, uncertainty amongst Sunni communities, such as in Anbar, grew exponentially. Combining political failures with worsening socio-economic conditions therefore helped trigger a new dynamic, not only causing sectarian schisms and anti-government sentiment, but disharmony amongst the Sunni Arab tribes themselves as they disagreed over the best way to confront the challenges ahead. Despite a hiatus during the Sahwa, these issues only simmered.

In order to create a clearer understanding of how ISIS emerged, this chapter will consider the role of tribal dynamics in politics in Iraq, with a particular focus on the tribe as a source of authority. Tribal survival depends on the ability of the tribes themselves to navigate, compete or adapt to the conditions, which as seen in Iraq's history has been influenced not only by local interactions (such as politics or sectarian tensions per se), but external actors like the Ottomans, Britain, the USA and Iran. Tribal elements that have failed to adapt have lost influence, but those that have done so have reaped the benefits. As tribes have evolved through a changing landscape, they have interacted with each other, the state and other groups including militias and militant organisations. The relationship between ISIS and Iraq's tribes will therefore be discussed in reference to this dynamic, identifying key actors and periods throughout modern history that have shaped the current conditions.

The chapter will focus on the origins of ISIS through Iraq's Arab tribes, and in turn the impact of ISIS on the Arab tribes themselves. While primarily focusing on tribes of a majority Sunni Arab denomination, it will, however, assess the broader impact on Shi'a Arab tribes, particularly in the south of the country. Nevertheless, it is important to note that in the Kurdistan region, while Islam has not had the same impact upon Kurdish tribal elements as it has in the Arab areas, the tribal structure has remained a prominent feature. The main tribes are Barzani, Dizai, Hamawandi, Herkki, Jaff, Sorchi and Zibari,[1] while there are also Kurdish tribes further south in predominately Arab areas, such as the Zargushi from the Himreen mountain ranges in Kirkuk province.[2]

As in other regional areas, then, the politics of Kurdistan, primarily through its leading political parties the Kurdistan Democratic Party (KDP) and the Patriotic Union of Kurdistan (PUK), draws influence and support from regional and tribal affiliations. Schisms have, however, arisen, exacerbated by competing interests, which at different times have also drawn on external relations, the Iran–Iraq War being an indicator of loyalties in the past, and to a certain extent the present. For Alheis,

> the failure of the creation of a Kurdish state in northern Iraq is primarily attributed to the continuous quarrel and struggle between Kurdish clans [...] As we see Arab tribes of the same ethnicity and sect infighting, the same process occurred between Kurdish tribes.[3]

There are of course ISIS members that originated from the Kurdistan region, and in all likelihood from its tribes as well; however, its relative autonomy and Kurdish identity has combined with its military prowess and coalition support to isolate it from ISIS; this despite an attempted ISIS incursion into Erbil province during 2014.

Iraq's tribal structure

Iraq's tribal networks have continued to evolve within the environment in which they exist. Dynamic change has therefore occurred as a consequence of a variety of internal and external factors. This has led to new relations, the shifting of alliances and the empowering of the tribal system or even the very few sheikhs at the head of a tribe. Different family names, clans or tribes have at times gained prominence, sometimes through a particular individual or through collective strength. At other times, these same names and their power have diminished as new elites, structures or policies governing the locality emerge. Despite these changes in Iraq, the values associated with the traditional tribal structure and the rules that govern it have largely remained. Tribal leadership and the use of tribal heritage as a cultural value have played a part in this, but so has the relative weakness of the Iraqi state. Changes to names, or, more accurately, changes in family or tribal prominence, have occurred over a much longer period. For example, between 1950 and 1990 a significant degree of tribal continuity existed in Iraq's geographical areas;[4] however, through periods of chaos where order has been removed – following 2003 for example – these changes have occurred at a much faster rate, as violence became a necessary part of survival.

The make-up of a tribe is not as complicated as *prima facie* glances suggest, and a person's tribal lineage can be found in their name, albeit more accurately in the male version.[5] As in the case of Iraq, a male born into a family will take the name of his father as his second name. For example, Saddam took the name Hussein from his. The families form part of a house or *bayt*, which once again in the case of Saddam Hussein was al-Majid, which itself formed part of the Albu Ghafur household. The Albu Ghafur stands as one of ten households of the Beijat clan (or *fakhd*), which in turn was one of six clans that made up the Albu Nasir tribe (*a'shira*). The Albu Nasir tribe forms part of a larger confederation of tribes, sometimes referred to as *qabila*, which in this case is al-Tikriti, the same name as the district in which these names descended. So in full, Saddam's name is Saddam Hussein Abd al-Majid al-Tikriti.[6]

Through a history of movement, marriages, wars, agreements and the favouring of some tribes over others, which have cumulatively caused a significant degree of blurring in some geographical areas in Iraq, there are at present ten major tribal confederations that have maintained a concentrated presence in specific regions.[7] Through various interactions, some of the confederations were spawned from the same ancestral tribe – the Dulaymi from the traditionally southern Arab Zubaydi tribe being an example; and several of the confederations also consist of Sunni and Shi'a tribes. The Dulaymi, as previously noted, are Sunni and are prominent in Anbar province. Other tribal confederations include al-Tikriti and Jabbouri in north-central areas (both having Sunni and Shi'a tribes), plus al-Shammar in the north. A large number of the Anizah confederation are concentrated in southern areas, as are the Khaza'l. The largely Shi'a

Zubaydi are mostly in south-central areas.[8] Depending on the nature of interaction, tribal structures are in constant fluctuation with the environment around them, and despite the survival of names and networks their power bases are not necessarily fixed.

Iraq's tribal dynamic: from empires to state

As with the majority of Arab tribal structures, locality and common interests have traditionally provided the bond for families, clans and tribes to work together as a means to survive, which has provided a semblance of order. On numerous occasions throughout pre-Ottoman history, such solidarity or *asabiyya* amongst the tribes in the Arab region led to territorial expansion or even the establishment of leadership over urban centres. While tribal patterns have mostly been nurtured on the periphery of cities and towns in the agricultural areas, they have at times accumulated enough strength to challenge and dominate central areas. However, as Ibn Khaldun (1332–1406), an Islamic philosopher, wrote,[9] this was more or less part of a cyclical process where the tribes and their leaders would sedentarise, which would eventually weaken the *asabiyya* under the influence of material luxuries and a desire, from the tribal leader per se, to hold on to power. Tribes on the periphery would take advantage of this fracturing, forging a new *asabiyya*, and challenge the central authority.

Under this process of local interaction, the tribal system in the Arab region remained largely stable, occasionally punctuated by external elements such as the Persian Sassanids during the early eighth century and Mongolian raids of the thirteenth century. Even during the creation of Islam from the seventh century, the forging of tribal bonds remained central to the establishment of the religion, which itself fractured as decisions related to leadership split along tribal lines (Quraish being the first tribe, followed by Abbasid and Umayyad). For Jabar,[10] however, it was not until the expansion of the Ottoman Empire into the Arab region that the effective functioning of this cyclical process ceased.

In the case of Iraq, much of the Ottomans' power was centralised in the *vilayats* of Mosul, Baghdad and Basra, and, although peripheral tribal areas proved difficult to govern during this period, the implementation of land reform policy and tax collection mechanisms fundamentally altered the tribal dynamic. Tribes were forced into a competition over land ownership, as the tenets of socio-economic development became ever more focused on private ownership, as opposed to the collective. This became further ingrained in tribal structures after 1918, following the fixing of state borders through the imposition of a British mandate. As Iraq's tribal structure became ever more enmeshed in the development of an Iraqi state, through migration, resistance and administration, galvanising factors such as the agricultural sector that had traditionally provided the tribes with independence and cause for solidarity diminished under greater industrialisation, and reliance on oil. In the decades under the Hashemite monarchy, attempts to appease tribal grievances under the new statist approach often benefited the few wealthy Sunni tribal leaders attached to the administration in Baghdad, for example. Land reform was, then, designed to secure the central rule of the state over peripheral areas, with economic reform designed to aid the state-building process, often at the expense of the local tribes.

Nevertheless, this did not always extend to the more impoverished south, where a large percentage of Iraq's Shi'a Arab tribes congregated. The prevalence of Shi'a belief in the south of Iraq increased in the eighteenth and nineteenth centuries as Persian religious scholars (*ulema*) migrated to the revered Shi'a cities of Karbala and Najaf, influencing and converting the southern populations. For Cline,[11] however, Shi'a belief did not pervade the social and moral values of the tribesman, whose alignment to traditional tribal structures remained. Religious and tribal sentiments have continued to intertwine in the south of Iraq, and on occasion the influence of one has superseded the other depending on circumstances. For example, tribal allegiance and influence gained prominence during the initial formation of modern Iraq as disagreements amongst the Shi'a *ulema* reduced its leadership capacity.[12]

Factors driving activity amongst Iraq's Shi'a Arab tribes, while appearing sectarian in nature, were largely related to political and socio-economic grievances. As previously noted, rebellions against the British in 1920 and against the Hashemite monarchy in 1933 drew much of their strength from the south's tribal sheikhs. Nevertheless, while Iraq's different rulers have created tribal schisms of both a socio-economic and sectarian nature through preferential treatment, tribal differences throughout history have also been curtailed most effectively through *Mudheef* justice, the bringing together of rival tribes before the point of escalation and onset of fighting. Bonds have also been forged through business arrangements and intermarriage. As noted, several tribal confederations consist of both Sunni and Shi'a tribes, and some tribes themselves have mixed families. The Hamdani tribe, for example, has both Shi'a and Sunni members spread across northern, western and southern areas in Iraq. Of course, in contemporary times these relations are largely based on lineage and cultural history rather than practical purpose. However, this can also be enough to maintain a bond, especially in the case of the Hamdanis who draw on a history that includes a major role in the 1920 rebellion against the British. Under the state of Iraq, these relations changed but the tribal link cannot be overstated. For example, senior former servicemen Colonel Saud al-Hamdani, a Shi'a from Basra, and Major Saad al-Hamdani, a Sunni from Anbar, met for the first time in 2014. A combination of business interests, military service and tribal heritage has created a strong relationship, with the latter even being a guest of the Hamdani tribe in Basra on several occasions, referring to each other as 'kin'.

Under Baathist rule, the traditional tribal structure was viewed as incompatible with the nationalist project, but in reality, despite the continued implementation of land reform policies and increased migration towards central areas, the state of Iraq has never been strong enough to maintain total control over its peripheral areas. Saddam Hussein recognised this, and for Yaphe[13] 'tribal values and loyalties as well as Baathist ideology and Arab nationalism were intended to enforce pride in his and the country's uniqueness' while giving him the 'tools' to reinforce his own power and control. Apart from employing members of his own tribe,[14] Saddam also utilised tribal symbols and lineage, while during the more difficult periods he even devolved power to tribal areas. For Jabar,[15] this overlapping effect of 'statist' and 'social' tribalism respectively, was dependent upon the state's ability to manage its affairs. In the first case, patronage networks are used to strengthen control over areas where problems are foreseen. For example, in the case of the Sunni Jabbouri 'many lands in the tribe's domain west of the Tigris, near al-Madain in south of Baghdad, were taken and given to other tribes.'[16] Saddam adopted a similar policy with 'Shammar Jarba in the Jazira, the Azza just north of the capital, and a few tribes between Baghdad and the Iranian border'.[17]

Patterns akin to social tribalism appeared more prominently during periods of hardship for the state, where the strain of war or economic sanctions led to a greater reliance on peripheral actors as a means to maintain order. Under Saddam, tribes within their own vicinities provided security and justice, even collecting tax on behalf of the state. This happened following the 1991 Gulf War, when Saddam turned to the tribes in an attempt to quash uprisings, even in Kurdish and predominately Shi'a areas. As Baram noted,

> near Samawa and Rumaytha (al-Muthanna province, south Iraq) a tribe (section of the Al Ribbat) helped the Baghdad division of the Republican Guard cross the river at Mishhuf and take Samawa after the bridge had been destroyed by the Allied air force. Their choice of sides may be explained by the fact that a member of the tribe, Major General al-Wahid Shannan Al Ribbat, was the divisional commander.[18]

Once again, tribal loyalty has crossed the sectarian divide and even dissected tribal confederations, not only because of the benefits enjoyed by certain tribal individuals or certain tribes, but because a number of their members had also been absorbed into the state's apparatus. However, tribes also benefited from the latter as it provided an avenue in which to gain favour from the state. Tribes that supported Saddam were rewarded for their loyalty, even heralded as bastions of the Iraqi state, which in the immediate aftermath of the 1991 Gulf War and under the strain of international sanctions became even more important as a means of maintaining stability. Saddam therefore, like the tribes, recognised the need to adapt in order to maintain power. He embraced the tribal system, including the Shi'a sheikhs who had been part of the uprising following the 1991 war.

Under these circumstances, Saddam helped to create a new tribal dynamic under his autocracy,[19] albeit one that allowed tribal elements a significant degree of autonomy within their own locality. Some from the Dulaymi, for example, used this flexibility for their own financial benefit, targeting and stealing from travelling groups on the Baghdad to Amman road in Anbar province.[20] For example, the Gaoud family of the Albu Nimr tribe and Dulaymi confederation had close links to Saddam Hussein, with Sattam al-Gaoud fronting a network of companies involved in smuggling for Saddam's regime.[21]

In a weak state that was created under colonialism and held together through authoritarian leadership, tribal structures maintained their legitimacy despite the loss of the traditional agricultural resource base. When the state was weak, tribes even gained in prominence and influence as they were asked to fill the power vacuum in peripheral areas. As chaos ensued following the 2003 invasion, the tribal dynamic was to change once again, but this time with greater intensity as the state of Iraq fragmented under the pressure of occupation, the establishment of new central powers, resistance and sectarian conflict.

Tribal dynamics post-2003

The overthrow of Saddam's regime by US-led forces saw the full removal of a fragile nationalist-based structure that had remained in place since 1958. This process entailed the demobilisation of the military and a process of de-Baathification, aimed at purging Iraq of Saddam's control and administrative legacy. As Iraq's sovereignty wilted, the occupation and ensuing violence created a chaotic environment. The collapse of order perpetuated uncertainty but also allowed peripheral actors the opportunity to stake a claim, provincially and nationally. Those who were previously on the periphery, particularly in Shia and Kurdish areas of influence, took advantage of this power vacuum, which was embodied in the formation of the provisional government in 2005. For Ucko,[22] the US approach did little to advance a sovereign solution and instead engendered a sectarian theme born out of a general acquiescence towards Shi'a and Shi'a militia leaders, who were at large viewed as part of a legitimate guerrilla campaign and brought into negotiations. Sunnis on the other hand were viewed with suspicion or as part of an insurgent threat, and largely placed on the periphery. The impact of this should not be understated. Once in government, militia leaders gained control over particular ministries and such ministries were then used to serve the interests of tribes and their leaders rather than of Iraq.[23]

In the south, the role of the tribe during this period appeared secondary to that of organisations such as JAM or the Mahdi Army (Sadr formed the now Saraya al-Salam or the Peace Brigades out of this), as well as the pro-Iranian Supreme Council for Islamic Revolution in Iraq and its military wing at the time, the Badr Brigades (now the separate Badr Organisation). Much of this was based on the view that tribal influence in the south had previously shown signs of dissipating under the Iraqi state, particularly in view of growing Shia political–religious party dominance.[24] In truth, however, tribal culture never went away. Tribesmen became part of the changing dynamic, interspersing in religious movements, political parties and resistance movements at both the local and national level.[25] While militias such as Muqtada al-Sadr's Mahdi Army drew strength from their followers, the resistance movement in the south was also energised by memories of the British mandate and the subsequent withdrawal of British troops in the 1930s. These factors also appealed to the Shi'a Arab tribal members.

The chaotic situation also resulted in an increase in local dynamics and greater competition amongst the various actors. Some Shi'a tribal members and tribes in the south, depending on their links, were presented with greater opportunities. Amidst a variety of rivalries, some joined government institutions, or even became part of the resistance movement; some even joined the ranks of the Shi'a militias while others contested for power. In one incident reported in August 2006, pro-Iranian death squads with links to the Iraqi Ministry of Interior in Basra reportedly killed Sheikh Faisal al-Khayoon of the large Beni Assad tribe, for his apparent opposition to the newly established authority.[26] Even to this day, disagreements between the tribes and militias over land, business and power spill over into inter-

or intra-tribal violence. For example, in May 2015, members of the Tamimi tribe in Basra province had an altercation with the prominent Shi'a militia Asaib al-Haq (AAH) over the latter's expropriation of land believed to belong to the former. Five people were killed and four injured during the incident.[27] Some of the militia belonged to a rival tribe who were able to draw on the militia's resources to exact their own justice. In some cases, it is difficult to see where the tribe starts and the militias end, but despite this blurring, the sense of loyalty to the tribe has remained. What is clear is that the importance of the tribal dimension, including the use of violence, seemingly with impunity, results in a complex set of relationships with the state.

Through fault and design, then, the emerging political order under the occupation created a new elite, one that placed those aligned with anti-Baathism, most of whom were Shi'a, at the centre, while former Baathists and, as time evolved, even those of Sunni identity were pushed to the periphery. There were of course anomalies, where some Sunni tribal members saw benefit in attaching themselves to the new authority, but many experienced Iraqis including former public sector workers, soldiers, officers and police members were essentially removed from the country's long-term plans. Those that could escape did, while the many who stayed searched for a means to support their families. A large number returned to their homes or family roots, while others joined the resistance.

The Sunni Awakening

Without order, tribal factors once again became important and the need to survive meant that Sunni Arab tribal members had to interact with their environment. As noted by John McCary, a former intelligence collector for the Iraq army in Anbar during 2003 and 2004, the situation led to a blurring where groups including insurgents, militias, death squads, security forces and local Al Qaeda could draw on 'many of the same individuals within the general populace to support their causes, from providing personnel to logistics support to navigating unknown territory'.[28] The fluidity of these networks meant that the creation of order – and ultimately re-establishment of a functioning, sovereign state – faced serious challenges.

In Anbar in particular, some of the tribal networks sought to maintain their businesses and even smuggling routes that had profited under Saddam's regime. However, as the tribes competed with one another for finance, they overlapped with those of the resistance movements, who, like most, also needed resources to sustain their struggle, Al Qaeda in Iraq (AQI) being one example. While AQI gained strength from foreign fighters through the relatively porous borders between Iraq, Syria, Saudi Arabia and Jordan, it also drew a lot of support from the local resistance movement, including the many Sunni Arab tribes faced with an occupation and sectarian struggle. To this end, some tribal members were coerced into joining the group, while others saw the benefit in using AQI's networks for the benefit of their businesses. Once more, the incentives for becoming involved in such a group and, moreover, for supporting them are multifarious.

Nevertheless, AQI did not appeal to all of the Sunni resistance, and their approach became increasingly divisive amongst and within the tribes themselves. A number of senior leaders fled to nearby countries such as Jordan, while those that stayed and confronted AQI put their lives at risk. In one particular case in Anbar, the highly influential Sheikh Nasr al-Fahdawi of the Albu Fahad tribe was killed in 2006 by one of his own tribesmen under the orders of AQI. Sheikh Nasr had taken part in discussions with Iraqi and US officials, which for some of his tribe meant he 'was a traitor who deserved to be killed'.[29] For others such as a senior Fahdawi and former general in Saddam Hussein's army, this was 'an act of war, and matter of pride'.[30] This tactic, commonly used by AQI, ensured that they were able to control and restrict tribal coordination, but it also paradoxically triggered the survivalist instincts of the tribes around them.

The Albu Fahad tribe[31] – of the Dulaymi confederation – had a considerable number of members who were part of the resistance following 2003, such as the leader of the 1920 Revolutionary Brigades, Mohammed Mahmoud Latif – or, as he is also known, Mahmoud al-Fahdawi. From the outset, AQI formed part of the resistance, even luring members from tribes such as the Albu Fahad.[32] Yet, in Anbar by 2006, this dynamic had begun to change. A combination of factors such as the influx of foreign AQ fighters, AQI's desire to control smuggling and other businesses, and their approach towards potential opposition, particularly senior tribal sheikhs, helped shift momentum, even leading to recognition of US support.

A term often used in Iraq to depict a shifting of support, particularly amongst older families and tribes, is *imshe ma al-roj*, which translated means 'walking with the waves' and suggests changing affiliations based on changing circumstances. Sheikh Sabah al-Sattam Fahran al-Shurji Aziz of the Albu Mahal tribe epitomised this trend. Sheikh Sabah originally fought on the side of the insurgency against US forces post-2003, with some even suggesting that he had links with AQI.[33] Despite this, influenced by the aforementioned factors, he eventually established his own anti-AQI tribal force in the western border district of al-Qaim, next to Syria. He was joined by members of the Albu Mahal, Albu Karabla and Albu Nimr[34] in forming Kataib al-Hamza (Hamza Batallion), which merged into the Albu Mahal Desert Protectors,[35] with intermittent support from US forces. However, the trust mechanisms between this grouping (particularly the Albu Mahal) and the Americans never fully developed, and without this support the Desert Protectors were unable to maintain control of al-Qaim.

The anti-AQI tribal movement only truly gathered momentum following the establishment of the Awakening or Sahwa in September 2006 and the formation of the Anbar Salvation Council, comprising a small number of senior sheikhs who had escaped the AQI cull, and other lesser-known figures. Prominent members included senior tribesmen Sheikh Wissam Hardan al-Aithawi and Sheikh Ali Hatem al-Suleiman, plus Hameed al-Hays Dhiyabi and Muhammad al-Hays Dhiyabi. It was a known smuggler by the name of Sheikh Sattar al-Rishawi from the Albu Risha tribe from the Ramadi area in Anbar (a smaller tribe within the Dulaymi) who emerged as the face of this tribal collective. Supported by the Americans, he managed to bring together 41 other tribal leaders in an alliance that would eventually provide a model for reducing AQI influence across the country. Despite not being a senior tribal leader, Sheikh Sattar was particularly knowledgeable about his surroundings and adept in bringing other insurgent groups and militants into the fold, even figures such as

Mohammad Mahmoud Latif of the 1920 Revolutionary Brigades.[36]
Sheikh Sattar's notoriety amongst his enemies led to his death in 2007
and his brother, Ahmed al-Rishawi, replaced him.

Sheikh Ahmed, or, as he is more commonly known, Abu Risha,
became a close ally of the US and Iraqi governments, but never really
had the tribal respect that his brother attained. Nevertheless, the
Awakening movement to some extent enabled the creation of local
solutions to an otherwise chaotic situation, allowing a degree of self-
organisation to emerge. Spearheaded by US General David Petraeus,
it was to form part of an overarching strategy to not only defeat AQI,
but provide a long-term security plan across Anbar by laying the
foundations for the strengthening of Iraqi sovereignty through the
eventual amalgamation of the Awakening movement into federal and
local security structures. This was agreed with the Iraqi prime minister
at the time, Nouri al-Maliki. America started paying monthly salaries
to the fighters, with the aim of handing this responsibility over to the
Ministry of Interior as well as responsibility for the orientation of the
movement's members into state mechanisms. In return, the USA
would continue to provide reconstruction funds for areas that were
able to remove AQI.[37] By the spring of 2008, the USA had paid out in
the region of US\$767 million towards the tribal programme.[38]

Some Sunni communities benefited greatly from the financial
initiative and the presence of local tribal security, particularly in areas
of high AQI activity such as the southern Baghdad belt area in Babil
province, often referred to by US soldiers as the 'Triangle of Death',
where soldiers were targeted. Here, senior sheikhs such as Qasem
Sweidan al-Janabi were able to utilise the programme for community
initiatives and employment opportunities. Fish farms and the
nurturing of agricultural land once more became a source of revenue
for local families. As a prominent community leader and senior tribal
sheikh, Sheikh Qasem had developed good relations with the USA,
but the struggle to rid the area of insurgents proved much more
difficult. According to a tribal liaison specialist in Iraq, John Harris,
'Sheikh Qasim had a long-term development plan, but unfortunately
he could not control the power struggles in Babil or the lasting
militancy.' Harris noted, 'take the fish farms for example, the pools
were occasionally used by insurgents to hide their weapons, which

forced US troops to adopt a blanket policy of draining the pools, even from those who did not have anything to hide.'[39] Because of this, and other incursions, many families lost their livelihoods.

There was an element of short-termism about the Awakening programme, for two primary reasons. First, as noted by Gonzalez,[40] the American approach bore all the hallmarks of an imperialist counter-insurgency programme, wherein tribes were rewarded for seeking out insurgents, a process akin to 'tribal renting'. Therefore, while long-term stability was bandied around at the political level, the operational focus was on achieving short-term security above all else. As noted by Wilbanks and Karsh, 'Being totally result-oriented, the coalition forces were primarily interested in having all checkpoints manned, arms caches uncovered, and the violence decreased, leaving the methods for achieving these goals at the sheikhs' discretion'.[41]

For US soldiers on the ground, then, it was about getting results, and this meant identifying influential local tribal actors who could turn the insurgency in their favour, which proved problematic considering the amount of money available and the lack of transparency. According to a former soldier who served in Anbar, 'young captains trying to make a name for themself would often be too easily impressed by anyone resembling a sheikh, or somebody who could communicate in good English'. The finances available did of course benefit those who were fighting AQI, but also opportunists who were able to propose grand schemes of development, on behalf of their communities or own self-interests. Another liaison specialist previously attached to a US-funded development programme during 2007 revealed, 'there were a lot of ghost projects, made up to win money [. . .] In some cases money was handed over to men who had no credentials whatsoever.'[42]

The second problem was related to the lack of a political solution and what was, and still is, the political–sectarian divide. By 2008, the Awakening had amassed a force of approximately 80,000 mostly Sunni Arab fighters, but this caused concern for the Shi'a-dominated government and al-Maliki in particular, who saw it as an emerging well-organised militia with political aspirations. Faced with economic difficulties, the government of al-Maliki was forced to choose how best to spend its finances. In November 2008, on taking mandate of the Sahwa from the USA, it announced a pay cut to its members, from an initial US$400–600 per month (which the USA had previously paid) to US$250 per month.[43] The plan to absorb Sahwa members into the security forces also faltered, and while approximately 30,000 were given (largely menial) public sector positions away from the security sector, not even 10 per cent of the 94,000 had been given jobs in the police or army by the proposed 2009 deadline.[44]

Tribal politics and the 'Sunni problem'

Although thousands of the Sahwa's members eventually joined the federal police and army within their respective provinces, their access to political functions remained limited. In essence, Sunni Arab tribes became part of the Sunni 'problem', struggling for power and resources, and divided over how to respond to the worsening political-economic conditions. Al-Maliki was able to use these schisms for his own benefit, playing Sunni groups and tribes against one another across his tenure. As Sunni Arab tribal politics interacted with politics at the national level, the identity of the tribal movement that had been briefly established during the Sahwa eroded, and the tribes once again became fractured. For instance, following the 2010 elections, Anbari tribal figures Rafia al-Issawi, of the Albu Issa tribe, and Jamal al-Karbouli of the Albu Karbala, both prominent Sunni figures in Eyad Illawi's Iraqiyya coalition, were touted as potential candidates for the minister of defence position under al-Maliki. Despite their credentials, al-Maliki named Sadoun al-Dulaymi, a member of the Unity Alliance of Iraq, a coalition that included Sheikh Ahmed al-Rishawi.[45]

By the end of 2010, the sectarian nature of al-Maliki's government was apparent, and with the Shi'a Islamist bloc forming part of his National Alliance (including the pro-Iranian Badr Organisation), he was able to control parliament, albeit by making concessions to non-secular and pro-Iranian interests. But as noted by Sowell, 'Maliki and his Shi'a Islamist allies controlled all key security posts and the vital energy sector.'[46] For tribal leaders, surviving in this landscape proved just as difficult, as not only did al-Maliki use his forces to quash dissonance, but the militant movement had never truly disappeared and was re-energised by the increasingly sectarian nature of al-Maliki's leadership. This was true of tribal fighters and militant organisations such as Jaysh Rijal al-Tariq al-Naqshabandi (JRTN), a group linked to the former regime and Baathist leader Izaat al-Douri and specifically more radical groups like AQI's subsidiary of the time, ISIS, who had continued a campaign of targeting potential opposition, including security and tribal personnel.

In 2011, amidst growing demonstrations in Sunni-populated areas, al-Maliki removed Sheikh Ali Hatem from his Baghdad offices,[47] and issued an arrest warrant for Sunni Vice President Tariq al-Hashemi, who was forced to flee to the Kurdistan region and then Turkey. Then in 2012 he went after the former defence minister candidate and at the time finance minister, Rafi Issawi, from Anbar.[48] By 2012, Sunni Arab tribes were divided over their support for the government and even the method of protest, peaceful or violent; by the end of the year, the pendulum had begun to swing towards the latter. Despite initial calls from Sheikhs Ali Hatem and Ahmed al-Rishawi to maintain the peace, by the end of 2013 even they had called their fellow tribal members to arms. This escalation was triggered by a series of events.

Firstly, demonstrations were targeted by security forces, and on 25 January 2013 five protestors were killed as security forces attempted to break up a gathering in Fallujah. In the immediate aftermath of this, militants targeted security forces in Fallujah's peripheral areas, and the following day Sheikh Ahmed al-Rishawi demanded the security personnel responsible for the killings of the protestors be handed over.[49] On 23 April, violence erupted when security forces attempted to dismantle a protest camp in Hawija,[50] a predominately Sunni Arab town in the northwest of Kirkuk province (southeast of Mosul). The government justified its actions on the grounds of rising violence in surrounding areas and the belief that militant groups had infiltrated the protest movement. Hawija had remained a stronghold for Sunni militancy during the occupation, with JRTN particularly prominent. At the very least, organisations linked to JRTN had called protestors to take up arms prior to this incident,[51] but al-Maliki's actions and rhetoric became something of a self-fulfilling prophecy.

Sheikh Ali Hatem, along with Sunni cleric Said al-Lafi, once again called for calm; however, in Ramadi and in response to the events in Hawija on the evening of 23 April, protestor Qusay al-Junabi, supported by the nephew of Ahmed al-Rishawi, Mohammed Khamis al-Rishawi, called for all tribes to mobilise and demanded the removal of federal forces from Sunni areas.[52] On Saturday 18 May, Iraq's security forces attempted to arrest Mohammed Khamis in connection with the death of five soldiers near Ramadi.[53] Mohammed Khamis had initially put himself at the front of the movement, with local sources from the Ramadi area even suggesting that 'he was working with Daesh',[54] the Arabic acronym for ISIS. This may have been the case, but the proximity to each other in which the various groups operated in Anbar made separation very difficult and it was more likely that Mohammed Khamis, like other tribal members, was trying to position himself in a place of power within the overarching movement.

On 30 December 2013, al-Maliki forced the closure of Ramadi's symbolic protest site, in what some might consider was the actual tipping point. In the background, the militant response was already gaining in strength as the political Sunni voice was extinguished. Survivalists by nature, Ali Hatem and Ahmed al-Rishawi, along with several other tribal leaders, had also shifted their positions and by the beginning of 2014 violence began to spread. The difference between tribes, resistance fighters and terrorists began to blur once more, with the state increasingly unable to differentiate between them, further adding to suspicion of Sunnis. In Anbar, Ahmed al-Rishawi and his nephew Mohammed Khamis had their own militia, as did Ali Hatem through his senior role in the Military Council of Anbar Tribal Revolutionaries (MCATR).[55] As they targeted security forces, al-Maliki tried to tarnish their names by using television confessions to link them to AQI.[56] This was all part of al-Maliki's pre-2014 election propaganda, but separation from the radical elements became increasingly difficult for the Sunni sheikhs.

In an attempt to buy support in Anbar and to compete with figures such as Ahmed al-Rishawi, al-Maliki turned to other Dulaymi members, with former Sahwa sheikh Wissam al-Hardan a notable ally. Nevertheless, little was achieved and tribal elements were once again enmeshed in the violence, dividing the tribes internally and the Sunni political movement in general. Ali Hatem maintained his defensive position, potentially viewing an alliance with the more radical elements such as ISIS as a necessary evil, or using their presence as a bargaining chip with the government. After all, in the early stages of 2014, ISIS was part of the broader movement and, for some, a controllable force.

Ahmed al-Rishawi, on the other hand, was eventually swayed by al-Maliki, for reasons of security but also the lure of power and financial benefits. Despite Mohammed Khamis al-Rishawi's initial hard-line position,[57] he too was brought back into the government fold by the summer of 2014. However, because of this he was subsequently killed during an Awakening patrol with security forces in June 2014, when a suicide vest wearer grabbed him at a checkpoint near Ramadi and detonated his device. Bearing all the hallmarks of ISIS, this attack symbolised the changing conditions. The AQI–ISIS campaign against tribal opposition had never really relented, and if anything, learning from past mistakes, their targeting became more ruthless.

Through its links to tribal elements and the resistance movement (including organisations such as JRTN, 1920 Revolutionary Brigades, Hamas in Iraq, Mujahideen Army, Islamic Army in Iraq and more), ISIS was able to utilise the conditions to cement footholds in Anbar province and Mosul prior to June 2014. By then it was in control of Anbar province's Syrian border town of Qaim, as well as Rawa, Hit, Rutbah, Karma and, perhaps most prominently, Fallujah. In the north, towns such as Sinjar, Hawija, al-Sharqat, Baiji and Tikrit came under their influence, which also reached even as far as Diyala and the Baghdad belt area. Their targeting of tribal opposition figures also escalated, and in Hit, where the Albu Nimr tribe attempted to resist ISIS advances, over 200 tribal members were executed. As noted by tribal member Sabah al-Haditheh, 'We put the responsibility on the government because they didn't respond [...] we were fighting ISIS with rifles, and it was fighting us with heavy machine guns.'[58]

With ISIS having nurtured a fighting army in Syria, acquired military hardware from successful campaigns and opened border routes for the access of logistic resources and foreign fighters, opposition tribal fighters struggled to hold their ground and large numbers of the military in both the north and west abandoned their positions. For example, Sheikh Ali Hatem, under pressure from al-Maliki's forces, had already fled to Erbil, and Sheikh Ahmed al-Rishawi, for fear of being targeted by the militants, established new homes in neighbouring countries, Jordan and the United Arab Emirates. Other senior tribal members followed, leaving a lack of structure and leadership that was evident during the Sahwa.

Despite troop withdrawals from Iraq, coalition forces still needed a reliable ally on the ground and Sheikh Ahmed tried to enable this once more by lobbying officials in Washington in January 2015. However, his intentions were never clear and his influence was already waning. When another tribal delegation visited Washington in May 2015, prominent Dulaymi tribal leader Sheikh Abdul Razzaq al-Dulaymi was quoted as saying 'My visit is not to talk about Abu-Risha (Sheikh Ahmed), but the man has lost his popularity.'[59] Former al-Maliki ally Sheikh Wissam al-Hardan had expressed similar sentiments, although his tribal credibility had also diminished because of his previous links and, according to a former intelligence office from Anbar, 'al-Maliki had only used Sheikh Wissam to teach Abu-Risha a lesson, but he was a thief and even al-Maliki discarded him [...] Sheikh Wissam has no support now'.[60]

The impact of ISIS

In February 2014, AQI officially distanced itself from ISIS,[61] but by the summer of 2014 ISIS had managed to stretch its influence across Anbar and most of the northern Iraqi provinces, including incursions into the Kurdistan region, south of Baghdad in northern Babil province and as far east as Diyala. Conditions in Sunni majority areas therefore enabled ISIS to build a network amongst the local resistance movements and tribes, feeding off the socio-economic grievances and political schisms that were never attended to, and of course an increase in sectarian tensions. ISIS became an extremely powerful movement and, with past experience to draw from, it knew how to subdue its opposition. Tribes once again fragmented, sheikhs and senior members fled their respective areas and those who didn't flee either adapted or were left to a worse fate. There were of course a number of tribal members who chose to fight.

In Anbar province, the Jaghayfi in Haditha, with support from the Albu Mahal and Albu Nimr, who had been largely forced out of Qaim and Hit respectively, continued to resist ISIS. A number of its fighters were members of the army or federal police force, although they did not receive salaries for most of 2015. With only US air support and humanitarian aid to provide substance, the scarcity of food and water impacted on living conditions. For these reasons, according to a local security officer based in Haditha, not all of the food received was distributed to the community in Haditha and a considerable percentage of it was sold to the black market to make money.[62] A worker from a humanitarian organisation in Iraq stated, 'we were even told of our food stuffs that were intended for the people of Haditha being sold in IS controlled areas'.[63] Despite the warring between the parties, intermediary groups are able to maintain trading channels. With ISIS controlling border areas and the majority of towns in Anbar, they are able to benefit from this activity by applying tariffs on all trading goods. This has also caused inter- and intra-tribal rivalry over the control of the smuggling routes. According to a federal police officer working in Haditha: 'The smuggling gangs will even target each other, sometimes using the name of Daesh to hide their real intentions.'[64] He also highlighted that the alliance between the Albu Mahal and Jughayfi in Haditha has suffered fractures as both 'compete with one another for the control of foodstuffs, military resources and money'.

ISIS has therefore intensified the dynamic within Sunni tribal areas, more so than AQI, particularly evident in Anbar. While much of the media tends to focus on international fighters coming into Syria and Iraq, also advertised by ISIS through social media, there is a tendency to neglect the locality of the cause and therefore the issues affecting the Sunni Arab tribes in Iraq. A member of the Albu Khalaf tribe, fighting in areas east of Ramadi in Khaldiyah and Husaybah, highlighted the locality of the situation: 'Our day-to-day battles on the frontline are fought with fellow Iraqis, people we know from nearby tribes and other men from the north. We only see foreign fighters or the senior commanders when there are big battles.'[65]

Iraq's lack of control over Sunni provinces, particularly Anbar in the west and Ninawa in the north, epitomises the fracturing of its sovereignty. Political failures and economic circumstances have precipitated this, but tribal elements through their own desire to survive have also contributed to the dynamic. For different reasons, the tribal dynamic in the south has also changed. The enduring conflict with ISIS has drawn both financial resources and security forces away from the southern provinces where both militias and tribesmen have taken advantage of this vacuum in an effort to support their own needs, leading to an increase in criminal activity and further fracturing the ability of the regime to maintain control across the state. According to Alex Atkinson,[66] an analyst who has worked in Iraq in both the military and private security sector over an eight-year period and has monitored this transformation in Basra province since 2014:

> Security capability in Basra province was damaged by the 2014 re-deployment of 14 Division Iraqi Army, and nearly all federal police to participate in the fight against IS. Because of this the remaining provincial police are unable to take effective action against tribal members involved in criminal acts, not only due to a lack of resources but because they live in the communities they work, and therefore especially vulnerable. The remaining federal forces are less vulnerable but nonetheless outgunned and outnumbered by tribes.

He went on to say:

> It is a combination of a weakened justice system and decreasing security capability in the province [Basra], which has amplified the significance of the role of tribes in society. In recent years more reliance is placed on tribal

dispute resolution, but under current circumstances, this has had little effect, and tribal and intra-tribal violence has increased significantly.

Issues that trigger tribal violence are often minuscule, but tend to evolve very quickly. In one case in Qarmat Ali, northern Basra province, two young men took offence at being covered in dust by a motorbike rider. In response they went to the individual's house and insulted him, prompting a rapid response from his immediate family. The two young men left and returned with members of their family and the situation quickly escalated in to an exchange of shots, killing at least one person. From a small incident, the consequences grew exponentially, establishing a blood feud – which in all likelihood would have to be solved through *Mudheef* justice.

***

Tribes in Iraq contribute to and are affected by the prevailing political, social and economic conditions across the state. In the current context, the Sunni Arab tribes have found themselves on the periphery, forced to adapt to less favourable conditions following over a decade of unbalanced policy making. However, the response has also contributed to the dynamic, particularly through its resistance and militancy. ISIS has grown through these conditions, a symptom of the tribal situation and other factors, including but not limited to policies of the regime and the US invasion. The war with ISIS has also drained financial resources and removed security from other areas, creating a vacuum that has allowed the southern tribes in particular to act with near-impunity. The emerging strength of the tribes is testament to a weak centre or government, and for the state of Iraq to be saved solutions that include incorporation of the Sunni Arab tribes into a long-term political solution will be needed. While ISIS emerged from the fracturing of the Iraqi state, capitalising on increasingly deteriorating political, social and economic conditions affecting the Sunni community, the fight against ISIS has worsened these conditions across the state as a whole. This has fed into a weakening of Iraqi sovereignty, providing more space for other actors to emerge and gain political traction.

5

The Roots of Sunni Militancy and its Enduring Threat in Iraq

In the autumn of 2003, Khaled, a former intelligence officer based in Baghdad, was witnessing his country turn into a war zone. He, like many of the other moderate Sunni men who had previously worked for the regime, was left on the periphery following Paul Bremer's process of de-Baathification. With a wife and small child to support, Khaled was forced to seek work outside of the government for the first time in his life. Despite finding low-paid work in a local shop, the conditions around Khaled and his family deteriorated, hastened by the emerging sectarian war in 2006 and 2007. During this uncertain period, whilst standing outside his place of employment, men claiming to be 'friends of a friend' approached him: 'We have been told that you are a good man, *Haji* [pilgrim – a respectful term for a man of Muslim faith]. We are going to Fallujah to join the resistance and would like you to come with us.'[1] The men, who were Sunni and all former military, had been asked by friends and resistance leaders in Anbar to collect as many Sunni ex-servicemen as possible for the 'fight ahead'. At a crossroads in his life, Khaled declined and explained to the men that he had his own personal 'jihad', one that involved the survival of his family.

Many others in Khaled's position chose a different path, including those who went on to be leaders in the resistance movement and, later, ISIS. One such was Abu Ali al-Anbari, a former general in the Iraqi army before joining the Wahhabi-inspired Ansar al-Sunna, AQI and ISIS. A similar timeline also applies to Fadel Ahmed Abdullah al-Hiyali, also known as Abu Muslim al-Turkmani, another former general with moderate religious views.[2] The turn to Sunni militancy was therefore a choice, one that was heavily restricted by the prevailing circumstances, but one nonetheless that was based on survival. The occupation therefore triggered a response from within an uncertain Sunni community, one that became enmeshed in a sectarian struggle regardless of choice.

The enduring threat of Sunni militancy in Iraq is rooted in the conditions from which it has emerged and evolved. Religion has long been used as a means of securing loyalty and as a mechanism of control, yet such efforts also have consequences for regional conditions and dynamics. ISIS is a symptom of these conditions and an organisation that has thrived on the factors already mentioned in this book. Therefore removing it as a main force from Iraq and its control over cities such as Mosul and Fallujah will only provide temporary respite, as the long-standing issues driving Sunni militancy will ultimately remain. To show this, this chapter will focus on the conditions and factors that influence Sunni militancy, building on the conditions across the state in the run-up to the 2003 invasion. The violence that was triggered via the invasion will be discussed with reference to Sunni militancy and the groups that helped forge the response. The second part will pay particular attention to ISIS and how a myriad of factors allowed it to establish its roots in Sunni communities across Iraq. The third part will highlight the enduring threat of Sunni militancy and the potential for future stability in Iraq. Quantitative data and qualitative research will be used to highlight the enduring threat of Sunni militancy amidst Iraq's fragmenting conditions.

The road to Sunni insurgency in Iraq

The foundations for Sunni Islamism and militancy had already begun before 2003. Irredentism, ethnic and sectarian tensions, social cleavages and political suspicions had long existed within Iraq's borders, but these factors were exacerbated following two Gulf wars and the imposition of economic sanctions. As Saddam's control over peripheral areas wilted, new actors emerged in the provincial areas. Tribal factors played an important role in organising communities, but religion also became a galvanising force. In an attempt to reinforce his own leadership, Saddam introduced *Hamla al-Imaniyya* or 'return to faith' in 1991, evoking Islamic values under the country's duress. However, without the necessary funds for public investment, economic conditions soon affected the very core of society. Saddam introduced Islamic schools and colleges in his name, but without finance even the education sector faltered. As Hashim[3] highlights, school enrolment between the years 1990 and 1994 decreased from 56 per cent to 26 per cent, while adult literacy was reduced from 89 per cent to 59 per cent between the years 1985 and 1995. Nevertheless, as a result of Saddam's policies new generations of religious Sunnis were created, one of whom was Abu Bakr al-Baghdadi, who attended the Islamic University of Baghdad.[4]

The turn to conservative religious values in periods of hardship is not uncommon, and despite Saddam's suppression of Sunni organisations such as the Muslim Brotherhood, there existed a trend for such a retreat into religious identities. It would therefore be plausible for Saddam to think that he could utilise religion for his own political gain. He was also aware of the challenge posed by the Shi'a political and religious opposition in Iraq and therefore he could use his own version of Sunni Islam to counteract the religious forces emerging from Shi'a communities. This was particularly evident in the southern provinces like Najaf and Karbala and across the southeast where the building of communities around mosques was an increasingly common theme. While there was little sign of a unified front amongst Shi'a political and religious circles, pro-Iranian opponents of the regime were nevertheless keen to take advantage of the apparent weakness of government. To this end, Saddam used violence and coercion to maintain control, but he also recognised the utility of religion as both a counter-narrative and a motivational tool. He used it to chastise Saudi Arabia and Syria during the second Gulf War[5] and even called Iraq the 'land of jihad' during a speech in 2002.[6]

While maintaining the basic tenets of Baathism, Saddam fused his interpretation of Iraqi nationalism with various religious groups and movements, attempting to maintain control in the peripheral areas, including the Kurdistan region, much as he did with the tribes. In an interview with two former military officers[7] who had served under Saddam's regime, they recalled how various beliefs were used as control mechanisms against potential threats or as a way of balancing against other religions. In one particular example, 'connections with Sufis in the north through Izzat al-Douri served a purpose during the early 2000s, but many of us (senior military officers) were uncomfortable with their practice, which seemed to be based on magic rather than religion'.

By the start of the Sunni insurgency, the roots of disaffection and the drivers of militant mobilisation had already been established, with several supporting a blend of Iraqi religious nationalism. For example, the Sufi-labelled Jaysh Rijal al-Tariqa al-Naqshbandia (JRTN) did not officially mobilise as an insurgent group until 2006, following the execution of Saddam Hussein; however, with Izzat Ibrahim al-Douri, the former deputy head of the Revolutionary Command Council under Saddam Hussein,[8] as the apparent leader of the organisation, a dynamic between Baathism and religion already existed. After 2006, the JRTN used these links to mobilise supporters within Sunni Arab communities in the provinces Kirkuk, Ninawa and Salahaddin in particular, while creating alliances with other similar religious–national organisations, such as the Islamic Army of Iraq (IAI). The IAI, led by Sheikh Ahmed al-Dabash, was also reportedly established before 2003,[9] but its ranks were bolstered by Sunni Iraqi nationals after the invasion, a number of whom also had links to the military. The IAI has also maintained a connection with prominent members of the large Jabouri tribe in particular, and thrived in areas north of Baghdad. IAI has purported a more nationalist version of Sunni Islam, but, under conditions exacerbated by the occupation and sectarian conflict, found commonalities with a number of other insurgent groups, many of whom were Islamist in ideology, such as AQI.

Supporting this growth in Islamism, foreign fighters were also able to take advantage of the porous borders, allowing them to travel to the region. At the time, Kurdistan was particularly isolated, a peripheral region in the north. Despite being composed predominantly of Kurdish and Iraqi Arabs, it became an ideal place for Salafis and foreign radicals alike,[10] some of whom were from Saudi Arabia and Yemen, while others came from further afield. This was noted by former officers who recalled information on 'Saudi-sponsored Salafis from the Caucasus and the Balkans',[11] many of whom had prior experience in places such as Chechnya, Bosnia and Afghanistan. Some Kurdish media reports even speculated that Saddam was sending arms to Salafis in the region, with Ansar al-Islam being a case in point,[12] following their creation in Kurdistan in 2001. Initially called Jund al-Islam, with links to Al Qaeda, it was also known as Ansar al-Sunna, a name that became apparent following a split within Ansar al-Islam in 2003.[13] It regrouped as Ansar al-Islam in 2007.[14]

As the occupation took hold then, other Sunni militant organisations emerged, drawing their energy from the sectarian conditions and uncertainty within the Sunni community, including religious advocates, former members of the army, and Sunni tribes and clans. One such example was the 1920 Revolutionary Brigades, led by Dr Mohammed Mahmoud Latif (also known as Sheikh Mahmoud al-Fahdawi). Latif, a Shariah Law scholar from Sofia near Ramadi in Anbar province, led the Revolutionary Brigades in the area referred to as the Sunni triangle, comprising Anbar, Baghdad (including its belt areas), Diyala,[15] and particularly in southern parts of Salahaddin province, in towns such as Tarmiya and Taji. Another organisation of Islamist leanings was Jaish al-Mujahideen or the Mujahideen Army (MA). According to its leader Abd al-Hakim al-Nuaimi, MA was a religious organisation before the occupation, and according to spokesperson Abdul Rahman al-Oaisi the group was even providing social services including religious education and charity.[16] It established its roots in central and eastern areas in Anbar province, in towns such as Karma, before becoming active in the insurgency in 2004.

Both Sunni national and religious organisations therefore joined the insurgency against the occupying forces, while rejecting the Shi'a-dominated government. In the early stages, AQI became the de facto leader of the insurgency, working alongside groups like IAI and Ansar al-Islam. In 2005, an organisation composed of AQI and several other groups, calling itself 'Islamic State in Iraq', took over the Sunni majority city of Mosul, in Ninawa province in the north of Iraq. In establishing its own rule, it benefited from kidnapping and extortion from local businesses, justifying it as a type of legitimate taxation.[17] However, as a consequence of their popularity both locally and globally, they also became the primary focus for US operations in the area. Despite not having a footing in Iraq prior to the 2003 invasion, conditions in the country drew in Al Qaeda and foreign Jihadists as they flocked to take part in a fight against the US-led forces, which they saw as a religious – and personal – duty. In an interview with *Atlantic Magazine* in 2006, known Palestinian–Jordanian jihadist, Huthaifa Azzam,[18] stated that:

> I was in Syria when the war in Iraq began [...] People were arriving in droves; everyone wanted to go to Iraq to fight the Americans. I remember one guy who came and said he was too old to fight, but he gave the recruiters $200,000 in cash. 'Give it to the mujahideen,' was all he said.[19]

When Abu Musab al-Zarqawi, AQI's Jordanian-born leader and one-time jihadist colleague of Azzam, was killed in an airstrike in 2006, it was considered a watershed moment. Yet AQI (or AQI–ISIS for that matter) were not the driving factors behind Sunni militancy, but as with ISIS, were a symptom of the circumstances that have emerged over a much longer period, triggered by the invasion in 2003. It was during this period that the landscape had changed and the majority of Iraq's Sunni Arabs found themselves on the periphery, facing increasing uncertainty under a majority Shi'a government and the growing strength of Shi'a militias. AQI and its affiliate, ISIS, were created under these circumstances and sought to take advantage amidst the chaos. AQI-ISIS established trade and financial networks, but as time elapsed, their desire to control the insurgency and finances in areas where it was established led to increased discontent amongst other Sunni Arab groups, tribes and communities. Yet in the short term, the group was able to draw support from the disaffected Sunnis who were struggling to meet their basic needs.

Breaking Al Qaeda

The Sunni insurgency was a melting pot of disaffected former soldiers, tribal members, Islamists – both local and foreign – and Baathists. The US-led forces approached the matter as a problem to be eradicated, conducting numerous military offensives and anti-terrorist operations, often in coordination with Iraq's newly founded security forces, which they themselves were involved in training. The Awakening or Sahwa programme with the tribes had an important role in this, and by late 2007 the tide against the insurgency had begun to turn. For example, Ansar al-Islam created an alliance with other Sunni and national militant groups such as IAI and MA in the hope of projecting a more moderate position than that of AQI without giving up on their position against the occupying forces and the Iraqi government.[20] The IAI itself officially announced its parting from AQI-ISIS in April 2007, and with evidence of momentum shifting in favour of the anti AQI-ISIS movement, Mishan al-Jabouri, a prominent former Baathist and tribal leader, used his IAI-affiliated media channel, al-Zawraa, to condemn AQI-ISIS.[21]

Other groups like the 1920 Revolutionary Brigades were more divided over their support for the insurgency. Although this organisation is Iraqi, its Islamist tendencies meant many of its members had much in common with AQI-ISIS. Yet being from Anbar, its leader Mohammed Mahmoud Latif was all too aware of the problems caused at the local level by AQI, and his rapprochement with the Sahwa movement through relations with Sheikh Sattar al-Rishawi epitomised the shift in balance. Nevertheless, those that did not support the Sahwa left the organisation and formed Hamas in Iraq.[22]

At the local level, being part of the Sahwa was paying dividends, an effective recruitment process for more organisations and individuals to join the cause. As momentum shifted, the Sahwa proved a highly effective short-term strategy and many of the insurgents that were not killed were either forced underground or placed in prison camps. Nevertheless, this did not remove the threat of Sunni militancy in its entirety. According to al-Bawaba, a Jordanian media outlet, following al-Maliki's military campaign to completely remove AQI-ISIS from Mosul in May 2008, the organisation merely adapted and, according to a contractor, they went underground and 'instead of targeting homes and businesses with explosive devices, al-Qaeda started kidnapping and assassinating'.[23]

Even in prisons, the legacy of internment created conditions that facilitated radicalisation, through the detainment of a number of

Sunni insurgents, ultimately proving favourable recruitment ground for groups like ISIS. During the occupation the USA reportedly detained 100,000 people in Iraq,[24] both Sunni and Shi'a. Of these, approximately 26,000 were based in Camp Bucca, a desolate facility near Garma in the south, close to the Kuwaiti border. Prisoners were divided along sectarian lines, and the inmates themselves implemented a code of Islamic law to govern their everyday lives. It is here that figures like ISIS leader Abu Bakr al-Baghdadi were groomed amidst an environment of radical insurgents and Islamists. Al-Baghdadi himself was incarcerated in 2004 but released in 2007,[25] after which he went on to join the AQI branch of Islamic State. A former intelligence officer[26] stated, 'there were many young men who were in these prisons already part of the insurgency, but when they were released and returned to their homes, they were now wearing beards and short trousers (in reference to the Salafi trend)'. He continued, 'That was one of our fundamental errors, we never monitored these guys. I remember a young man I use to know, from a good family, but when he was released he returned to little Fallujah [Adhamiyah district, a predominately Sunni area in Baghdad], where he became attached to a mosque known to be linked to al-Qaeda.'[27]

Insurgent detainees were being released before the end of 2009, and several of the prison camps including Camp Bucca were closed. Despite this, there was little in the way of a reintegration programme for former prisoners and, as Thompson and Suricot note, 'Poor record-keeping, limited language skills, detainee obfuscation and the pressure to cut costs prohibited the effective evaluation of prisoners.'[28] Due to resource limitations, neither the US nor the ISF were able to control the situation and, while some of the worst insurgents were moved to other prisons, those that were freed re-entered the same uncertain society that had governed Sunni communities since 2003, where there was very little in the way of political or socio-economic improvements.

The 'purge', as it has been referred to by the Americans, proved successful in reducing the Sunni militant threat and, by the time US forces left in December 2011, it is estimated that AQI-ISIS had diminished to approximately 10 per cent of its peak capacity during the insurgency.[29] However, the failure to introduce political and economic reform across the sectarian divides never materialised under the government of Nouri al-Maliki, and while the unbalanced conditions existed the threat of Sunni militancy was unlikely to disappear. Added to this, a number of the hardline radicals and Islamists (such as ISIS leader al-Baghdadi) were merely pushed underground, but they never went away and instead continued their asymmetric campaign against the government of Iraq and any opposition. As the situation slowly deteriorated and protests escalated in Sunni communities, tribal organisations (as noted in the previous chapter) and militant factions mobilised, and by 2012 a new war was beginning.

Making ISIS in Iraq and Syria

Although AQI-ISIS continued to operate in Iraq, the conflict in Syria, which began in March 2011, provided the chaotic conditions for the organisation to regroup and ultimately flourish. Porous borders and a reduction in sovereign control allowed for the influx of weapons and foreign fighters into Syria openly supported by countries opposed to Assad's regime. Al Qaeda affiliates Jabhat al-Nusra and other groups such as the Saudi Arabian-backed Jaish al-Islam[30] acted quickly to capitalise on grievances in predominately Sunni areas, filling the power vacuum east of Assad's control. However, as the war evolved it was the emergence of ISIS that began to command most of the attention. By the end of 2013, despite the success of aligned rebels and other Sunni militant groups, ISIS had managed to embed itself in cities, towns and villages spanning from Aleppo in the west to Raqqa in the east (its Syrian stronghold) and the border areas with Iraq, gaining control of oilfields and trading networks in the process. In slowly establishing the tenets of what it believed to be an Islamic State, ISIS's actions brought it into direct confrontation with other anti-regime groups including Jabhat al-Nusra, with which it had aligned at the onset of the conflict. As with other organisations in the past such as Al Qaeda in Iraq, ISIS knew the benefit of controlling resources and trade routes. By the end of 2013 it had 'alienated most of the rebel groups by creating smothering checkpoints, confiscating weapons and imposing its ideology on the local population'.[31] In

February 2014, Al Qaeda officially distanced itself from ISIS, claiming it 'is not a branch of the al-Qaeda group' and 'does not have an organizational relationship with it and [Al Qaeda] is not the group responsible for their actions'.[32] Such tensions also arose between Al Qaeda and AQI under the leadership of al-Zarqawi.

Nevertheless, the appeal of ISIS to Sunni communities in Syria bore similar traits to AQI after 2003. ISIS infused itself amongst the tribal networks in peripheral areas, and as Dukhan and Hawat[33] note, a combination of economic strength, the instilling of fear and presenting itself as a valid alternative to the threat posed by Assad's regime (one could even include its supporters Iran in this), it was able to offer a semblance of order amidst increasing uncertainty and chaos. Indeed, with control of logistic routes and oilfields spanning across both Syria and Iraq, ISIS has been well placed to provide economic incentives and socio-economic support. Beyond their defined military objectives, Stephen McGrory, a security and humanitarian consultant, notes that a number of actors in the Syrian conflict implicitly recognise the importance of garnering local support and seek to achieve this through the provision of social services:

> The regime has prioritized the steady supply of flour and fuel to bakeries in areas still under government control, while attempting to disrupt this in opposition areas. A pattern has emerged over the past four years of the regime specifically targeting bread supply – bakeries, fuel, wheat flour supplies and entire wheat crops – in areas where it has lost territory.[34]

As McGrory notes, however, anti-Assad elements are equally adept in this process.

> ISIS and Jabhat al-Nusra have replicated the regime's focus on bakeries by an equivalent prioritisation on the distribution of cheap bread as a critical enabler to establishing, and maintaining, popular support from 'liberated' communities [...] ISIS in particular has a clear, patient and long-term policy of promoting bread as

a critical social service by distributing flour and fuel to functioning bakeries, and actively supporting the reconstruction of damaged bakeries and supply lines once an area has been taken. In addition, there is evidence of bread being distributed for free, by fighters, and often deliberately provided to the most vulnerable, poor and food-insecure groups within contested communities.'

For McGrory, ISIS capitalised on the vacuum in governance to consolidate its control and ultimately legitimise the Islamic Caliphate, presenting itself as a long-term solution to the region's uncertainty. To guarantee this foothold, it also applied a basic fiscal policy, applying taxation to material items, businesses and salaries, while simultaneously regulating trade. ISIS has therefore utilised local workers and networks to generate its income via general acquiescence. For example, oil from ISIS-controlled areas has reportedly been sold to local businesses, Assad's regime[35] and even to neighbouring countries such as Turkey.[36] It is precisely this complex network of actors that makes removing ISIS extremely difficult. Air strikes against its oil convoys for example may reduce ISIS profits, but at the same time they also remove the livelihoods of the local tribes and communities who rely on the work for their own sustenance, simultaneously weakening ISIS and deepening the grievances amongst the very communities that the West seeks to empower.

By June 2014, political and security conditions in Iraq had decreased sufficiently to allow ISIS to cross from Syria to Iraq in considerable military force, with little in the way of resistance. Once again utilising local networks and the efforts of other Sunni militant organisations, it eventually assumed de facto control of western border areas and main cities and towns. Firstly, it established its presence in Anbar province, in populated areas such as Qaim, Rawa, Rutbah, Hit, Fallujah, Karma and other smaller areas and, following this, to the north in Sinjar, Tal Afar, Mosul, Hawijah, Baiji and Tikrit. They even established footholds in the Baghdad belt areas, notably in the mixed populated provinces of Diyala, Babil and Salahaddin. Control over much of this territory and the logistic routes enabled ISIS to obtain a degree of financial autonomy and, with it, to offer a degree of protection and welfare to those in its territory. It is estimated that ISIS has generated in the region of US$80 million per month from its financial activities in both Syria and Iraq, with approximately 50 per cent obtained through taxation and the confiscation of items, and oil trade accounting for 43 per cent.[37]

Between two fragmented states, ISIS has projected itself as the custodian of an Islamist utopian society and at the vanguard of a fundamentalist Sunni Islamist movement, dedicated to violently defending its beliefs. This has been presented to an international audience through social media, causing shock, outrage and demands for a military response. Nevertheless, it is important not to lose sight of the circumstances and conditions that have combined to forge the situation where ISIS has emerged. The fragmentation of both Syria and Iraq is a consequence of a much more complex set of interactions that have occurred over a longer period of time. It is therefore through this melange of interactions that we have arrived at the current landscape, where the conditions for Sunni resistance and militancy have been cultivated.

Sunni militants re-energised in Iraq

By the summer of 2013, Iraq's major Sunni towns and cities were in open revolt against the Shi'a-led government.[38] Deteriorating socio-economic conditions along with a worsening security landscape enabled groups such as ISIS to grow in popularity and to establish footholds in Sunni communities, particularly in the western border areas of Anbar province. The border with Syria had been notoriously difficult to control, with a legacy of smugglers and tribes profiting from the lack of security and even applying their own form of governance. Controlling the border areas within the province, particularly Syria and Jordan, while maintaining tribal networks across the borders was – and remains – vital to preserving the trade and logistic routes vital to sustaining a programme of self-sufficiency.

By the summer of 2013, ISIS fighters in Iraq had asserted their authority on routes and towns near the borders in Anbar. In August of the same year, a YouTube video was posted showing the killing of three truck drivers of reported Alawite origin in the border area of western Anbar, on the main route to Baghdad.[39] The man who led the execution of the Syrian drivers wore long hair, a beard and combats, in the style now synonymous with ISIS fighters. Highlighting ISIS's ideology and radical militancy, the video also showed how ISIS used its local leverage to operate in strategically important areas, with impunity.

The man who conducted the executions was Shakir Waheeb al-Fahdawi, formerly of AQI and a Camp Bucca detainee, having been arrested by US soldiers in 2006 while fighting in Anbar. Being from the al-Fahdawi tribe (Dulaymi confederation), Waheeb's roots are in Anbar province or more specifically al-Madhaiq, a small village east of Ramadi where most of his family still reside. According to a source from al-Madhaiq 'Waheeb was a normal boy from a good family' but was drawn to the resistance movement and became more radical following his experiences of war and imprisonment, apparently threatening 'he would kill his own family for not supporting Daesh'.[40] Following the closure of Bucca, Waheeb was transferred to Tikrit where he was to await his own execution; however, he escaped following an attack on the prison – a strategy regularly employed by ISIS fighters – in 2012. Since then, he has become somewhat of a poster figure for ISIS and, according to sources in Anbar, instrumental in organising offensives in Fallujah and Ramadi during ISIS's large-scale conquests.

Shakir Waheeb's timeline offers a useful case study of how domestic conditions have produced a local ISIS fighter, but it also highlights failures in Iraq's security apparatus. Nevertheless, in 2013 ISIS was only one of many groups vying for a foothold in Iraq and their violent actions had already drawn much criticism from within Sunni tribal and political quarters. In response to the changing conditions, alliances developed once more and in January 2014 al-Majlis al-Askari li-Thuwar al-Asha'ir al-Iraq, or Military Council of Iraqi Tribal Revolutionaries (GMCIR), officially announced its formation on Twitter. The GMCIR was composed of a network of tribes, former military personnel, Sunni militant group members and religious leaders such as Sheikh Harith Sulayman al-Dhari of the Muslim Scholars Association. The grouping had been under formation since the summer of 2013, but projected itself as a legitimate leadership council for revolutionary groups of Sunni denomination across Iraq.[41] According to research conducted by Heras,[42] there were 75,000 fighters associated with the GMCIR concentrated in the provinces of Anbar, Salahaddin and Ninawah, with armed affiliates in Baghdad, Diyala, Kirkuk and amongst the predominately Shi'a provinces Karbala, Dhi Qar and Maysan in the south of Iraq. It also drew on external networks in Jordan, Turkey, Lebanon, Saudi Arabia and the United Arab Emirates, many of whom were also able to tap into networks in their residing countries that had similar issues with the pro-Iranian agenda in Iraq.

At the local level, prominent members of the GMCIR included former Baathists within the JRTN,[43] who had established a strong presence in the emerging resistance movement in Kirkuk and Ninawah provinces in the north of the country. The majority of the GMCIR's members were tribal fighters, many of whom had participated in the Sahwa programme and took up arms once more as uncertainty in their communities heightened. Some of these former Sahwa members joined other local councils, several of which overlapped with the GMCIR through its members and affiliates. For example, across the provinces of Anbar, Salahaddin and Ninawah, a number joined the Military Council of the Tribal Revolutionaries (MCTR). Many of these same fighters and others in Anbar chose to join Sheikh Ali Hatem al-Suleiman's Military Council of Anbar Tribal Revolutionaries (MCATR), including fighters from within the Dulaymi confederation of tribes, such as the Albu Nimr and Albu Issa as well as members from the al-Jabbouri and al-Janabi.[44] While calling for autonomy, these groups targeted government security forces in what they believed to be part of a legitimate resistance movement. They were joined by the Fallujah Military Council (FMC), a non-GMCIR aligned (but with affiliations) collection of militant groups led by the Salafist Abu Abdullah al-Janabi, a former senior member in the Mujahideen Shura Council of Fallujah post-2004 that had AQI as a part of it.[45] This time around, the FMC included former members of the 1920 Revolutionary Brigades via the new title of Hamas in Iraq, the Islamic Army of Iraq and, of course, ISIS.[46]

Despite evident ideological and strategic tensions between the various councils and particularly ISIS, there existed a common goal and a strong enough network between the tribes and various militant groups to establish an operational understanding. For example, as members of the Sunni insurgency in Anbar consolidated their control over its villages and towns, the ISIS-led attack on Mosul in June 2014 further stretched Iraq's security forces. In an interview in June 2014, Ahmed al-Dabbash, leader of the IAI, declared this was part of a larger movement: 'Is it possible that a few hundred ISIS jihadists can take the whole of Mosul? No. All the Sunni tribes have come out against Maliki.'[47] However, al-Dabbash, like many of the other factions involved with the large-scale assault, believed its relationship with ISIS was one of convenience in what was supposed to be an holistic effort to establish an autonomous region, and therefore a relationship that could be controlled considering the relative size of ISIS's organisation compared to the combined councils. Al-Dabbash even stated the IAI were 'not extreme like ISIS', were 'one of the biggest factions fighting' and would accept 'western military support to stop Maliki'.[48]

During the early summer months of 2014, operational partnerships continued to bear fruit, particularly as the Sunni movement gained momentum heading south through Kirkuk, Salahaddin and Diyala, towards the Baghdad belt areas. Two former Iraqi generals associated with both the JRTN and GMCIR were placed in strategic positions in Anbar and Salahaddin,[49] and other militant factions including IAI, the MA and Ansar al-Islam, along with other tribal fighters, formed part of the offensive, securing areas from the government. As suggested by Hassan Hassan,[50] it was a failure to politically engage these other non-ISIS forces during their period of formation that allowed for the more radical elements to emerge.

On 12 June 2014, ISIS executed what initially appeared to be hundreds of mostly Shi'a army recruits from Camp Speicher near Tikrit, in Salahaddin province. More recent evidence has suggested that this number is closer to 1,700,[51] emphasising the brutality and scale of ISIS violence but also affirming the sectarian trajectory of the conflict. With Iraq's military evidently weak, on 13 June 2014 Ali Sistani called upon all Shi'a men who were able to do so to join the fight against ISIS, which led to the establishment of the Hashd al-Shabi, or popular movement. This was followed by rhetoric from al-

Maliki on 17 June 2014, who evoked Shi'a narratives when he called for a military campaign in Anbar, akin to 'the followers of Hussein and the followers of Yazid', a reference to a seventh-century defining Shi'a battle. Such calls from Sistani and al-Maliki would only deepen sectarian grievances across the state. From this point, not only did Sunni communities have to contend with the government's forces, but also those of a popular Shi'a movement that contained a number of prominent Shi'a militias whose violent actions against Sunnis had been well documented during the mid- to late 2000s.

ISIS slowly gained control of the Sunni insurgent movement, but by the end of summer 2014 disagreements between it and other groups had intensified. In August 2014, the GMCIR accused ISIS of trying to hijack the 'revolution' following its attack on the Yazidi community near the northwestern town of Sinjar, which brought about international condemnation. Such actions precipitated the divide between ISIS and other insurgent groups, but this did not stop ISIS in their efforts to establish a caliphate. ISIS targeted dissonant Sunni factions and potential opposition, killing over 200 members of the Albu Nimr tribe as part of its attempts to establish authority in Anbar, during October 2014.[52] This strategy, coupled with the threat of international reprisals, caused groups such as IAI, JRTN and MA to break ties with ISIS. In the case of MA, in August 2014, it refused to either pledge allegiance to ISIS leader al-Baghdadi or leave Karma (in east Anbar province), which led to ISIS kidnapping MA members, shelling and detonating the homes of MA members and even refusing tribal mediation.[53] MA, like many of the other insurgent groups that were part of the initial offensive, either withdrew, fractured (many members even joining ISIS) or operated under the ISIS banner. ISIS were, however, able to pay salaries to their fighters through an intricate network of financing that included the sale of oil, taxation and the maintenance of local industry; this enticed many to join their ranks, a public relations opportunity ISIS was able to capitalise on. For instance, despite Ansar al-Islam openly rejecting ISIS's advances in Iraq, in August 2014 it was reported that 50 of its leaders had declared allegiance to ISIS, a statement that was rejected by Ansar al-Islam,[54] and approximately 90 per cent of its fighters also joined ISIS.[55] It is not known whether this claim was entirely true, and Ansar al-Islam have continued in some capacity to resist ISIS in the north of Iraq. It is likely, however, that they lost much of their strength following ISIS's gains in the summer of 2014.

Although ISIS gained control of much of the territory and the logistics routes that linked these territories following the 2014 offensive, opposition from a number of the factions still remains. Indeed, low-level fighting between the supporters of JRTN and ISIS is well documented in Kirkuk, with reports of attacks and reprisals by ISIS across the province. In one particular case on 1 December 2015 and in response to previous attacks, ISIS reportedly kidnapped 35 members belonging to JRTN and Ansar al-Islam in the south of Kirkuk province.[56] It is likely that the fate of those kidnapped will be execution, consistent with ISIS's strategy of making its surrounding Sunni areas in Iraq subservient to its demands. Nevertheless, persisting resistance from other factions also shows a degree of disharmony and the potential for the development of a larger resistance movement, akin to the Sahwa. Sunni tribes and communities have little faith in the Iraqi government, though, and because of fears of retribution, working with the USA and other coalition forces will take time to develop, particularly to the level of synergy witnessed in the Kurdistan region, where a degree of unity amongst the Kurdish factions enabled a coordinated response against ISIS. Moreover, Shi'a actors have also lost faith in the government, in part led by the Al Sadr, resulting in the storming of parliament on 30 April 2016.

The inability of the Iraqi government to confront ISIS as a unified entity is indicative of its fragmentation over a longer period of time. In addition, security failings were also furthered by a political system that had failed to provide the appropriate opportunities and mechanisms to allow for greater Sunni participation. By doing this ISIS has not only isolated a large bulk of its society, capable of aiding its development as a state, but contributed to the country's chaotic circumstances.

Failing Iraq and the security apparatus

As previously noted, the Sahwa programme generated short-term success but the political and sectarian issues that had helped drive the insurgency following the 2003 invasion were never truly resolved. Initial signs were positive; after all, the USA had agreed to withdraw by 2011 and inclusivity was aided by the drafting of Sunni Arabs from communities and tribes into the security forces, particularly in Anbar where the local and federal police forces were bolstered. Despite this, the majority of Iraq's Sunni Arab communities remained on the periphery.

From 2006 up to the summer of 2014, al-Maliki's own ambition, along with his power bargaining with hard-line Shi'a nationals only managed to increase the schism between Sunni communities and the Shi'a Dawa-dominated government. Much like under Saddam, patronage networks were built and loyalty was rewarded through governmental positions, benefiting a number of hard-line Shi'a figures and Shi'a militia members in particular. As a former member of the Iraqi intelligence service between 2007 and 2010 noted, 'They [hard-line Shi'a] wanted to control all functions of government, to protect their power and gain financially, but in doing this they undermined or removed experienced technocrats.'[57]

For example, Iraq's intelligence service was re-established in 2004 under US supervision. The Iraqi National Intelligence Service (INIS), as it became known, was first led by a former officer in Saddam's army, General Mohammed Shahwani, a Sunni Arab who had fled Iraq in the 1990s before becoming part of an attempted CIA-led coup against Saddam Hussein in 1996.[58] In order to counter US influence and assert control, al-Maliki and the Dawa party sought to challenge the INIS, even creating a parallel intelligence network as part of the Ministry of State for National Security Affairs (MSNS).[59] Shahwani retired from his position in 2009, reportedly in response to al-Maliki's misuse of intelligence leading up to 'Black Wednesday',[60] when four large bombings in Baghdad by Sunni militants killed 183 people. Politicisation of the security sector has remained a theme and its inherent dysfunction was further aided by a political quota that has enabled the appointment of 'incompetent individuals to leadership position on the basis of political loyalties rather than ability and national needs'.[61] Drawing on Iraq's sectarian cleavages and internal power struggles, this process has entrenched mistrust between the various groups and, in doing so, removed the mechanisms needed for coordination and intelligence gathering in particular, causing a fundamental weakening in security, a legacy of al-Maliki's tenure that has proved difficult to overturn.

Favouritism and the buying of loyalties also affected the military. Experienced Sunni officers were removed from their high-ranking positions and replaced with Shi'a commanders who were given authority to 'run battalions, brigades, or divisions as personal fiefdoms extracting revenues from procurement deals or collecting "taxes" from subordinate ranks'.[62] Iraq's military was already a skeleton of its former self and, in reality, international donors had no intention of investing in the creation of a strong force post-2003. Nevertheless, as part of the development programme, finances were made available. By 2012, the USA had made $US25.26 billion available to Iraq's government for the training, equipping and sustaining of the ISF, and for the infrastructure of the Ministry of Defence and Ministry of Interior.[63] However, by 2008 both the police force and army were already finding it difficult to recruit and were witnessing an increasing number of members failing to turn up, with 3 per cent of the military absent without leave (AWOL) on a monthly basis.[64] To counteract this trend, former Sunni officers were drafted in to make up for the 30 per cent depletion in leadership numbers, and while a small number of the thousands approached were given official positions, the majority that did sign up had no orders. A former Iraqi army general said 'we were asked to attend work at an airbase in Baghdad, but it was soon very clear that it was all for show'.[65]

Iraq's military expenditure had more than doubled from 1.9 per cent of GDP in 2006 to 4.3 per cent in 2014, but the security sector in general was unprepared to deal with the assault. In response to these flaws, the new prime minister, Haider al-Abadi, set about purging the security sector of its corrupt and incapable officials, including many supporters of al-Maliki.[66] Dozens of military commanders were removed from their posts and even the Minister of Interior, Adnan al-Asadi, was replaced. In December 2014, al-Abadi revealed 50,000 'ghost soldiers' were still receiving salaries from the government despite not having any record of attendance. Many of these ghost soldiers were missing, deserters, retirees or dead, but the commanding officers had not removed their names from the payroll. According to

Iraqi army sources, 'The commanders did not report the real numbers to keep getting the [ghost soldiers'] salaries, so no one could do anything to stop the collapsing of troops at that time.'[67] So when ISIS and its affiliates secured control of areas in Mosul and the provinces of Anbar and Salahaddin, this was because the 'battalion or brigade has to have at least two-thirds of its boots on the ground to attack [...] but because of the corrupted commanders, the fighting capability of the Iraqi troops was no more than 20 per cent'.[68]

By the summer of 2014, the security apparatus was much weaker than initially assumed and, as a consequence, was unable to respond to the ISIS-led summer offensive. Security forces were ill-equipped, untrained and unmotivated to deal with the situation, all the more obviously when compared to the response in the Kurdistan region from Kurdish forces despite their own political fractures. ISIS social media accounts and YouTube uploads captured evidence of their forces taking villages, towns and cities and, in some cases, ISF fleeing checkpoints and positions on roads and highways. Such videos helped to cultivate a climate of fear that would surround the group and increase perceptions of its military prowess. ISIS took security vehicles and stockpiles of military weapons along the way, accumulating an armoury and enough momentum to support a long-term struggle with the government of Iraq. What security forces remained were relatively small in number, limited in supplies and often without pay.

Sunni Arab tribal leaders and other political figures from within Sunni communities called for the government to arm their fighters to confront ISIS; however, both al-Maliki and al-Abadi showed reluctance to do so. Much of this was related to the way in which the second Sunni revolt emerged, where former Sahwa fighters and others who had supported the anti-AQI movement turned on the government and its security forces. Weapons were readily available and the Iraqi government had procured a considerable number of them. According to a local source from Ramadi, at the beginning of the revolt in 2012 'some groups (militant factions) were already buying up the weapons from the villages and towns', adding, 'You can't blame them; they needed the money'.[69]

In addition to this, documents seized by US forces in Mosul during 2010 also linked a number of senior Sunni political figures to ISIS,[70] who at this point in time had established itself a network for smuggling and other illegal activities in Mosul. Some of the officials cited in these documents can be considered political opportunists, who also sought financial gain from the illegal activity of groups such as ISIS. For instance, following ISIS gaining control of Mosul, one such name was the former Ninawa province governor, Atheel al-Nujaifi[71], who called for the devolution of power in Iraq and the creation of a Sunni Arab army to confront ISIS.[72]

While mistrust and corruption are evident, another reason affecting the government's support for a Sunni Arab army was the worsening economic conditions. With its finances dependent on the price of oil, which took a dramatic downturn during 2015, bottoming out at US$28 per barrel, the government has been forced to cut public expenditure significantly. In October 2015, an officer from a border crossing in Anbar and a federal police officer based in the western Anbar town of Haditha, a town which is constantly under attack from ISIS forces, declared they had not received their salaries for 'six months'.[73] Following the near collapse of Iraq's army in the summer of 2014, much of the funding available was diverted to the *Hashd al-Shabi* (or people's movement), the Shi'a-dominated popular forces that were established under government supervision following Sistani's call to arms in June 2014. The *Hashd* are led by the pro-Iranian Badr organisation's leader, Hadi al-Ameri, who is deputised by leaders of prominent Shi'a militias, Qais Khasali of Asaib al-Haq and Abu Mehdi Muhendis of Kataib Hezbollah.

The *Hashd al-Shabi*, which consists of people from predominately Shi'a but also Sunni, Turkmen, Yazidi and even Christian communities, was established to defend Iraq, but most of its strength is drawn from the trained and more experienced pro-Iranian Shi'a militias. A number of these groups, such as Asaib al-Haq (AAH)[74] and Kataib Hezbollah (KH), have gained notoriety for their attacks against US forces post-2003, their confronting of Sunni militant organisations such as AQI and the sectarian targeting of Sunnis. In a growing trend since 2013, some Shi'a militias are reported to be complicit in the 'cleansing' of mixed ethnic areas in Babil province, Diyala province and Baghdad, while claims of attacks against Sunnis have also been made in Kirkuk and Salahaddin province.[75] This has included abductions, killings and extortion of Sunni individuals and families, a situation that has worsened since the summer of 2014.

Uncertainty in Iraq is indicative of its fragmentation, further fuelled by the inability of its government to provide security for its entire population across ethnic and sectarian divides. This has allowed forces at the radical end of the spectrum to fill the vacuum left by the weakened government, which, in turn, has itself looked towards the Shi'a militias for support. In essence, this has resulted in the establishment of parallel security infrastructures, condoned by the state. This has created further mistrust in Iraq's Sunni Arab communities, where galvanised by political rhetoric from Shi'a hard-liners and the actions of the Shi'a militia, it has provided cause for the mobilisation of militant factions. Such conditions have allowed both AQI and ISIS to take advantage of the situation, once more perpetuating the sectarian schism and the fragmentation of Iraq. Without the appropriate curtailing of these political and ideological forces, even with the removal of ISIS militarily, the conditions for civil conflict and Sunni militancy will remain.

Enduring Sunni militancy

Groups such as ISIS do not represent the majority of Sunnis in Iraq, nor do Shi'a militias represent the Shi'a community. Yet in conditions where a weak government and uncertainty across both Shi'a and Sunni communities is prevalent, the struggle for power and ensuing violence is likely to remain. The power vacuum has therefore allowed for the emergence of armed militant factions who wield considerable authority in their respective localities and, in the case of the Shi'a militia in particular, at the national level, and often with impunity.

The role of the Shi'a militias has proven pivotal in re-establishing government momentum against ISIS, but this success has come at a cost. A thirst for revenge for the loss of family and loved ones exists amongst the Shi'a population and this has tended to feed the sectarian dimension of the struggle. In doing so, it has provided the more radical elements of the *Hashd al-Shabi* with justification for their actions, not just against militants but Sunni communities as well. There are stories of families in the predominantly Shi'a south of the country demanding – and receiving – the heads of Sunni militants as reparation for the loss of family members in conflict, and war souvenirs are also increasingly common.[76] Such issues will only serve to perpetuate the cycle of violence and the sectarian mistrust. The 'cleansing' of areas by Shi'a militias is unlikely to have a positive sustainable impact on the security situation across the state, as witnessed in the mixed sectarian provinces of Babil and Diyala.

Since 2003 the security conditions in the north of Babil province have caused problems for first the occupying forces and subsequently the Iraqi government. As a former Baathist stronghold directly south of Baghdad, the area became synonymous with its pockets of resistance and vibrant Sunni militancy, earning the label 'Triangle of Death' from the US military. Its predominately Sunni population has suffered from the same political and socio-economic conditions that engulfed many other Sunni areas following the removal of Saddam Hussein. Factoring in its past, this has increased its susceptibility to radical elements of Sunni Islam, such as AQI, as it did in presenting itself as an ideal location for ISIS to embed its core fighting forces, an event that eventually justified a full-scale Iraqi security force and *Hashd al-Shabi* (albeit mostly established Shi'a militia) operation in October 2014.

The deployment of Shi'a militias into northern Babil was a hugely controversial move, yet despite this, it led to the removal of ISIS's core fighting force by the end of October 2014. Nevertheless, as a consequence of these actions, Sunni Arab communities were systematically removed from their land, causing an increase in the number of internally displaced persons (IDP), placing an increasing economic burden on the state and ultimately causing greater uncertainty across the region. Through the creation of these conditions, the government has become complicit in the proliferation of sectarian tension, explored in more detail in Chapter 5. As the following statistics highlight (Graph 5.1), even after the expansion of ISIS in the summer of 2014 and the subsequent government-militia security operations in the autumn of the same year that removed ISIS's main force, statistics indicate that Sunni militant activity remained in the early months of 2015, albeit low-level asymmetric activity, which nonetheless questions the limits of the clearance strategy.

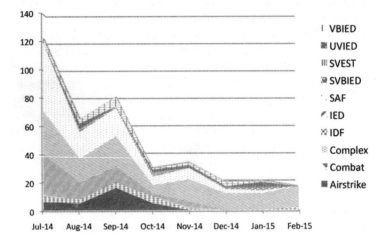

Graph 5.1 Number of incidents in Babil province between July 2014 and February 2015. (The thickness of the line denotes the actual number of a particular type of attack relative to the number of incidents in total.)[77]

The security operations in the north of Babil were successful in that they removed ISIS as a core fighting force, and over time reduced logistic routes into the capital Baghdad. Statistics also show a marked improvement in security when comparing the current situation to the period between July and October 2014. This is, of course, related to the end of security operations, and the reduction in combat and other attacks such as airstrikes, mortars and artillery rockets (commonly known as indirect fire or IDF) and small arms fire (SAF). Incidents reported therefore decreased from 123 in July 2014 to 17 in February 2015 (see Graph 5.1).

Nevertheless, despite the reduction in conventional warlike methods, an asymmetric threat has persisted, affecting the lives of the remaining provincial population. Shi'a Arab civilians, Shi'a militia and security forces in what were predominately Sunni but mixed areas like Jurf al-Sakhar, Latifiya, Iskandariya, Yousifia and Mahmudiya continue to be targeted on a consistent basis by improvised explosive devices (IEDs).[78] Indeed, on reviewing the statistical information we can see that IED attacks have remained at a relatively high rate since August 2014 when security operations began, becoming the main form of attack following the end of the more conventional form of fighting. This suggests that Sunni militancy continued despite the removal of ISIS's core fighting force. Secondly, on viewing the data collected in Graph 5.2, it reveals that the targeting of civilians has also remained constant since the end of the government-militia security operations in the province during November 2014.[79] This is particularly evident when compared to the targeting of Sunni militants (marked AOG) and government aligned forces (marked GAF). Between November and February, civilians were targeted; 17, 17, 22 and 15 times respectively.

The cleansing of areas in northern Babil had a significant impact upon Sunni communities in both the province and across Iraq, adding to the insecurity in the longer term. Evidence of the damage caused

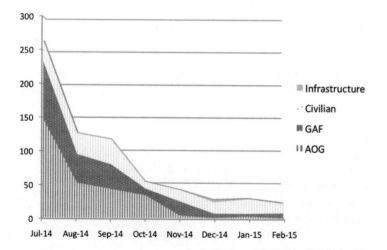

Graph 5.2 Attack targets and estimated casualty numbers during the period July 2014 to February 2015. (The thickness of the line denotes the number of a particular target casualty relative to the number of attacks in total.)[80]

can be seen in Jurf al-Sakhar, a predominately Sunni town in northern Babil that bore the brunt of government-militia security operations.

Jurf al-Sakhar,[81] like most of its surrounding areas, is known for its historical links to the Baath party but, after 2003, to Sunni militancy. Its location, approximately 35 km south of Baghdad's city parameters on the banks of the Euphrates and 30 km northeast of the city of Karbala, makes it a strategically important area for the launching of attacks against government and Shi'a interests. Following the expansion of ISIS's main fighting force into Iraq, Jurf al-Sakhar became a natural stronghold.

Government forces had made a number of efforts to take control of the town dating back as far as 2013, forcing a majority of the 80,000 residents to flee. By the end of October, government and militia forces had established control. This involved the total clearing of the town and surrounding rural areas, leading to the confiscation of land and the separation of families. Women and children were placed in compounds while the fate of a number of their men has not yet been determined. According to an Iraqi security spokesperson, the 'families were harbouring Islamic State [...] The judicial system will decide their fate.'[82] Unfortunately, the reality has not been as transparent. The distinction between 'Jihadi' and 'Sunni' became blurred amidst the security operations, and reports of militias Asa'ib Ahl al-Haq and Kataib Hezbollah active in the area,[83] and it is likely that a blanket security policy became the norm. Jurf al-Sakhar remains dormant, its buildings destroyed and emptied. In addition to this, despite initial indications from the government that those with no ties to Sunni militants would be allowed to return to their land, it has still not happened. It has even been mooted that the area may be used as a forward operating base for future offensives in Anbar.

A similar pattern of violence emerged in Diyala province in the summer of 2014, when a small number of its Sunni Arab villages and towns came under the influence of ISIS and other affiliated groups. Following clearance operations, which peaked in November 2014, both incident numbers and the scale of attack decreased. However, following this relative success and the redeployment of some security forces to other combat areas, asymmetric attacks, particularly IEDs, have persistently targeted Shiʻa Arabs and security forces and since March 2015 there has been a notable increase in the level of violent attacks.

Looking at Graph 5.3, the data between August 2014 and June 2015 reveals a trend that only asymmetric violence increased and violence intensified, thus suggesting a return to the conditions witnessed in the summer of 2014. This potentially opens the door to high-impact attacks and an escalation of violence between both Shiʻa and Sunni Arab communities, as witnessed on 17 July in the southwest of Diyala province, when a suicide vehicle attack (SVBIED) in a market area of Khan Bani Saad, in the largely Shiʻa populated district of Baquba, killed at least 100 people and injured many more during an Eid gathering.[84]

Diyala province is a flashpoint area, given its mixed Shiʻa and Sunni population. Since late summer 2014, Shiʻa militias have maintained a

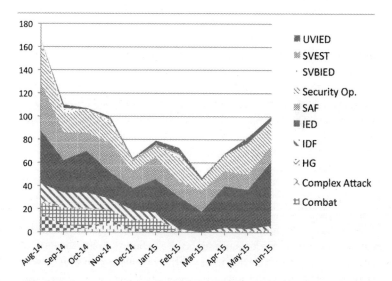

Graph 5.3   Number of incidents in Babil province between August 2014 and June 2015. (The thickness of the line denotes the actual number of a particular type of attack relative to the number of incidents in total.)[85]

strong presence in Diyala, which Human Rights Watch suggests has led to an increase in kidnappings, execution-style killings and the forced removal of Sunni populations.[86] In Muqdadiyah alone, which is in the centre of the province just east of the River Diyala, Human Rights Watch states that at least 3,000 (mostly Sunnis) fled their homes following June 2014, many of whom have since been unable to return. One person declared that 'when we tried to return home, our house was being used by somebody else. We are sure they are a Shi'a family, but what can we do? The government is not on our side.'[87]

A local police officer working in the area also said, 'many Sunnis have lost their homes, but some have fought back, sometimes with guns and sometimes using roadside bombs and placing bombs outside of buildings. Most of them are not Daesh, but they are desperate.'[88]

While we cannot be sure about the specific number of attacks in Diyala that are linked to ISIS, a number of the attacks are conducted by locals and driven by local issues. This again has the potential to form part of something much bigger, to become part of the larger struggle that continues to be proliferated by the extreme sectarian elements. Throughout 2015, retaliatory attacks continued and in January 2016 the escalation of violence caused Sistani to condemn the activity of Shi'a militias acting outside the law, while Prime Minister al-Abadi called for calm.[89] However, with both a weak government and the pro-Iranian Badr and militia Asaib al-Haq maintaining a strong presence in Diyala, any peaceful resolution would have to include the involvement or acquiescence of the latter two, an issue unlikely to be supported by the Sunni communities at large.

The long-term threat of Sunni militancy

While Sunni communities have been targeted in an effort to remove the threat of ISIS, this has also served as a pretext for the more radical elements of the Shi'a militia to assert their power in the state. As the previous statistics have shown, such strategies have failed to enhance human security, as asymmetric attacks persist in and around the areas that have been targeted as part of government-militia operations. Policies that continue to cause the displacement of people or cultivate fear are therefore unlikely to reduce militant activity beyond the removal of ISIS and other related groups as a core fighting force. Events similar to those witnessed in northern Babil and Diyala have also been evident in other provinces across Iraq, even Sunni majority provinces such as Anbar and Salahaddin. For example, following the involvement of Shi'a militia in areas such as Habbaniyah, Husaybah and Khaldiyah in Anbar province during the first quarter of 2015, a number of incidents involving the looting and blowing-up of Sunni Arab homes were reported. A police officer from Anbar was quoted saying, 'These militias broke into empty homes and stole cars. In one example, my cousin's car was stolen from his house, and later reported in Baghdad, where it was being sold.'[90]

Financial profiteering in an environment of such economic insecurity is also fuelling crime and sectarian tensions. An Iraqi journalist in Baghdad added to this: 'In Sadr City, there is a market under a bridge that people call "Daesh" market (Souk al-Daash). On the market they sell cars, electrical and other consumer items stolen from Sunni houses in Baghdad and from other provinces.'[91]

In the north of Iraq, similar concerns have been raised regarding Sunni Arab communities near ISIS strongholds Hawija and Mosul, particularly as Kurdish[92] forces consolidate and advance their own regional borders that cut across Ninawa, Kirkuk and (north) Diyala provinces. The situation in the north is even more fluid as it draws national, ethnic and sectarian cleavages into the struggle within the context of the fight for Kurdish autonomy.

Since August 2014, reports have documented the establishment of 'security zones' by Kurdish forces to hold Sunni Arabs displaced from areas near the Kurdistan regional border in the conflict with ISIS.[93] Amnesty International has also reported the displacement of thousands of Sunni Arabs and destruction of numerous villages previously populated by Sunni Arabs.[94] Even in the Yazidi[95] majority town of Sinjar in Ninawa, close to the Syrian border, tensions have escalated following the removal of ISIS by Kurdish-led forces in November 2015. Kurdistan region president and leader of the KDP, Masoud Barzani, had his Peshmerga forces lead the assault, but they were also joined by rival Kurdish factions the Kurdistan Workers Party (PKK) and its Yazidi and Syrian Kurdish affiliates known as the Sinjar Resistance Units (YBS) and People's Protection Units (YPG) respectively.[96]

According to one Yazidi fighter known as Mr Ceedo, ISIS 'took the honour of Yazidis' and, referring to Sunni Arabs in general, there was 'no way' they would be welcomed back.[97] The suffering of the Yazidi community at the hands of ISIS has led to retribution and blaming of Sunni Arabs for ISIS's discretions. This hostility is highlighted in a personal account of a Sunni Arab male reported by Amnesty International:

> After the Peshmerga and the Yezidis and the PKK recaptured the area in December 2014 we were told by Peshmerga officers that we would be able to go back home within a few days. But then we started to hear that Yezidis and PKK militias were staying in our village and would attack any Arabs who went there [...] A few days later our village was burned down. Three weeks later the Yezidis and the PKK burned several other villages nearby and killed several villagers.[98]

Such actions against Sunni communities are unlikely to herald stability, and could even contribute to sustained acts of violence, as shown in Diyala and Babil provinces. As highlighted by an aid worker in Sinjar, 'Now the Yazidis have become just like Daesh [...] If our rights will not be given back, we will fight them.'[99]

Under Barzani, the Kurdistan region has assumed responsibility for the security of Sinjar and its surrounding villages and towns. Controlling this area allows them to monitor logistical routes used by ISIS, but it also broadens the borders of the Kurdistan region. Despite their own internal political schisms, the Kurdish regional government has used the weakening of Iraq's sovereignty following ISIS advancements to assert its control over its border areas, thus strengthening its claim for independence. In the long term, this is likely to trigger a response not only from Sunni Arabs, but Shi'a Arabs and Turkmen as well, a microcosm of which is being played out in the mixed ethnic and sectarian province of Kirkuk.

Iraq's complexities are highlighted in the provincial border between Salahaddin and Kirkuk, where despite the existence of an anti-ISIS alignment, tensions between Sunni Arabs, Turkmen of both

Shi'a and Sunni faith, and Kurds continue to typify the country's historical creation and current fragmentation. In Tuz Khurmatu on 12 November 2015, low-scale fighting erupted between Kurds and Shi'a Turkmen as local disagreements over property and land led to the targeting of one another, the burning of shops and the involvement of both Kurdish Peshmerga forces and Shi'a militias. As noted by Adnan Abu Zeed, the disruption to this area which had remained relatively calm between 2003 and 2014, was caused by the withdrawal of Iraq's security forces from northern areas following the summer of 2014 and the subsequent land grab by Kurdish forces,[100] who claim their historical roots in the area of Tuz Khurmatu.

***

As this chapter has shown, Sunni militancy and the emergence of groups such as ISIS in Iraq is a symptom of the conditions that have been created, where sovereignty has slowly eroded and fragmentation of the state increased. These issues themselves are part of a dynamic historical process that has included international intervention, tribal relations and sectarian differences amongst many other interactive layers of overlapping influences. This chapter has also sought to highlight that stability in the region cannot be enhanced through land grabs or the targeting of particular ethnic or religious groups. As the statistics in the mixed Sunni–Shi'a Arab provinces have shown, strategies that have attempted to remove the threat of militancy through the cleansing of Sunni Arab majority areas have failed to enhance human security, as asymmetric attacks persist in and around the areas that were targeted. Policies that continue to cause the displacement of people or contribute to generating fear are therefore unlikely to reduce militant activity beyond the removal of ISIS as a core fighting force, and this should also be taken into account in the northern areas, where Kurdish forces have sought to take advantage of Iraq's fragmentation. Uncertainty, particularly in Sunni Arab majority areas and provinces, can be alleviated by projections of prosperity and access to decision-making processes. However, this will require considerable political and economic concessions and ultimately greater regional autonomy, which in creating a more stable environment could lead to further fragmentation.

6

The Human Tragedy

> Politics is concerned with the administration of home
> or city in accordance with ethical and philosophical
> requirements, for the purpose of directing the mass toward
> a behaviour that will result in the preservation and
> permanence of the (human) species.[1]

As Ibn Khaldun notes, politics is inherently about people. Be that at a
domestic, national or international level, politics is about the
administration of organisations, by people, for people. The case of Iraq
is no different. At the heart of this exploration into the fragmentation
of the Iraqi state and the rise of ISIS are people, whose lives have been
decimated by the failure of several regimes to fulfil their obligations to
citizens and by the ensuing manipulation of a vacuum that has allowed
groups to act in their own interests at the expense of others.
This chapter considers the impact of these actions on the Iraqi people.
As noted in earlier chapters, the responsibility of a sovereign state
includes protecting those people defined as citizens. In doing so, it
engages in the administration of governance over a particular area in
accordance with, as Khaldun notes, 'ethical and philosophical
requirements'. At the heart of this administration are existential
questions about the survival of the particular form of political
organisation.

A sovereign state also possesses a monopoly on the use of force,
demonstrating its power, authority and, technically, legitimacy. Yet
the monopoly over the use of force also serves to protect the citizens of
the state from others who may seek to exercise force over them. In the
case of Iraq, as noted in Chapters 2 and 5, the existence of strong
militias challenges the state's monopoly of the use of force, as
demonstrated by the rising violence from sectarian militias.[2]

The failure of the state to curb the power and influence of militias has had a serious impact upon the people of Iraq, creating an increasingly violent sectarian schism, driven in part by geopolitical considerations, with Iraqis caught at the heart of it. Clearly, this has not just resulted in large numbers of deaths, it has had an impact upon the displacement of peoples, seeking to find sanctuary free from the threat of violence or discrimination.

Despite the ruminations as to how best to resolve the crisis, find a diplomatic solution to the conflict and prevent the implosion of state infrastructure, this is fundamentally a story of human suffering on a regional level. While the crisis in Syria has affected over half the population, with an estimated 250,000 people dead, 4 million refugees and 7 million people displaced internally, the case of Iraq is equally tragic.

This chapter maps out the extent of the human tragedy in Iraq from the 2003 invasion to the present day. While previous chapters have dealt with the nature of high politics, this chapter focuses upon the impact of these high politics upon people. The chapter begins by outlining human rights violations under the CPA. It then considers the prime ministerships of Nouri al-Maliki and Haider al-Abadi, before unpacking the human cost of the rise of ISIS in Iraq. Across these sections, four themes are explored: deaths, displacements, structure and economy.[3] The chapter concludes by considering the ramifications of the Iraq conflict in the Middle East, but also internationally, given ISIS's ambitions and the number of foreign fighters in Iraq and Syria. In doing this, it draws upon personal accounts from Iraqis affected by the crises,[4] along with official reports from the United Nations, Human Rights Watch, Amnesty International and the International Crisis Group.

The CPA and transition

The chaos that emerged in the aftermath of the 2003 invasion was hardly surprising. Fuelled by the action of insurgents and the ensuing counter-insurgency programme, the situation across Iraq quickly deteriorated. Allegations of war crimes were rife, with reports suggesting that US soldiers had murdered incapacitated Iraqi combatants, forced civilians into battle zones and used unnecessary force against civilians.[5] The implications of this for quality of life were clear, with a dramatic impact upon women and children as the fabric of the Iraqi state was torn apart.

With the establishment of the CPA, a Law of Administration for the State of Iraq for the Transitional Period was introduced, which contained a bill of rights for Iraqi citizens.[6] The CPA also introduced emergency legislation enabling Prime Minister Ayad Allawi to declare martial law for periods of up to 60 days. It also allowed for the imposition of curfews, limited public gatherings, allowed for surveillance of communications, the closure of roads, sea lanes and air space, along with wide-ranging stop and search powers.[7] The CPA also reintroduced the death penalty, for 'certain crimes affecting internal state security, public safety, attacks on means of transportation, premeditated murder, drug trafficking and abduction'.[8] Yet at the same time, the judicial system was in dire need of reform, with the vast majority of defendants not having access to lawyers before trials, experiencing torture during the detentions (with confessions extracted under torture permissible[9]) and summary trials lasting less than 30 minutes. Perhaps most worryingly, there was no requirement that guilt be proved beyond reasonable doubt.

In 2005 violence increased, leading to large numbers of displacements across the state increasingly taking on a sectarian dimension, as noted in Chapter 5.[10] It is alleged that security services were behind hundreds of disappearances, although it is important to note that uniforms were easily available and often obtained by militias.[11] Regardless of who was responsible, these actions eroded faith in the security services and state institutions more broadly. The continuation of counter-insurgency operations resulted in damage and disruption to key infrastructure including water and electricity, and the destruction of homes.[12]

Clearly though, ongoing military action impinged on attempts to rebuild this infrastructure and boost the economy.[13] By 2005, it was estimated that women and children constituted 20 per cent of civilian deaths.[14] The emergence of Al Qaeda-affiliated organisations in

Anbar led to an increase in the number of violent incidents, with civilians particularly targeted.[15] Attacks were aimed at a number of different targets, including government officials, politicians, judges, journalists, humanitarian aid workers, doctors, professors, and those believed to be collaborating with the foreign forces in Iraq.[16]

On 17 July, over 98 civilians were killed and approximately 150 people were wounded in an insurgent attack in Baghdad.[17] While elections were planned to take place in January, voters faced an environment of insecurity and turmoil, along with a climate of fear,[18] with a marked increase in violence in the run-up to the elections.[19] This would be a recurring theme over the coming decade, as various actors sought to shape the nature of Iraqi politics through a 'bullet and ballot box' strategy. Judicial concerns also increased, particularly in light of anti-terrorism legislation and a broad definition of terrorism, along with the extension of the death penalty to new crimes, such as complicity.[20]

Discrimination also occurred along ethnic lines, with representatives of particular communities experiencing arbitrary detention amidst allegations that they were 'terrorists'. Furthermore, Sunnis complained about profiling and victimisation by security forces.[21] While US treatment of detainees has been well documented, detainees in Iraqi custody were also a serious issue, with incidents connected to the Ministry of Interior or Ministry of Defence.[22]

As the situation in Iraq deteriorated in 2006, taking on an increasingly violent sectarian dimension, civilians began to be targeted by militias.[23] This action was predominantly undertaken out of reciprocity or a failure to engage with grievances, or a sense of impunity for human rights violations.[24] The number of IDPs rose dramatically, with the figure in 2006 standing at 470,094.[25] Those displaced faced serious problems, namely, lack of shelters, food assistance, personal safety, access to school, health and other social services and economic resources.[26]

The al-Maliki and Abadi regimes

On 6 April 2005, the Iraqi National Assembly elected Jalal Talabani as President and nominated Nouri al-Maliki as prime minister.[27] Shortly after taking office, al-Maliki announced a 24-point plan in an attempt to reconcile the Iraqi state, which included provisions for amnesty, compensation for victims, a review of de-Baathification processes, punishment for war criminals and terrorists and the creation of the Supreme Committee for Dialogue and National Reconciliation. Despite this, during al-Maliki's tenure as prime minister, Iraq descended into a cycle of sectarian violence as long-standing grievances resulted in people turning to militias as the state failed to offer them protection.

The new regime also sought to restrict freedom of expression, both through legislation and harassment.[28] Academics and students were also affected, resulting in a number of academics leaving Iraq.[29] The judicial process continued to be problematic, with issues to do with overcrowding within the system and a limited capacity to investigate acts of violence across the state.[30] Human Rights Watch also documented how the judiciary was obstructed through intimidation, particularly when involved in cases of militia activities.[31]

The execution of Saddam Hussein in December 2006 heightened the suspicion with which many Sunnis viewed the Shi'a government.[32] As sectarian violence rose, the number of displaced people reached 4.4 million, with sectarian identity being cited as a key source of threats to their safety.[33] The failure to respond adequately to the displacement problem would be a recurring theme across the next eight years.[34] Tragically, a UN High Commissioner for Refugees (UNHCR) report articulates how Syria had admitted 30,000 Iraqis a month, many of whom would flee fighting in Syria four years later.[35]

In the aftermath of the 22 February attack on the al-Askari mosque in Samarra, reciprocal attacks on Sunni mosques were carried out.[36] Allegations that militia elements had joined the security services increased,[37] reducing confidence in state institutions and forcing people to turn to militias in order to ensure their security needs were met. These concerns were furthered by allegations of human rights violations including restrictions on freedom of movement, excessive use of force, theft during raids of private homes, and the demolition of houses.[38] Furthermore, the redistribution of ethnic groups to redraw the ethnic balance of a community only served to divide communities further, consolidating sectarian division.[39]

In addition to the sectarian dimension, militia-driven violence also resulted in the targeting of ethnic minorities,[40] along with public figures. Reflecting this increase in violence, between March and April, the Medico-Legal Institute in Baghdad issued 2,449 death certificates.[41] The precarious situation would also have a serious impact upon non-governmental organisation (NGO) activity,[42] resulting in several aid groups being threatened for helping people from different ethno-religious backgrounds.[43] Women and children were not exempt from the increasing violence, with honour crimes and kidnapping increasing[44] and many experiencing harassment and intimidation if they didn't conform to traditional dress codes.[45] The increase in violence against symbolic targets such as mosques and churches only served to fuel grievances between sects, with reciprocal acts of violence carried out across the state, resulting in many civilian casualties.[46] The deteriorating security situation also resulted in many changing their name in an effort to avoid associations with particular communities.[47]

From a range of sources, it is clear to see that the al-Maliki regime's control over events in Iraq was at its weakest in 2006–7, as noted earlier with the Sunni insurgency. As militias responded to attacks with their own, civilians were disproportionately affected. On 14 and 15 April, attacks in Karbala and Baghdad left hundreds dead.[48] Between July and September 2007, some of the deadliest since 2003 took place across Iraq. On 7 July an attack was carried out by what would later become known as vehicle-borne improvised explosive devices (VBIED), as a suicide truck bomb was detonated in Amerli, killing 160,[49] and on 14 August VBIEDs were used to target the Yazidi community, killing 350 and injuring 400.[50] As groups retreated into their sects and the militias took on more of a role in protecting communities, more hard-line views on the behaviour of actors within these communities were developed. One consequence of this was a marked increase in gender-based violence, which is grossly under-reported and often remains uninvestigated.[51] Since 2003, the number of reported rape cases has increased, but victims are considered of 'little value' and are likely to be killed by their families or subjected to reconciliation with their rapists.[52] A number of female bodies were found with notes accusing women of adultery or 'un-Islamic' conduct, signed by groups operating under the banner of *al-Amr bil-Ma'ruf wal-Nahi 'an al-Munkar* (The Propagation of Virtue and the Prevention of Vice).[53]

While the security situation improved in 2008 with a significant drop in violent, high-casualty attacks,[54] human rights violations remained unaddressed. The position of Iraq's displaced peoples was equally dire, with 2.8 million people displaced internally and a further 2 million abroad, predominantly in Syria and Jordan.[55] The situation was worsened by 11 of the 18 governorates preventing IDPs from accessing public services and aid and many struggling for work.[56] The introduction of Order 101 improved the situation for IDPs, allowing them to regain control of their occupied houses. This helped to improve the security situation and allowed almost 150,000 to return home.[57] One of the main reasons for the improved conditions in Iraq was the ceasefire called for by Muqtada al-Sadr.[58] Despite this ceasefire, suicide bombings continued to plague Iraq. In the first six months of 2008, suicide bombers in Baghdad, Karbala and Dyala perpetrated 13 attacks.[59] In the second six months, suicide bombings were combined with the widespread use of IEDs and magnetic bombs.

The fragmentation of the Iraqi state and its loss of control over the periphery during this period is perhaps best seen in Anbar province. Since 2003, Anbar has become a stronghold for resistance against both the occupation and the government, with Sunni militancy, including Al Qaeda, thriving in cities such as Fallujah and Ramadi. Much of this violence had subsided by 2011, with the US-sponsored 'Awakening' movement and sufficient Iraqi finances directed towards key tribal leaders, buying a modicum of stability. This was, however, only a temporary fix, as the worsening socio-economic conditions across Iraq invigorated protest movements. Militant organisations, including the 1920 Brigades and ISIS were able to take advantage of the situation, increasing their support base amongst disenchanted Sunnis.

The failure of the al-Maliki government to merge the Awakening movement into the national security infrastructure, coupled with a failure to improve economic conditions on the ground, furthered this opposition. The lack of greater political inclusion only served to fuel the grievances of those in Anbar, leading to increased insecurity, with senior figures such as tribal leaders and security personnel targeted.[60] Without the support of Baghdad, those who had been given authority by al-Maliki fragmented and dispersed, with several prominent tribal leaders seeking safe havens in Baghdad, Kurdistan, the Emirates or Jordan, furthering the power vacuum. One of the best examples of this is the case of Ahmed Abu Risha, the brother of Abdul Sattar Abu Risha, one of the founding members of the Awakening movement. Ahmed Abu Risha now spends most of his time in the Emirates, living off money from businesses established following the influx of money during the Awakening, or Sons of Iraq programme.[61] The deterioration of the security situation across Anbar continued in 2009, where 1,100 members of the ISF were killed, with the majority of the attacks occurring in Mosul, Baghdad and Anbar.[62]

In the six weeks after the US withdrawal of 30 June, a series of coordinated bomb blasts, seemingly carried out by Sunni insurgents, struck Shi'a targets including refugees, children, pilgrimages, weddings, funerals and hospitals, killing more than 700 Iraqis.[63] More elections were held in March 2010, but the Supreme National Commission for Accountability and Justice disqualified more than 500 candidates over alleged links to the Baath party.[64] Nouri al-Maliki's State of Law Coalition won 89 of the 325 seats, while Ayaad Allawi's al-Iraqiya list won 91,[65] yet a coalition was not formed until November and, once more, a political stalemate allowed militias to gain support.[66]

Even five years into al-Maliki's rule, civilians still lacked access to basic humanitarian services and were often denied the right of assembly, freedom of expression and religion, and protection from discrimination.[67] Armed groups continued to use tactics that deliberately targeted civilians, aimed at cultivating fear amongst the population, with religious festivals and processions increasingly targeted. In addition, militias increasingly resorted to criminal activity to fund their activities, further adding to instability. The overarching conclusion of this appears to stress the Iraqi government's failure to meet its obligation to ensure the security of its people.[68]

These problems re-emerged in the following years. In late March 2012, ISI – the Islamic State of Iraq, a precursor to ISIS – claimed responsibility for a number of suicide attacks that killed 71 people and injured more than 100.[69] The group also claimed responsibility for a number of other VBIED attacks in predominantly Shi'a public spaces across 2012.[70] While the motivations for ISI and Sunni militant attacks are, as argued previously, diverse, including the pursuit of a sectarian agenda, attacks were also carried out against other minority religious and ethnic groups.[71] Across the year, Sunni militias attacked Shi'a religious festivals, pilgrims and funerals.[72] An additional motivation, however, was to undermine government credibility, achieved through attacking the police and other facets of state infrastructure.[73]

State infrastructure was also challenged by the need to provide welfare and security to all those in the state. The escalation of the Syrian conflict had a dramatic impact on Iraq in 2013, when 206,137 people had fled the fighting, mostly to the Kurdistan region.[74] The impact on public services and local infrastructure was undeniable. Emboldened by the gains made by similar groups in the Syrian conflict,[75] Al Qaeda affiliated organisations in Iraq carried out nearly daily attacks against civilians.[76] The intensity of the violence is reflected in the number of civilians killed in 2013, which the United Nations Assistance Mission for Iraq (UNAMI) puts at 7,818 people, and a further 17,981 injured,[77] making it the deadliest year since 2008.[78] On 20 May, 46 incidents took place across Iraq, resulting in 102 casualties and 350 wounded. Of the 46, 19 took place in Baghdad alone.[79]

The following year saw elections for local councils across Iraq. Much as in previous years, candidates were targeted in the run-up to council elections, held in April, with 17 candidates killed.[80] In an effort to shape the outcome of elections, polling stations were also targeted in an attempt to intimidate people from voting, resulting in 11 civilian casualties and 90 injuries.[81] Yet the most seismic event in Iraqi politics that year would take place only four months later. On 14 August, 2014, Nouri al-Maliki announced his resignation, paving the way for Haider al-Abadi to become his successor. Frustrated at the al-Maliki regime's policies and the political stalemates that followed, coupled with concerns at the emergence of ISIS only two months earlier, a change was necessary at the head of Iraqi politics.

One of the first successes of the al-Abadi regime was to create a unity government to fight ISIS, drawing on figures from both Shi'a and Sunni parties. The results were immediately felt, with some tribal leaders falling into line but also followers of Muqtada al-Sadr also seeming to be in favour of the deal, with some suggesting that al-Abadi could bring about serious political reform.[82] In the summer of 2015, a year into his term, al-Abadi was able to pass reforms that would reduce tensions across Iraq. Facing power shortages that left some areas with only a few hours of electricity each day and allegations of corruption, al-Abadi was also able to eradicate the quota system that entrenched sectarian divisions within the political system.[83]

Ultimately though, the reforms enacted by al-Abadi occurred too late. The reciprocal attacks across Iraq post 2003 served to fuel and increase the divisions between community groups across Iraq. The implementation of a representative democracy allowed Iraq's Shi'a majority to gain power for the first time in Iraq's history but the divisive policies embraced by first al-Maliki then al-Abadi, who, despite his best efforts, has largely been unable to end the reciprocal violence. Many Sunnis found themselves stuck between a state that discriminated against them and seemingly did little to protect them and the militias that conducted violence against them.

The emergence of ISIS

[T]he spark has been lit here in Iraq, and its heat will continue to intensify – by allah's permission – until it burns the crusader armies in Dabiq.

(Abu Mus'ab al-Zarqawi)[84]

The emergence of ISIS in the summer of 2014 is undoubtedly a consequence of many of the grievances explored in the preceding chapters, and, while al-Zarqawi's spark is an obvious reference to the 2003 invasion, the previously documented events across Iraq could also be taken to be such a spark. While the policies of al-Maliki prioritised Shi'a over Sunni and failed to offer protection to Sunnis across the state, meaning that the Iraqi state had failed in its basic responsibility over its people, the roots of the emergence of the group are much deeper. The remainder of the chapter explores the continuation of many of the patterns identified earlier in the chapter. The impact upon people is clearly felt across ISIS-held areas, but also across Iraq broadly, as fear of the group spreads.

In the year since Abu Bakr al-Baghdadi declared the caliphate, it is estimated that ISIS is responsible for the deaths of 11,303 people with a further 18,627 injured.[85] Anecdotal reports suggest that a number of these deaths came as a result of civilians refusing to support the group, or its own supporters[86] refusing to fight. In cultivating a climate of fear across Iraq, ISIS was responsible for systematic killings and abductions, predominantly amongst people who opposed the group, or who posed a threat to it, such as members of ISF, the police, government officials, former members of Sawha, figures of authority from religious or tribal backgrounds, journalists, lawyers and doctors.[87] Military strategy placed fighters amongst civilians or within civilian areas, which is an infringement on several international laws,[88] often leaving the area mined when retreating.[89] The UNAMI/OHCHR (Office of the UN High Commissioner for Human Rights) is also aware of a number of mass killings carried out by ISIS, verified by the discovery of a number of mass graves. By 21 July, the IOM totalled the number of Iraqis displaced internally since the beginning of 2014 at 3,112,914, including some 250,000 from Ramadi since April 2015.[90] This poses severe challenges for providing shelter and welfare to those displaced. The IOM suggests that 67 per cent are sheltered in private locations,[91] 20 per cent are in dangerous shelters[92] and 8 per cent in temporary camps.

Attacks were carried out against a wide range of people, but predominantly against individuals from other ethnic and religious backgrounds, notably Christians, Yazidis, Turkmen, Shabk, Kurds, Shi'a and anti-ISIS Sunnis. This process typically involves the denial of fundamental rights and subjugation to abuse that is aimed at suppressing – and ultimately expelling – non-Sunni Muslims from ISIS-held territory, framed as a requirement to expel infidels from the caliphate. Although Christians are known as 'people of the book', which offers them a degree of protection in comparison with other religious groups, they have also been victims of forced displacement and the seizure and destruction of property. In addition, they are expected to convert to Islam. Failure to do so will result in them being subject to taxes, being expelled or killed.[93] Shi'a Muslims are expected to repent for their sins – as apostates – or to face penalties, including death. Other faith communities are expected to convert to Islam or be killed.

This systematic campaign against ethnic and religious minorities has led the UN to accuse ISIS of genocide and war crimes, arguing that this behaviour demonstrates an intent to 'destroy the Yazidi as a group'.[94] This allegation is given more credence when delving deeper into ISIS treatment of the Yazidis, where it is estimated that between 3,000 and 3,500 women and children, most of Yazidi descent, remain in ISIS captivity. Those who managed to escape reported gross violations of human rights while in captivity, along with calls to convert to Islam. Those who converted were married to ISIS fighters, and those who refused were subjected to sexual slavery; men who refused to convert were killed.[95] Furthermore, a UN report reveals eyewitness accounts of how hundreds of Yazidi men over the age of 14 were led to ditches and executed.[96]

The plight of women and children who are captured is especially tragic. They are often subjected to sexual violence while in captivity, with numerous testimonials reporting that ISIS fighters raped girls on a daily basis. A market for the sale of abducted women was created in the al-Quds area of Mosul, where women and girls were evaluated according to their age and beauty. After this, women and girls were given as 'gifts', or sold to ISIS fighters. Married women who converted were told that previous marriages were not valid under Islamic law and were given as wives.[97] A UN General Assembly report outlined how 'Girls would then be prepared for "marriage" (rape), involving, in some cases, full body searches. Mission investigators met with victims as young as 11 years of age.'[98] It continues:

> The mission obtained credible reports about the rape of young girls, including a 9-year-old and 6-year-old. The former was raped for three days by an ISIL fighter in Tel Qaseb, Ninawa governorate. A witness stated that she

could clearly hear the girl being assaulted and screaming out her name for help. The girl told the witness that she was blindfolded, handcuffed, beaten and repeatedly raped. Eventually, her 'owner' sold her to another ISIL fighter from the Syrian Arab Republic. In the same house, a 6-year-old girl was raped by another ISIL fighter. A witness heard the child screaming. She was reportedly sold to an ISIL fighter in the Syrian Arab Republic.[99]

After experiencing such horrors, the rise in suicides and attempted suicide is hardly surprising, with survivors displaying 'visible signs of trauma and depression'.[100]

What is immediately clear from these testimonials is that sexual violence is a tactic often used by the group to advance strategic priorities, namely: recruitment; fundraising, achieved through the sale of women and girls, along with ransom payments from families; the enforcement of discipline and order by punishment of dissenters or family members; to advance its ideology.[101] The al-Khansaa brigade notes how the most important way that women can aid the ISIS cause is by serving as wives and mothers and by introducing the ISIS ideology as early as possible.[102]

Life in ISIS-held territories is run in accordance with a strict interpretation and implementation of the Shari'a. These laws extend into everyday life, regulating speech, dress and travel. One reason for the number of foreign fighters wishing to join ISIS rather than other Islamist groups in the Syrian conflict is their strict adherence to the Qur'an and Shari'a. Punishments for breaking these laws are harshly enforced, including by torture and death sentences. UNAMI has recorded 165 executions carried out under the orders of 14 ISIS established courts.[103] These death sentences have resulted in public executions, usually by firing squad and conducted at times of day selected to ensure the highest possible turnout. Those executed included lawyers, doctors and parliamentary candidates, who were individuals with social influence.[104]

Socially, men are required to grow beards of a particular length and women are expected to wear the abaya when out in public; they are also expected to be in the company of a related male chaperone.

Within the confines of Mosul, civilians are free to move, although a bail system is in place for those wishing to leave. The need for a restriction demonstrates the ISIS leadership's concern at people leaving to join the resistance movement established by the governor of Mosul.[105]

It is important to note that, however unpalatable, some in ISIS-held territories are thankful for the group's presence. In Mosul, many had experienced persecution and discrimination along sectarian lines, under officials affiliated to Baghdad. The group has also eradicated crime within its territories, under the threat of draconian punishments. As Patrick Cockburn notes in a prescient work that began documenting the rising Sunni insurgency in Iraq, life in ISIS-held territory before the group seized it was tough for Sunnis, who faced discrimination from Baghdad.[106]

The extent of ISIS penetration of everyday life in parts of Iraq can be seen in the story of Omar. Omar lives in Baghdad with his family. He is a former senior intelligence officer who spent over 20 years working for the Ministry of Interior. He views himself as an Iraqi national first and foremost, but is also proud of his Anbar roots. He is a Sunni Muslim but his tribe, most of which is present in the west and south of Iraq, has both Sunni and Shi'a members. In the summer of 2014, Omar and his teenage son, Ahmed, fled Baghdad following an escalation in Shi'a militia activity in the vicinity of his neighbourhood. Reminiscent of the sectarian conflict that emerged post-Saddam, the militias had taken tens of Sunni men. With obvious sectarian overtones, such actions by the militias were also related to power and control as they sought to remove past influences or challenges to the new status quo. The militias are sought to target current and former security personnel, particularly those associated with the former Baathist regime, something that Omar was all too aware of. In light of these events, Omar and his son travelled to the west of Anbar where he has family, in Hit and Haditha. While Anbar is almost exclusively Sunni, there are a number of political, tribal and family factions, which have ensured that both uncertainty and issues of trust remain.

While sitting on a minibus waiting to leave Abu Ghraib in west Baghdad, the driver asked if anyone on the bus worked for the security forces as he had heard that groups of armed men had set up checkpoints on the main routes and were actively seeking such personnel.[107] Neither wanting to go the long way around, nor to raise suspicions of his background, Omar remained quiet, trusting no one on the grounds of the fluidity and dynamism of local politics in Anbar. The main road that links Anbar to Baghdad travels through a walled-town called Hit and was under ISIS control. Before reaching Hit, the minibus was stopped by men who identified themselves as Daesh.[108] Upon seeing Omar's identification, which identified him as a former employee of the Ministry of Interior, they asked him to come with them for further questioning. Fearing the worst, Ahmed followed his father.

In the following hours, Omar and Ahmed were driven to a house around 20 km from Hit, whereupon they confiscated Omar's phone and began to ask a series of questions, predominantly to ascertain if he still worked for the government. As is standard practice across the region, the men looked through Omar's phone and called several numbers to test the veracity of his story. At the same time, Ahmed was taken into a separate room to be questioned alone. Ahmed was given two options: the first involved him telling them everything, which would allow him to return to his mother; the second was to say nothing and die with his father. Ahmed's response was nothing but courageous: 'I have nothing to tell you, but even if I did, how could I return to my mother and look her in the face knowing that I had abandoned my father.'

Following several hours of interrogation, Omar and Ahmed were told they could leave; however, Omar refused and asked if he could stay the night, as it was dark outside and he knew that there would be no transport. While this seems a curious decision, Omar later explained that 'I know these Wahhabis, I know how they think. If we were to leave there and then, they would be suspicious.'[109] Instead, Omar and Ahmed stayed and ate with the ISIS members, who by this point numbered approximately ten. They were all Iraqi and the several that spoke to Omar directly had 'northern accents', identified as potentially being from Mosul. The following morning, Omar and Ahmed left for their destination; however, in the following months, the situation in Anbar deteriorated. Omar and his son eventually returned to Baghdad.

Omar's story sheds a great deal of light on the actions of ISIS across Iraq. Concerned both with the decimation of the *ancien régime* and the consolidation of its territorial gains, the ISIS security apparatus ensures compliance with al-Baghdadi's rule. While news of the treatment of ethnic minorities, people of other religious denominations and faiths, women, homosexuals and prisoners shows the brutality of the group, the governance of territory – and methods used to ensure compliance – demonstrates the impact upon everyday life across Anbar. Dissent from the religious, ideological view of the group is not tolerated, to the point where identities and symbols are destroyed to pave the way for the expansion of the ISIS view. As part of this process of rewriting history to shape the future, places of religious and cultural significance have been destroyed. Places that are considered to be un-Islamic are typically looted, then destroyed, with artifacts often sold on the black market.[110]

Of course, as Omar's story highlights, not all in ISIS-controlled territory are complicit in the continuation of ISIS rule, and a number of opposition groups have engaged in acts of resistance against the group. The blog Mosul Eye sought to record life under ISIS and the acts of resistance conducted against the group.[111] It documented the ISIS-directed destruction of Mosul's heritage, along with the brutality of governance, which appears tantamount to criminal enterprise. It regularly noted the punishments handed out by the group for breaking the law while also detailing the problems with uprisings against ISIS, noting the extent of penetration of everyday life and the climate of fear that has been created.

At the international level, it is important to distinguish between security and the welfare of people. In recent months, the number of people fleeing the Middle East to go to Europe has provoked serious debate, with an outpouring of support for those making the harrowing journey across land and sea. Yet security implications are also emerging from the fragmentation of Iraq and the rise of ISIS. Two serious issues concern the international community: the apparent fragmentation of the Middle Eastern states system, and the number of foreign fighters travelling to the region to join ISIS. In the five years following the Arab Uprisings the chaos emerging from the fragmentation of regime–society relations has drawn in actors from across the region, leaving national identities at the whims of sub- and supra-state identities and, ultimately, challenging the states system.

Adding to this complexity, the recent nuclear deal signed by Iran and the P5 + 1, comprising the five permanent members of the UN Security Council and Germany, has added to the growing tensions across the region. While ISIS has few friends, save some ideological ties to the Wahhabist *ulemma* in Saudi Arabia, the domestic ramifications of the group's ascendance is hard to ignore. The declaration of *wilayats* across the region[112] and attacks across Egypt and in Kuwait have further divided the region along sectarian grounds. The group has been especially clever in Saudi Arabia, where it has forced the al-Saud into a dilemma over whether to protect the Shi'a targets of the Eastern Province and, in doing so, stressing a collective identity at the expense of the Wahhabi clerics, or to side with the more hard-line clerics against the Shi'a.[113] For Western states, however, the main concern is the radicalisation of citizens, who either present a 'home grown threat',[114] or who travel to Iraq and Syria to become 'foreign fighters'. The number of foreign fighters in Syria and Iraq is difficult to ascertain accurately; however, estimates from the International Centre for the Study of Radicalisation (ICSR) put this figure in the region of 20,000 at the turn 2015, from over 100 nations.[115] Of this number, a small yet significant percentage are women.[116]

While it is clear that there are multifarious factors involved in causing an individual to travel to Iraq and Syria, including an interaction of push and pull factors,[117] there are a number of common themes. In particular, to explore the drive to join the group there must be a sense of commonality, a sense of belonging, or, as we have previously discussed, a sense of *asabiyya*. Yet unlike the *asabiyya* constructed across a region, this is a sense of *asabiyya* constructed internationally, via contemporary communication technologies.

***

Over the course of this chapter, the extent of the Iraqi government's failure to uphold its responsibility to protect peoples living within its borders has been documented. Government after government has failed in its responsibility to protect those people residing within the borders of the state. Ultimately, this failure to protect people and pursue policies that are inclusive rather than exclusionary has forced people to turn elsewhere to ensure that their needs – both welfare and security – are met. The inability to curb the influence of militias and uphold a monopoly of the use of force has meant that divisive politics is inherent within the very fabric of the Iraqi state. Since the emergence of ISIS, it has become clear that attempts have been made to create unity; however, the marginalisation of communities and ensuing persecution has created a cycle of violence that created a fertile breeding ground for ISIS to grow.

Recognising the failure of the Iraqi government to adhere to its obligations, in December 2014 Zeid Ra'ad al-Hussein, the UNHCR, made an impassioned plea:

> Accountability is of paramount importance to address past and prevent future violations of international law. The Iraqi Government should consider accession to the Rome Statute of the International Criminal Court, and as an immediate step, consider accepting the exercise of the International Criminal Court's jurisdiction with respect to the specific situation facing the country pursuant to Article 12(3) of the Rome Statute.[118]

What is clear, given both analysis and al-Hussein's remarks, is that the situation in Iraq cannot be resolved by the Iraqi government alone. The involvement of external actors in shaping the nature of political dynamics across Iraq has escalated the situation beyond Baghdad.

Ultimately, though, it is the people of Iraq that are suffering and this suffering has been a direct consequence of the pursuit of power across the state since its inception. The desire to seize – and hold – power has excluded many and has also led to the abuse of positions of authority. To combat ISIS, an inclusive politics must be designed that gives all groups an input into the running of the state, for the good of Iraq, not for one sect above the other. While al-Abadi's reforms have the capacity to bring people together, it is too early to ascertain the success of such strategies. The illusion of an Iraqi nationalism remains in the minds of the Iraqi people, but this illusion must become a reality, or forever be lost.

Conclusions

A day after the publication of the Chilcot Inquiry, the British inquiry into the Iraq War, Philip Hammond, the British foreign secretary, stated that mistakes made in the de-Baathification process directly caused the emergence of ISIS. He argued that the process left thousands of trained soldiers unemployed, who were forced to turn elsewhere in order to feed their families.[1] Hammond suggested that many of the problems seen in contemporary Iraq stemmed from this process. The same day, Tony Blair expressed regret at mistakes made in the run-up to the Iraq War:

> I can regret the mistakes and I can regret many things about it, but I genuinely believe not just that we acted out of good motives and I did what I did out of good faith, but I sincerely believe that we would be in a worse position if we hadn't acted that way. I may be completely wrong about that.[2]

The Chilcot Inquiry, an incredibly thorough examination of the UK's involvement in the 2003 Iraq War totalling 2.6 million words with an executive summary of 150 pages, offered a damning indictment of British policy in Iraq and the mismanagement of the post-conflict situation in Iraq. The findings of the inquiry echo a number of the arguments in our book, particularly that the de-Baathification process was mismanaged and resulted in thousands of people having to turn elsewhere to provide for their families and to ensure that basic needs were met. The failure of postwar reconstruction and the inability to establish a non-sectarian political system has contributed heavily to the emergence of an increasingly divided Iraqi society.

In October 2015, Blair began the process of framing the Chilcot Inquiry by giving an interview to CNN. During the interview he offered a mea culpa, apologising for aspects of the Iraq War including 'the mistakes in planning and, certainly, our mistake in our understanding of what would happen once you removed the regime'.[3] For many, Blair did not go far enough on either occasion, failing to apologise for the removal of Saddam Hussein or, indeed, for the war itself. In a number of interviews in the run-up to – and after – the publication of the inquiry, he spoke of the culpability of coalition forces in the creation of ISIS, acknowledging that the Iraq War played a part in the group's emergence. For Blair, while the Iraq War played a part, other factors were also to blame: 'It's important also to realise, one, that the Arab Spring which began in 2011 would also have had its impact on Iraq today, and two, ISIS actually came to prominence from a base in Syria and not in Iraq.'[4]

Blair is correct to assert that the Arab Uprisings fractured regime–society relations across the region, but when speaking of this disjuncture, the removal of Saddam Hussein and the Baath party infrastructure achieved this in Iraq almost eight years before the onset of the Arab Uprisings. Indeed, the destruction of key institutions left thousands of people unemployed, and growing existential concerns forced people to retreat back into their local identities, be they of a tribal or religious nature. Yet understanding the rise of ISIS in Iraq requires engaging with the emergence – and interaction – of a range of factors, endogenous and exogenous to Iraq and the Middle East broadly. While Blair is right to acknowledge that ISIS seized territory in Iraq from a base in Syria and that Raqqa is the capital of the self-proclaimed caliphate, the group emerged from the embers of Al Qaeda in Iraq, is led by an Iraqi theologian and was able to draw upon much of the Sunni dissatisfaction across Iraq, so to attempt to reduce it to a Syrian phenomena is infelicitous.

Across the book we have argued that the rise of ISIS is firmly rooted within the fabric of the Iraqi state, and to understand one you have to understand the other. The history of assimilation and marginalisation of identity groups across Iraq goes some way to aiding our understanding of the frustrations that helped the group grow. The story of Iraq in the twentieth century is a story of the efforts to build a state and, within the confines of this state-building, the quest to build a nation. While many blame the legacy of Sykes–Picot for much of the Middle East's ills, this narrative is misleading and inaccurate. Despite this, the perception of colonial interference is powerful and Britain's actions and influence in Iraq in the early part of the twentieth century only served to fuel these perceptions.

Inherent within the attempts at state- and nation-building are exclusionary politics, traced back to the establishment of the British mandate in Iraq in the 1920s. The legacy of colonialism is keenly felt in Iraq, embedded within the social structures of the state up until 2003. Moreover, the culmination of this long history of Shiʻa exclusion from Iraqi politics can be seen in the actions of successive Shiʻa governments in the aftermath of 2003. In this time, Shiʻa governments sought to secure their own power at the expense of an inclusive, Iraqi identity, reversing the policy of exclusion towards the Sunnis.

In post-2003 Iraq, the state fragmented, with power becoming increasingly decentralised and formal power structures becoming less influential in the face of the growing influence of informal power structures, mobilised to provide safety and security in the face of increasing chaos across the state. Moreover, the ability of Baghdad to secure its borders and to maintain autonomy over the affairs of the state demonstrated the failings of the idea of Iraq as a sovereign nation. The penetration of the state by a range of different actors with differing motivations was all too often seen as a threat, resulting in people retreating back into the strongest unit available to them, which, typically, was either the tribe or the religious group.

The story of the rise of ISIS also tells us a great deal about the importance of political organisation and ideas of citizenship, authority, territoriality and autonomy, the concepts that constitute sovereignty. Conceptually, using sovereignty to unpack and explore political dynamics across Iraq elucidates the changing nature of political organisation within the state. The marginalisation of groups over the course of the history of Iraq can tell us a great deal about the rise of political violence across Iraq but it can also help to trace the ebbs and flows of communal loyalties. When facing existential threats, people typically turn to an identity group to ensure their survival and, as a consequence of the growing threat from Shiʻa militias and the apparent impunity of their actions, Sunnis typically turned to their tribes for organisation and protection.[5] This was predominantly as a form of strength in numbers, but it also reveals a great deal about historical forms of political organisation and responsibility, which historically lay with tribal leaders. From this, ISIS was quick to appeal to the tribes to demonstrate their respect.

In the first edition of *Dabiq*, the magazine speaks of the:

> extensive history of building relations with the tribes within its borders in an effort to strengthen the ranks of the Muslims, unite them under one imam, and work together towards the establishment of the prophetic Khalifa. Its practice of attending tribal forums, addressing the concerns of the tribal leaders and accepting their bay'ah is regularly met with success.[6]

These comments implicitly acknowledge the work of Ibn Khaldun, in particular the need to construct *asabiyya* amongst a group of people. For ISIS, this is to be achieved through religion, yet facilitated by the cultivation of tribal dynamics.

One can see the emergence of ISIS through looking at the fragmentation of the sovereign Iraqi state. The failure of successive Iraqi governments to secure the key component parts that constitute a sovereign state, namely territoriality, governance, citizenship and autonomy, left the state open to the ideological and geopolitical currents cross-cutting the region. This failure to secure the territorial borders and to define the exceptions to sovereign rule is perhaps best seen in the nature of external involvement in the Iraqi state post-2003. As Chapter 5 documents, the penetration of the Iraqi state in the years following the overthrow of Saddam Hussein dramatically shifted the nature of Iraqi politics, deepening sectarian divisions across the state.

Yet despite the support provided by Iran to a range of Shiʻa groups across Iraq and the wider Middle East, this did not ensure coherence amongst the Shiʻa of Iraq; nor did it create an Iranian satellite, under the auspices of a system of *veleyat-e faqih*. The diplomatic cables released by Wikileaks document the extent of the Iranian penetration of the south of Iraq, feeding into a narrative of

Iranian – and Shi'a – manipulation of Iraqi affairs. This narrative of an external manipulation of Iraqi affairs fuelled the grievances felt by the Sunni communities across Iraq and also demonstrated the extent of the penetration of Iraqi sovereignty. The cables also highlighted the proximity – and tensions – within the Shi'a communities, reflected by the tensions on the street between Badr and JAM. The rising prominence of Shi'a organisations, taking on an overtly sectarian dimension, served to antagonise the previously dominant Sunni minority, with clashes between the different militias over power and a struggle for survival being shaped by decades of political marginalisation.

Clearly, the consequences of this existential struggle for the heart of the Iraqi nation are wide-reaching. In Chapter 6, the ramifications of this struggle were documented, with a focus not only on the loss of human life, but the structural violence committed by a range of actors across the post-2003 landscape in Iraq. In part, it is the structural violence occurring across the state that helped to create a fertile ground for ISIS to take root. The failure of state infrastructure to combat this structural violence, coupled with instances of state-led structural violence, reduced confidence in the state, forcing actors to turn elsewhere to ensure their survival.

While ideas of citizenship are inherent within discussions of sovereignty, the notion of bare life, as conceptualised by Giorgio Agamben, helps to tease out a nuanced form of marginalisation within this concept of citizenship. Within the Iraqi state, the politicisation, marginalisation and securitisation of sectarian identities contributed to the climate of fear emerging in Iraq at this time. The violence conducted by Shi'a militias against Sunni communities with apparent impunity was done largely by Iraqi citizens against Iraqi citizens. From this, while notions of citizenship are useful in terms of understanding the state-building project, further exploration is needed to engage with the intra-citizen violence, stressing the divided nature of loyalties within Iraq. Clearly, this is not a problem unique to Iraq; rather, it is one that can be found across Middle Eastern states, where loyalty to the state is tempered by loyalty to the sect or to the tribe. Despite the problems of intra-citizen violence, understanding sovereignty helps to identify many of these tensions, which allows for a much more nuanced understanding of political dynamics within the state. Using such a conceptual approach can also be useful when understanding the emergence of violent groups more broadly. While a range of other approaches have been used to understand and track the emergence of terrorist groups, engaging with questions about sovereignty also helps us to traverse levels-of-analysis problems that are pertinent across the Middle East.

The political climate across Iraq has resulted in fertile conditions for ISIS to grow. The fragmenting sovereignty of Iraq and Syria has left both states open to external interference, often at the expense of citizens of these states. As such, despite not necessarily agreeing with the ideology or the methods of the group, facing threats from the state and Shi'a militias, ISIS provided a form of protection for Sunni tribes against these other actors. To this end, it is imperative to differentiate between the different types of support that one talks about when discussing the group and to differentiate between active and passive supporters. Such a distinction can help when creating strategies to defeat the group.

From this, it is clear that ISIS is a symptom of the conditions in Iraq and the broader region, where a history of intervention, war, politics, economic failings and the unleashing of identity forces have combined to both form and fragment its sovereignty. Following the 2003 invasion, local dynamics in Iraq intensified following the removal of Saddam's regime, where power struggles and sectarian agendas have become all too familiar, providing cause for external involvement whether needed or not. The majority Shi'a Arab community has benefited from these circumstances while the once favoured Sunni Arabs are largely on the periphery, with limited access to political and economic functions. Dissent and violence towards the government within a number of these Sunni Arab communities have persisted amidst worsening socio-economic conditions, which in reality only saw a brief respite during the existence of the Sahwa movement. The less affinity that Sunni Arabs have to Iraq as a state, the more they have sought alternative outlets, whether legitimate or not.

The weakened government has therefore been unable to respond through its proper functions or appropriate policy, allowing both Shi'a militia to gain greater authority and groups such as ISIS (and other affiliated groups) to take advantage of the power vacuum caused by the chaos. Using the situation in neighbouring Syria, ISIS has utilised local networks, resources and the porosity of Iraq's borders to establish its kind of authority over swathes of land that has connected Sunni Arabs between Iraq and Syria. Its posturing as a protector of Islam for Sunnis has appealed to international followers, and its violent actions, many of which are visible through social media, have created an aura of invincibility. There is a stoic willingness within ISIS's belief that enables them to continue fighting until the end point of a caliphate is established. Military victories are celebrated, while losing appears only temporary as they continue to regroup and attack. Nevertheless, resources are not infinite and its actions have only managed to increase military responses towards it. So while its military conquests along with its use of resources and economic planning have been impressive to date, the longevity of its current strategy, which involves the holding of towns and cities, will increasingly come under pressure as opposing forces focus their strengths on reducing its logistic capabilities. However, as we have stressed in this book, this does not mean the end of Sunni Arab militancy or violence in general, as the issues generated by Iraq's fragmentation require a much more holistic approach.

In promoting solutions to Iraq's current conditions it is necessary first of all to acknowledge that while ISIS as a major military force may only be a temporary issue, Iraq's fragmentation is likely to continue. Historically, Iraq's sovereignty has always been in question, as addressed in this book by referring to its many complex layers of influence, but after the 2003 invasion the break-up became a reality. For example, this provided an opportunity for the Kurdistan region to seek a path towards independence, while also empowering the Shi'a Arab majority over Sunni Arabs, which has reduced faith in Iraq's government. Iraq's Dawa-dominated government is therefore also responsible for the country's continued degradation. By restricting the participation of sections from its once semi-coherent state, particularly members of the former Baathist regime and Sunni Arabs in general, it has only furthered its decline by removing experience and knowledge from its institutions (as seen in the security sector) and industry, compounding the issue of a brain drain.

The level of mistrust and uncertainty engendered throughout these years will be difficult to overturn, especially as the economic situation worsens and rival factions become enmeshed in a struggle for power and resources. However, this does not mean that the fragmentation of Iraq has to be violent. The government and its benefactors should realise that long-term investment in its peripheral communities (such as in Anbar and parts of Salahaddin) is preferable to long-term conflict, at least for human and economic cost reasons, as seen in the conflict with ISIS. Baiji's oil refinery (Salahaddin) would be secured,[7] and there are also benefits to be had from the gas field in western Anbar.[8] Peripheral areas, particularly the Sunni Arab areas, could also benefit from the investment of a stronger central authority and its expertise, however short- or long-term this may be. This does not necessarily mean that the end goal is regional autonomy, but a process whereby healthy interaction between local and central parts allows for participation and mutual benefits. To reduce the level of uncertainty, there is a need to ease the chaotic circumstances while allowing stable networks between local actors and Iraq's central authority to emerge, a process that also needs to be supported by other regional and international actors. Reducing tensions between core and periphery is essential in (re-)establishing a coherent state.

There is, of course, no denying that a greater participation from Iraq's various communities and their interaction with one another will require time and significant investment, something that is becoming increasingly difficult for the Iraqi government. The World Bank has taken strides to alleviate the situation by providing loans to promote fiscal stability and soften the impact of the reduction in oil prices[9], but this is a short-term fix. To resolve the human crisis, huge investment is required, which the Iraqi government will struggle to finance alone. Investment in infrastructural repairs and development is required, so a concerted international effort towards establishing such a fund should be made. Interference in the management of Iraq's domestic affairs should be minimalised. Again, this may appear somewhat idealistic, but if there is a desire to end conflict and the emergence of groups such as ISIS, to minimise human cost and ultimately increase stability, then there are strategies that could be considered. To this end, we advocate that these strategies be predicated on the principle of self-organisation, or by allowing Iraq's local parts to establish their own development path, with guidance and support replacing overt interference.

A framework for self-organisation

Firstly, if we view Iraq systemically, we can make more sense of its chaotic circumstances. After all, chaos refers to a level of unpredictability, which has occurred through a set of circumstances that has produced non-linear outcomes.[10] Essentially, the Iraq that was once itself a system with relative stability, albeit under the highly regulated authority of Saddam's regime, is now operating without sufficient boundaries (physical and legal). This means its many endogenous (tribal and political) and exogenous (other countries/actors) factors, along with those of the non-physical (such as identity and psychology), affect the population's ability to establish more stable patterns of interaction. Iraq's sovereign decline, which was precipitated by the 2003 invasion, has therefore unleashed forces difficult to control or predict, which in turn has reduced order, increased uncertainty and allowed external actors to contribute to the chaos, including countries such as the USA, Iran, Saudi Arabia and Turkey. To this end, while immediate solutions may not be realistic, we can still offer parameters for stability (see C. 1), where sufficient space can be provided for Iraq's uncertain population to interact, ultimately aiding the long-term removal of threats such as ISIS.

External factors

As a starting point, there is a need to reduce the number of actors contributing to Iraq's chaotic circumstances, and in the first instance this can be aided through the containment of Iraq's issues within its own physical borders. The level of porosity and the reasons for it do however differ on each geographical side of Iraq. For example, on the northern border between the Kurdistan region and Turkey, Turkish concerns over Kurdish separatism across the region but also within their own borders (particularly the PKK) have led to its maintaining troops in Iraq since 1997, a situation that has the support of President

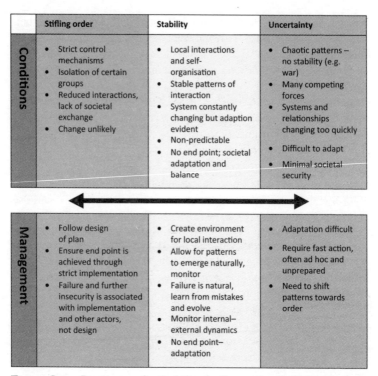

	Stifling order	Stability	Uncertainty
Conditions	• Strict control mechanisms • Isolation of certain groups • Reduced interactions, lack of societal exchange • Change unlikely	• Local interactions and self-organisation • Stable patterns of interaction • System constantly changing but adaption evident • Non-predictable • No end point; societal adaptation and balance	• Chaotic patterns – no stability (e.g. war) • Many competing forces • Systems and relationships changing too quickly • Difficult to adapt • Minimal societal security
Management	• Follow design of plan • Ensure end point is achieved through strict implementation • Failure and further insecurity is associated with implementation and other actors, not design	• Create environment for local interaction • Allow for patterns to emerge naturally, monitor • Failure is natural, learn from mistakes and evolve • Monitor internal–external dynamics • No end point–adaptation	• Adaptation difficult • Require fast action, often ad hoc and unprepared • Need to shift patterns towards order

Figure C.1   Parameters for Stability by Promoting Self-Organisation in Iraq

Masoud Barzani's KDP. This has not only caused friction between the Kurdish parties, however, but also, more recently with the Iraqi government and its aligned Shi'a militias who have shown particular concern over Turkish troop presence and their movement near Mosul, much of which is related to Turkey's alleged links to ISIS.[11] While such an allegation is grounded within geopolitical considerations, Turkey's presence in the north, particularly Mosul district, has created a dynamic that has contributed to Iraq's instability, leading to calls from US President Barack Obama in December 2015 for it to withdraw.[12] At present, a full withdrawal is unlikely and Turkish forces will continue their air campaign against Kurdish separatists in the Kurdistan region's northernmost mountainous areas. Nevertheless, engaging in dialogue with Turkey over this matter is preferential to hostile rhetoric and violence.

Iraq's western border with Syria is more problematic as sovereignty has diminished on both sides. ISIS now controls the majority of crossing areas and routes between Syria and Iraq, leaving the respective governments with little to negotiate over. To secure this border requires both military action and engagement with local actors in the border areas on both sides. This could involve a role for the coalition forces (potentially NATO) that could use both aircraft and ground troops to maintain control in the short term. Of course, this is problematic and would also call on the willingness of nations to contribute human resources to a highly unstable area. An increased role for aircraft (including drones) is perhaps more realistic and could act as a deterrent along the border while allowing ground operations in Iraq to concentrate on seizing key logistic routes and areas. In the medium to long term, local engagement by the Iraqi government will be required, preferably with international monitoring. This will help avert humanitarian situations such as those witnessed in Sinjar, where revenge attacks against local Sunni Arabs following the removal of ISIS resulted in escalated tensions, on Iraq's northwestern border with Syria, following successful Kurdish-led operations against ISIS in the latter part of 2015. Furthermore, as documented in the cases of Babil and Diyala provinces in Chapter 4, the removal or cleansing of populations is not a sustainable solution and, from this, methods of accountability will need to be established.

Considering Iran's proximity to Iraq on the eastern border, along with its increasing influence, stemming from financial support and shared religious and cultural bonds, removing it as an actor in Iraq is unlikely. Yet it is in the best interest of Iran to have a stable Iraq, and while it may believe that its current strategy is sufficient, one that appears to involve the creation of a Shiʻa buffer against any Sunni Arab incursions, in the long term this will not improve its physical security or geopolitical relations. Visa regulations between the two countries exist, but these have become difficult to uphold given the numerous smuggling routes that exist, along with the constant flow of goods and people. During the religious ceremony of Arba'een in November 2015, tens of thousands of Iranians wanting to commemorate the occasion in the Shi'a holy city of Karbala broke through Iraq's border without contest.[13] Such incidents highlight the lack of sovereign functions in Iraq, while for its Sunni Arab community this case and Iran's overriding influence increase the levels of uncertainty and mistrust.

Iran's involvement in Iraq's affairs is ultimately difficult to mitigate, especially considering the physical, religious and political connections, not to mention the sponsoring of Iraq's Shi'a militias.[14] In establishing and enforcing a border policy with Iraq, however fluid it may be, Iran would be exercising its leadership in supporting Iraq's sovereignty and therefore setting an example to countries such as Turkey and even Saudi Arabia in the process. Removing its influence from Iraq's political functions is, however, much more complicated.

Internal factors

For healthy interactions to emerge, the basic tenets of security are needed at the local level, for both Shi'a and Sunni. The current situation in Iraq shows a lack of order, which has allowed external actors to influence local dynamics and, in doing so, to add to the chaotic circumstances. For example, while the USA was overt in establishing Iraq's current governmental mechanisms, Iran, through its support of individuals in the political movement Dawa and organisations such as Badr and Shi'a militias, has set about influencing these very same mechanisms in a covert manner. While this influence is significant, a number of Iraq's Shi'a elite have also sought to use Iran to bolster their own credentials and power; al-Maliki being a case in point, having both been in and out of favour with Iran.[15] Similarly, hard-line Shi'a in Iraq have also utilised these networks, including Shi'a militias whose well-documented actions in Babil and Diyala provinces have fed into the deepening sectarian schism. Controlling these factors may indeed require Iran to stop supporting Iraq's hard-liners and its more radical militias, while somewhat paradoxically using their influence to bring them into line. Senior militia leaders will undoubtedly have to be accommodated at the national level, as they already are, but the fallout of this will also have to be managed to assert a degree of control over non-adhering militia factions. Senior Shi'a clerics such as Ali al-Sistani can also use their influence to exert boundaries, but even this is tentative considering the wealth of support that the militias receive from Iraq's Shi'a population, in many cases more than does the government[16]. It is also a cause of debate amongst Shi'a groups as to the extent to which clerics should be involved within the political sphere.

There is some hope that figures such as Muqtada al-Sadr, with his popularity and position as a pro-Iraqi militia leader of the Peace Brigades, may provide some balance, but as economic uncertainty envelops most of the country, asserting control over more radical elements is likely to become increasingly difficult. This is highlighted by militia involvement in criminal activity, notably kidnappings and robbery[17]. In the long term, legitimate economic opportunities could reduce the growth in militias and their illegal activity, but in the short term, the government must be able to assert its authority and provide security for all of Iraq's population.

This could be aided by constructive engagement with Sunni Arab communities, within majority Shi'a areas and provinces such as Anbar and Salahaddin, where a degree of local autonomy will need to be supported. This includes provisions for the establishment of local security as well as healthcare and education, while intervention from both the government and particularly the Shi'a militias will need to be avoided. Access to political and economic functions will provide incentives, but it will also require strong and transparent leadership from within the Sunni Arab communities, which has so far been elusive due to factors such as the targeting of local leaders (a tactic used by AQI, ISIS and Shi'a militias, for example), political and economic opportunism, and the lack of opportunity to participate in Iraq's political functions. As we have argued, we cannot refer to Iraq's Sunni Arab community as a homogeneous entity, and violent sectarian elements are likely to persist with their objectives, but in providing opportunities for participation at the local level there is potential for greater interaction and the emergence of improved representation. Local security, with support from the government, can help in fighting an asymmetric campaign, but such attacks should not be viewed as a failure, rather part of a long-term process that needs to be managed.

Such proposals would require considerable funding and a high degree of acquiescence from all actors concerned, both exogenous and endogenous, which makes such a process appear idealistic. These examples are merely used as guidelines to establish parameters in which threats such as ISIS can be eradicated in the long term. A degree of order is therefore required, not one that stifles interaction or universal participation (such as dictatorships), but one that provides security and an inclusive approach to dealing with the issues while ensuring that basic needs are met. The goal is to reduce the current chaos and implement a more flexible and pragmatic approach to the situation, in line with local capabilities and needs.[18] International actors can, of course, aid this approach through guidance, observation and financial support. Their involvement, however, should also recognise the potential impact of their work, and therefore avoid any unnecessary controlling mechanisms that might reduce the government's ability to respond, as and when it is needed, or one that favours one group over another. Stopping ISIS militarily is not a cure for Iraq's ills, and therefore a more holistic approach will be required if the violence is to subside. The story of the rise of ISIS is a long story of human suffering and exclusion, underpinned by the struggle to meet basic needs. Understanding this existential struggle is at the very heart of understanding how to defeat ISIS, yet it is a story that is all too often missed from accounts of the rise of the group. A growing number of people are struggling to meet their basic needs while also opposing ISIS, putting themselves in serious danger. We end this book by dedicating it to those brave people who, even in the struggle for survival, challenge the brutality of ISIS and, in doing so, continue to fight for what they believe in.

Notes

Introduction

1. *Dabiq* 1, 'The return of Khalifah' (5 July 2014).
2. The Sykes–Picot agreement of 1916 enabled the implantation of borders over the geographical Middle East. It was negotiated by the French diplomat François Georges-Picot and Britain's Sir Mark Sykes, with input from Russia. See James Barr, *A Line in the Sand: Britain, France and the Struggle that Shaped the Middle East* (London: Simon & Schuster, 2011).
3. 'ISIS – The End of Sykes–Picot', presented by spokesperson Abu Saffiya from Chile (29 June 2014), www.youtube.com/watch?v=YyM0_sv5h88.
4. G. Wood, 'What ISIS really wants' (14 March 2015), www.theatlantic.com/magazine/archive/2015/03/what-isis-really-wants/384980/.
5. Roula Khalaf, 'Abu Bakr al-Baghdadi, Isis leader', *Financial Times* (4 July 2014), www.ft.com/cms/s/0/ec63d94c-02b0-11e4-a68d-00144feab7de.html#axzz36WPWiRgC.
6. Simon Mabon, *Saudi Arabia and Iran: Soft Power Rivalry in the Middle East* (London: I.B.Tauris, 2013).
7. It is estimated that Shi'a account for approximately 10–15 per cent of Saudi Arabia's population. Pew Research (7 October 2009), www.pewforum.org/2009/10/07/mapping-the-global-muslim-population/.
8. 'Saudi refutes UK media claims of "ISIS support"', *Al-Arabiya News* (10 July 2014), http://english.alarabiya.net/en/News/world/2014/07/09/Saudi-Arabia-refutes-UK-media-allegations-of-supporting-ISIS-.html.
9. Patrick Cockburn, 'Iraq crisis: how Saudi Arabia helped Isis take over the north of the country', *Independent* (21 July 2014), www.independent.co.uk/voices/comment/iraq-crisis-how-saudi-arabia-helped-isis-take-over-the-north-of-the-country-9602312.html.
10. Madawi Al-Rasheed, 'The shared history of Saudi Arabia and Isis' (20 November 2014), www.hurstpublishers.com/the-shared-history-of-saudi-arabia-and-isis/.
11. Simon Mabon, 'ISIS: sectarianism, geopolitics and strong/weak horses' (10 April 2015), www.e-ir.info/2015/04/10/isis-sectarianism-geopolitics-and-strongweak-horses/.

12. 'Profile: Islamic State in Iraq and the Levant (ISIS)', *BBC News* (16 June 2014), www.bbc.com/news/world-middle-east-24179084.
13. David Remnick, 'Going the distance', *New Yorker* (27 January 2014), www.newyorker.com/magazine/2014/01/27/going-the-distance-davidremnick.
14. The term cystISIS was created by *The Last Leg*, a British television comedy show fronted by Adam Hills, in an attempt to use humour as a counter-narrative against the group. The name was also designed to defetishise the group.
15. Matthew Rosenberg and Eric Schmitt, 'In ISIS strategy, U.S. weighs risk to civilians', *New York Times* (19 December 2015), www.nytimes.com/2015/12/20/us/politics/in-isis-strategy-us-weighs-risk-to-civilians.html?_r=0.
16. Michael Weiss and Hassan Hassan, *ISIS: Inside the Army of Terror* (New York: Regan, 2016).
17. Jason Burke, *The New Threat from Islamic Militancy* (London: Bodley Head, 2015), pp. 57–8.
18. William McCants, *The ISIS Apocalypse: The History, Strategy, and Doomsday Vision of the Islamic State* (New York: St Martin's Press, 2015).
19. Graeme Wood, 'What ISIS really wants', *The Atlantic* (March 2005), www.theatlantic.com/magazine/archive/2015/03/what-isis-really-wants/384980/.
20. While the book focuses primarily on human interaction, there is also ground within the theory of complexity to apply other attributing factors such as environmental conditions. After all, the development of the Iraq people would be lesser without the water sources provided by the Tigris and Euphrates rivers.
21. David Byrne, *Complexity Theory and the Social Sciences: An Introduction* (London; New York: Routledge, 1998), p. 50.

Chapter 1   Sovereignty, Political Organisation and the Rise of ISIS

1. Jarrett Murphy, 'Text of Bush Speech', *CBS News* (1 May 2003), www.cbsnews.com/news/text-of-bush-speech-01-05-2003/.
2. The Peace of Westphalia comprised two peace treaties, signed at Munster, between the Holy Roman Empire and France, and at Osnabruck, between the Holy Roman Empire and Sweden.

3. Stephen Krasner, 'Compromising Westphalia', *International Security* xx/3 (1995–6), pp. 115–51. Although it is worth noting that the Peace of Westphalia is perhaps not as responsible for the development of sovereignty as many would hold. Derek Croxton unpacks how the Peace of Westphalia should not be considered as the foundation of modern understandings of sovereignty 'on the basis of having [not] granted sovereignty to the individual German estates, because no one believed that it actually did so'. Derek Croxton, 'The peace of Westphalia of 1648 and the origins of sovereignty', *International History Review*, xxi/3, p. 574.

4. Ibid., p. 115.

5. 'Charter of the United Nations', www.un.org/en/documents/charter/chapter1.shtml.

6. Stephen Krasner, 'Sharing sovereignty: new institutions for collapsed and failing states', *International Security*, xxix/2, p. 87.

7. Hugo Grotius, *De Jure Belli ac Pacis* (1625), trans. F. Kelsey (1925).

8. Max Weber, 'Politik als Beruf', *Gesammelte Politische Schriften* (Muenchen, 1921), http://media.pfeiffer.edu/lridener/dss/Weber/polvoc.html.

9. Max Weber, *The Theory of Social and Economic Organization* (New York: The Free Press, 1947), p. 154.

10. Lisa Anderson, 'The state in the Middle East and North Africa', *Comparative Politics*, xx/1 (1987), p. 2.

11. James Caporaso, 'Changes in the Westphalian order: territory, public authority, and sovereignty', *International Studies Review*, ii/2 (2000).

12. Stephen Krasner, 'Compromising Westphalia', p. 119.

13. This is typically what Migdal refers to as a strong society, but a weak state, although there are counter-arguments to this, where rulers have been successful in state-building processes, despite the challenges posed by strong societies. A prime example of this is Saudi Arabia, where, despite the existence of strong tribal networks, the al-Saud dynasty has been able to create a strong state.

14. James Caporaso, 'Changes in the Westphalian order'.

15. This is a criticism that can be levied at International Relations theory as a whole.

16. CIA: *World Fact Book: Syria* (21 July 2014), https://www.cia.gov/library/publications/the-world-factbook/geos/sy.html.

17. Simon Mabon, *Saudi Arabia and Iran: Soft Power Rivalry in the Middle East* (London: I.B.Tauris, 2013).

18. 'CIA: World Fact Book, Iraq' (20 July 2014), https://www.cia.gov/library/publications/the-world-factbook/geos/iz.html.

19. Hussein D. Hassan, 'Iraq: tribal structure, social, and political activities', CRS Report for Congress (15 March 2007), http://fpc.state.gov/documents/organization/81928.pdf.

20. Derek Harvey and Michael Pregent, 'Who's to blame for Iraq crisis?', *CNN News* (12 June 2014), http://edition.cnn.com/2014/06/12/opinion/pregent-harvey-northern-iraq-collapse/?c=&page=0.

21. Suadad Al-Salhy and Tim Arango, 'Iraq militants, pushing south, aim at capital', *New York Times* (11 June 2014), www.nytimes.com/2014/06/12/world/middleeast/iraq.html?_r=1.

22. According to some Arab sources, al-Batawi's early release was coordinated by Saudi intelligence. For example see http://faceiraq.com/inews.php?id=229533.

23. Quoted in Ruth Sherlock, 'Islamic Army of Iraq founder: Isis and Sunni Islamists will march on Baghdad', *Telegraph* (20 June 2014), www.telegraph.co.uk/news/worldnews/middleeast/iraq/10914567/Islamic-Army-of-Iraq-founder-Isis-and-Sunni-Islamists-will-march-on-Baghdad.html.

24. Daniel Dombey, 'Iraq crisis: Turkey's Erdogan warns on air strikes against ISIS', *Financial Times* (19 June 2014), www.ft.com/intl/cms/s/0/ae101292-f7b0-11e3-90fa-00144feabdc0.html#axzz38Yh5ieU7.

25. Osama Al-Sharif, 'Jordan shaken by threats from ISIS, Iraq, Syria', *Al-Monitor* (25 June 2014), www.al-monitor.com/pulse/originals/2014/06/jordan-isis-anbar-iraq-salafi-jihadist-maan.html#ixzz36a4HAX2R.

26. For a detailed analysis of this situation see Nir Rosen, *Aftermath: Following the Bloodshed of America's Wars in the Muslim World* (New York: Perseus Books, 2010).

27. Franklin Lamb, 'ISIS now recruiting in Palestinian camps in Lebanon', *Foreign Policy Journal* (30 June 2014), www.foreignpolicyjournal.com/2014/06/30/isis-now-recruiting-in-palestinian-camps-in-lebanon/.

28. Asmaa al-Ghoul, 'Gaza Salafists pledge allegiance to ISIS', *Al-Monitor* (27 February 2014), www.al-monitor.com/pulse/en/originals/2014/02/isis-gaza-salafist-jihadist-qaeda-hamas.html#.

29. Ibid.

30. Jack Moore, 'Gaza crisis: Isis pledge to join the Palestinian fight against "barbaric Jews', *International Business Times* (31 July 2014), www.ibtimes.co.uk/gaza-crisis-isis-pledge-join-palestinian-fight-against-barbaric-jews-1459190.

31. It is estimated that 1,000 fighters are on the full payroll of al-Baghdadi's organisation, receiving between US$300 and US$2,000 per month (See Paul Crompton, 'Can ISIS maintain its self-declared

caliphate?', *Al-Arabiya News* (16 July 2014), http://english.alarabiya.
net/en/perspective/analysis/2014/07/16/Can-ISIS-maintain-its-self-
declared-caliphate-.html). As it continues to grow, though, it is likely
that this number has more than quadrupled.

32. Quoting Channel 2 news in Israel Arutz Sheva, 'ISIS: fighting
"infidels" takes precedence over fighting Israel' (8 July 2014), www.
israelnationalnews.com/News/News.aspx/
182632#.U7uLApSSw00.

Chapter 2   Political Organisation and the State in Iraq

1. Angus McNeice, 'Police launch investigation into Chilean–Norwegian
jihadist in Syria', *Santiago Times* (3 February 2014), http://santiagotimes.
cl/police-launch-investigation-chilean-norwegian-jihadist-syria/.

2. 'The End of Sykes–Picot' (28 June 2014), https://www.youtube.com/
watch?v = i357G1HuFcI.

3. *Dabiq* 1.

4. Extrapolating from this, many have also rejected the application of
universal claims inherent within International Relations theory, arguing
that the discipline needs to develop non-Western strands to reflect
diversity and subjectivity.

5. Toby Dodge, *Inventing Iraq* (New York: Columbia University Press,
2005), p. 13.

6. Toby Dodge, 'Can Iraq be saved?', *Survival: Global Politics and Strategy*,
56:5 (2014), pp. 7–20.

7. Dodge, *Inventing Iraq*, p. 13.

8. A full exploration of the application of *bare life* to the case of Iraq is
beyond the scope of this work; however, the concept helps to elucidate
the marginalisation and persecution experienced by various actors across
the history of the Iraqi state. See Georgio Agamben, *Homer Sacer:
Sovereign Power and Bare Life* (Stanford: Stanford University Press, 1998).

9. See Dodge, *Inventing Iraq*, and 'Can Iraq be saved?'; Charles Tripp,
A History of Iraq (Cambridge: Cambridge University Press, 2007);
Adeed Dawisha, *Iraq: A Political History from Independence to Occupation*
(Princeton: Princeton University Press, 2009); Liam Anderson
and Gareth Stansfield, *The Future of Iraq: Dictatorship, Democracy, or
Division* (New York: Palgrave Macmillan, 2004) amongst others.

10. Peter M. Holt, *Egypt and the Fertile Crescent: 1516–1922* (Ithaca, NY:
Cornell University Press, 1996), pp. 250–1.

11. See Amal Vinogradov, 'The 1920 revolt in Iraq reconsidered: the role of tribes in national politics', *International Journal of Middle East Studies*, 3:2 (1972).

12. Ibid. See also Tripp, *A History of Iraq*, pp. 40–5.

13. Kristian Coates-Ulrichsen, 'The British occupation of Mesopotamia, 1914–1922', *Journal of Strategic Studies*, 30:2 (2007), p. 350.

14. Ibid., pp. 351–2.

15. Gertrude Bell, quoted in Vinogradov, *The 1920 Revolt in Iraq Reconsidered*, p. 135.

16. Vinogradov, *The 1920 Revolt*.

17. Arnold T. Wilson, *Mesopotamia, 1917–1920: A Clash of Loyalties* (London: H. Milford, 1931), pp. 273–6.

18. Elie Kedouri, 'Reflexions sur l'histoire du Royaume d'Irak (1921–1958)', *Orient*, 11:3 (1959), pp. 55–79.

19. Fariq al-Mizhar al-Fir'aun, *al-Haqa'iq al Nasi'a* (Baghdad, 1952).

20. Vinograd, *The 1920 Revolt*, p. 125.

21. Aylmer Haldane, *The Insurrection in Mesopotamia, 1920* (Edinburgh: Blackwood, 1922), p. 331.

22. Dodge, *Inventing Iraq*, pp. 20–1.

23. Tripp, *A History of Iraq*, p. 47.

24. Ibid., p. 48.

25. T.E. Lawrence, 'Faisal's Table Talk', report to Colonel Wilson, 8 January 1917, FO 686/6, p. 121. Faisal's remarks are also quoted in Hanna Batatu, *The Old Social Classes and the Revolutionary Movements in Iraq* (Princeton, NJ: Princeton University Press, 1978), pp. 25–6.

26. Adeed Dawisha, 'National identity and sub-state sectarian loyalties in Iraq', *International Journal of Contemporary Iraqi Studies*, 4:3 (2010).

27. Dawisha, *Iraq: A Political History*, p. 72.

28. The state-building process in Saudi Arabia was facilitated by the *Ikhwan*, but their power was curtailed by Ibn Saud in 1930 after an ill-fated rebellion.

29. Tripp, *A History of Iraq*, pp. 48–50.

30. This strategy of questioning the loyalty of Shi'a groups across the region has long been a prominent feature of states with sectarian fault lines.

31. See, Dawisha, *Iraq: A Political History*, p. 245, and Tripp, *A History of Iraq*.

32. Tripp, *A History of Iraq*, p. 75.

33. Ibid., pp. 81–2.

34. Ibid.

35. Ibid., p. 100.

36. Charles Issawi and Muhammed Yeganeh, *The Economies of Middle Eastern Oil* (New York: Praeger, 1962), pp. 143–7.
37. Amatzia Baram, 'Neo-tribalism in Iraq: Saddam Hussein's tribal policies 1991–96', *International Journal of Middle East Studies*, 29:1 (1997) p. 3.
38. Adeed Dawisha, 'Identity and political survival in Saddam's Iraq', *Middle East Journal*, 53:4 (1999), p. 554.
39. Baram, 'Neo-tribalism in Iraq', p. 1.
40. Ibid.
41. Dawisha, 'Identity and political survival', p. 563.
42. Hanna Batatu, 'Iraq's underground Shi'i movements' (MER102, 1981), www.merip.org/mer/mer102/iraqs-underground-shii-movements.
43. Soren Schmidt, 'The role of religion in politics: the case of Shia-Islamism in Iraq', *Nordic Journal of Religion and Society*, xxii/2 (2009), p. 129.
44. L. Carl Brown, *Religion and State: The Muslim Approach to Politics* (New York: Columbia University Press, 2001).
45. Soren Schmidt, 'The role of religion in politics', p. 137.
46. Judith Yaphe, 'Tribalism in Iraq, the old and the new', *Middle East Policy* vii/3 (2000), p. 54.
47. Edward Luttwak, *Coup d'Etat: A Practical Handbook* (Cambridge, MA: Harvard University Press, 1979).
48. James Quinlivan, 'Coup-proofing: its practice and consequences in the Middle East', *International Security*, xxiv/2 (1999), p. 133.
49. Ibid.
50. Simon Mabon, 'Kingdom in crisis', *Contemporary Security Policy*, xxxiii/3 (2012).
51. Quinlivan, 'Coup-proofing', pp. 139–40.
52. See Joost R. Hilterman, *A Poisonous Affair: America, Iraq, and the Gassing of Halabja* (Cambridge: Cambridge University Press, 2007).
53. In the aftermath of the new constitution and reflecting a pragmatic shift in policy, the group's name would change to ISCI.
54. Other notable groups established at this time with Iranian assistance include Hizballah and the International Front for the Liberation of Bahrain.
55. Schmidt, 'The role of religion in politics', p. 128.
56. Amatzia Baram, 'The radical Shi'ite opposition movements in Iraq,' in Emmanuel Sivan and Menachem Friedman (eds), *Religious Radicalism and Politics in the Middle East* (Albany: State University of New York Press, 1990), pp. 108–9.
57. *Al Thawra* (Baghdad), 18 September 1980, quoted in Dawisha, *Iraq: A Political History*, p. 554.

58. Although weapons were supplied to Saddam Hussein by Western states in an attempt to contain Iran. See Joost Hilterman, *A Poisonous Affair: America, Iraq, and the Gassing of Halabja* (Cambridge: Cambridge University Press, 2007).

59. The name of this conflict is contestable, with others referring to it as, for example, the Persian Gulf War, the Kuwait War and the First Iraq War.

60. Lawrence E. Cline, 'The prospects of the Shia insurgency movement in Iraq', *Journal of Conflict Studies*, xx/1 (2000).

61. Human Rights Watch, 'Endless Torment: The 1991 Uprising in Iraq and Its Aftermath' (1992), www.hrw.org/reports/1992/Iraq926.htm.

62. Ibid.

63. 'Full text: State of the Union address' (30 January 2002), http://news.bbc.co.uk/1/hi/world/americas/1790537.stm.

64. 'Text of Bush Speech' (1 May 2003), www.cbsnews.com/news/text-of-bush-speech-01-05-2003/.

65. Mark Thompson, 'Seeking a legacy, Bush cites security' (12 January 2009), http://content.time.com/time/nation/article/0,8599,1871060,00.html.

66. United Nations Security Council, 'Resolution 1511' (2003), https://www.iaea.org/OurWork/SV/Invo/resolutions/res1511.pdf.

67. Tripp, *A History of Iraq*, p. 280.

68. Al-Khoei was a member of one of the most prominent Shi'a families and was a leading figure in the Iraqi exile community. His obituary in the *Guardian* is here: Michael Wood, *Abdul Majud al-Khoei* (12 April 2003), www.theguardian.com/news/2003/apr/12/guardianobituaries.iraq.

69. John Chilcot, *The Iraq Inquiry*, Volume 8 (2016), p. 8.

70. Ibid., p. 14.

71. 'Coalition Provisional Authority Order Number 1: De-Ba'athification of Iraqi Society' (2003), http://nsarchive.gwu.edu/NSAEBB/NSAEBB418/docs/9a%20-%20Coalition%20Provisional%20Authority%20Order%20No%201%20-%205-16-03.pdf.

72. 'Coalition Provisional Authority Order Number 2: Dissolution of Entities' (2003), www.iraqcoalition.org/regulations/20030823_CPAORD_2_Dissolution_of_Entities_with_Annex_A.pdf.

73. Ibid.

74. Tripp, *A History of Iraq*, p. 282.

75. Chilcot, *The Iraq Inquiry*, Volume 8, p. 23.

76. Christopher M. Blanchard, 'Al Qaeda: Statements and Evolving Ideology' (CRS Report for Congress, 2007), https://www.fas.org/sgp/crs/terror/RL32759.pdf, p. 7.

77. Martin Chulov, 'Isis: the inside story', *Guardian* (11 December 2014), www.theguardian.com/world/2014/dec/11/-sp-isis-the-inside-story.

78. Nicholas Krohley, 'Opportunity in chaos: how Iraq's Medhi Army almost succeeded – and why it matters', *Foreign Affairs* (26 September 2015), accessed 11 December 2015, https://www.foreignaffairs.com/articles/iraq/2015-08-26/opportunity-chaos.

79. 09RIYADH447_a COUNTERTERRORISM ADVISER BRENNAN'S MEETING WITH SAUDI KING ABDULLAH (22.03.14), https://wikileaks.org/plusd/cables/09RIYADH447_a.html.

80. Triggered by the self immolation of the Tunisian street vendor, Mohammad Bouazizzi, whose frustration at socio-economic conditions across the country, coupled with the perceived corruption of the Ben Ali regime, pushed him to such drastic action. This act proved to be the catalyst for the fragmentation of regime–society relations across the Middle East. Previously embedded autocratic rulers were also overthrown in Egypt and Yemen while protest movements gained momentum in Syria, Yemen and Bahrain. The fragmenting of regime–society relations opened schisms for external actors to manipulate. This is perhaps best seen in Syria, with Saudi Arabia and Iran capitalising on the fragmentation of regime–society relations to pursue their own interests in the state. As noted in Chapter 5, the Saudi–Iranian rivalry is increasingly seen in zero-sum terms, but always at the expense of those caught in the fighting.

81. Anderson and Stansfield, *The Future of Iraq*, p. 118.

82. Haider Al-Abadi, 'We have heard the Iraqi people', *Wall Street Journal* (8 September 2015), www.wsj.com/articles/we-have-heard-the-iraqi-people-1441754816.

83. Dodge, 'Can Iraq be saved?', p. 16.

84. The White House, Office of the Press Secretary, 'Remarks by the President and First Lady on the End of the War in Iraq' (14 December 2011), https://www.whitehouse.gov/the-press-office/2011/12/14/remarks-president-and-first-lady-end-war-iraq.

Chapter 3   The Sectarian House of Cards?

1. Some suggest that the Shi'a comprise around 60 per cent of the Iraqi population.

2. Roy Wallis, *Sectarianism: Analyses of Religious and Non-religious Sects* (London: Peter Owen, 1975), p. 9.

3. Lawrence Potter, *Sectarian Politics in the Persian Gulf* (London: C. Hurst & Co., 2013), p. 2.
4. Ibid., p. 3.
5. Jacqueine Ismael and Tareq Ismael, 'The sectarian state in Iraq and the new political class', *International Journal of Contemporary Iraqi Studies*, iv/3 (2010), p. 340.
6. Fanar Haddad, 'Sectarian relations in Arab Iraq: contextualising the civil war of 2006–2007', *British Journal of Middle Eastern Studies*, xl/2 (2013), p. 118.
7. Benedict Anderson, *Imagined Communities* (London: Verso, 1983), pp. 6–7.
8. Darryl Champion, *The Paradoxical Kingdom: Saudi Arabia and the Momentum of Reform* (London: C. Hurst & Co., 2003), p. 64.
9. Khalil Osman, *Sectarianism in Iraq: The Making of State and Nation since 1920* (Abingdon: Routledge, 2014), p. 2.
10. Ismael and Ismael, 'The sectarian state in Iraq', p. 341.
11. Justin Gengler, 'Understanding sectarianism in the Persian Gulf', in Potter, *Sectarian Politics in the Persian Gulf*, p. 64.
12. Adham Saouli, 'Syria's predicament: state (de-) formation and international rivalries', *Konrad Adenauer Stiftung* (15 December 2014), www.iai.it/pdf/Sharaka/Sharaka_RP_10.pdf and Steve Bruce, *Politics and Religion* (Cambridge: Polity Press, 2003).
13. See Simon Mabon, *Saudi Arabia and Iran: Soft Power Rivalry in the Middle East* (London: I.B.Tauris, 2013).
14. Michael Barnett, *Dialogues in Arab Politics* (New York: Columbia University Press, 1998).
15. See Mabon, *Saudi Arabia and Iran*.
16. Shahram Chubin and Charles Tripp, *Iran–Saudi Arabia Relations and Regional Order* (London: Oxford University Press for IISS, 1996), p. 9.
17. Mabon, *Saudi Arabia and Iran*.
18. Ibid.
19. Con Coughlin, *Khomeini's Ghost* (London: Macmillan, 2009), p. 274.
20. *New York Times*, 'Excerpts from Khomeini speeches' (4 August 1987), www.nytimes.com/1987/08/04/world/excerpts-from-khomeini-speeches.html.
21. Simon Mabon, 'FPC briefing: constructing sectarianisms' (2014), http://fpc.org.uk/fsblob/1614.pdf.

22. 'Israel warns Hizbullah war would invite destruction', Reuters (10 March 2008), www.ynetnews.com/articles/0,7340,L-3604893,00.html.

23. Frederick Wehrey et al., 'Saudi–Iranian Relations since the Fall of Saddam: Rivalry, Cooperation, and Implications for U.S. Policy' (Santa Monica: Rand Corporation, 2009), pp. 81–2.

24. 'French weapons arrive in Lebanon in \$3 billion Saudi-funded deal', Reuters (20 April 2015), www.reuters.com/article/2015/04/20/us-mid-east-crisis-lebanon-army-idUSKBN0NB0GI20150420.

25. Simon Mabon, 'The battle for Bahrain', *Middle East Policy*, ix/2 (2012).

26. This was predominantly a legacy of the failed *coup d'état* in 1981, orchestrated by the International Front for the Liberation of Bahrain (IFLB). The IFLB received both ideological and logistical support from actors in Iran. For an in-depth study of this see Hasan T. Alhasan, 'The role of Iran in the failed coup of 1981: the IFLB in Bahrain', *Middle East Journal*, lxv/4 (2011), pp. 603–17.

27. Robert Smith, 'UK Ambassador Accuses Iran, Gulf Digital News' (25 March 2013), www.gulf-daily-news.com/NewsDetails.aspx?storyid=350071.

28. 06RIYADH9175_a SAUDI MOI HEAD SAYS IF U.S. LEAVES IRAQ, SAUDI ARABIA WILL STAND WITH SUNNIS (26 December 2006), https://wikileaks.org/plusd/cables/06RIYADH9175_a.html.

29. Ibid.

30. As reflected in the abandonment of the Arabian Gulf Games in 2013, over a dispute over the name of the body of water.

31. A misleading assumption that a number of scholars and practitioners adhere to.

32. As noted in Chapter 2, many of these assumptions are inaccurate.

33. Fanar Haddad, 'Sectarian relations in Arab Iraq: contextualising the civil war of 2006–2007', *British Journal of Middle Eastern Studies*, xl/2 (2013), pp. 115–38, p. 2.

34. Dodge, *Inventing Iraq*.

35. Namely family, tribe and sect.

36. International Crisis Group, 'The next Iraq War? Sectarianism and civil conflict', *Middle East Report*, No. 52 (2006), www.crisisgroup.org/~/media/Files/Middle%20East%20North%20Africa/Iraq%20Syria%20Lebanon/Iraq/52_the_next_iraqi_war_sectarianism_and_civil_conflict.pdf.

37. Known as Tandhim al-Qa'ida fi Bilad al-Rafidayan.

38. For a detailed breakdown of this, see International Crisis Group, 'The next Iraq War?'.

39. Mariam Fam, 'Militias growing in power in Iraq' (7 November 2005), www.washingtonpost.com/wp-dyn/content/article/2005/11/07/AR2005110700977_pf.html.

40. International Crisis Group, 'The next Iraq War?'.

41. International Crisis Group interview with a prominent Iraqi human rights activist

42. International Crisis Group interview with a young Sunni.

43. International Crisis Group, 'Make or Break: Iraq's Sunnis and the State, Middle East Report', No. 144 (2013), www.crisisgroup.org/~/media/Files/Middle%20East%20North%20Africa/Iraq%20Syria%20Lebanon/Iraq/144-make-or-break-iraq-s-sunnis-and-the-state.pdf.

44. Ibid., p. i.

45. Sabrina Tavernise and Andrew W. Lehren, 'Detainees fared worse in Iraqi hands, logs say', *New York Times* (22 October 2010), www.nytimes.com/2010/10/23/world/middleeast/23detainees.html?_r=0.

46. Andrew Wander, 'Left to die in jail', *Al Jazeera* (24 October 2010), www.aljazeera.com/secretiraqfiles/2010/10/20101022163052530756.html.

47. Perhaps a pseudonym.

48. 05BAGHDAD2547 ISLAMIC HUMAN RIGHTS ORGANIZATION ALLEGES IRAQI FORCES DETAINEE ABUSE IN NINEWA (16 June 2005), https://wikileaks.org/plusd/cables/05BAGHDAD2547_a.html.

49. Ahmed S. Hashim, 'Military power and state formation in modern Iraq', *Middle East Policy*, x/4 (2003), p. 29.

50. James Quinlivin, 'Coup-proofing: its practice and consequences in the Middle East', *International Security*, xxiv/2 (1999), pp. 131–65.

51. Coalition Provisional Authority Order Number 2.

52. Thom Shanker and Edward Wong, 'US troops in Iraq shifting to advisory roles', *New York Times* (5 December 2006), www.nytimes.com/2006/12/05/world/middleeast/05strategy.html?pagewanted=print&_r=0.

53. James A. Baker and Lee H. Hamilton (co-chairs), *Iraq Study Group Report* (New York: Vintage Books, 2006).

54. Edward Wong, 'U.S. faces latest trouble with Iraqi forces: loyalty', *New York Times* (6 March 2006), www.nytimes.com/2006/03/06/world/americas/06iht-military.html?pagewanted=all.

55. 'Coalition Provisional Authority Order Number 91: Regulation of Armed Forces and Militias within Iraq' (2004), www.iraqcoalition.org/regulations/20040607_CPAORD91_Regulation_of_Armed_Forces_and_Militias_within_Iraq.pdf.

56. Jeremy M. Sharp, 'The Iraqi Security Forces: The Challenge of Sectarian and Ethnic Influences' (Congressional Research Service Report, 2005), https://www.fas.org/sgp/crs/mideast/RS22093.pdf.

57. Walter Pincus, 'US military urging Iraq to rein in guard force', *Washington Post* (25 December 2006), www.washingtonpost.com/wp-dyn/content/article/2006/12/24/AR2006122400551.html.

58. Sharp, 'The Iraqi Security Forces: The Challenge of Sectarian and Ethnic Influences'.

59. Iraq Study Group Report, December 2006.

60. Although young, at 29 when the invasion took place, al-Sadr had a great deal of influence across Iraq, in part because his grandfather had been Grand Ayatollah until 1999, when he was assassinated by Saddam Hussein. See Patrick Cockburn, *Muqtada al-Sadr and the Fall of Iraq* (London: Faber and Faber, 2005).

61. Also known as the Badr Brigades.

62. Greg Bruno, 'Badr vs. Sadr in Iraq', council on foreign relations (31 March 2008), www.cfr.org/iraq/badr-vs-sadr-iraq/p15839.

63. 05BAGHDAD3015_a BUILDING A HOUSE ON SHIFTING SANDS – IRAN'S INFLUENCE IN IRAQ'S CENTER-SOUTH (20 July 2005), https://www.wikileaks.org/plusd/cables/05BAGHDAD3015_a.html.

64. Ibid.

65. Ibid.

66. *Veleyat-e Faqih* – Regency of the Jurist – is the system of government developed by Ruhollah Khomeini, to rule in the absence of the 12th Imam. See 05BAGHDAD3015_a.

67. 08BAGHDAD239_a "THE STREET IS STRONGER THAN PARLIAMENT:" SADRIST VOWS OPPOSITION TO LTSR (27 January 2008), https://wikileaks.org/plusd/cables/08BAGHDAD239_a.html.

68. 08BAGHDAD1105_a SADRIST CONFIDANTE WARNS OF BAD PRESSURE BUILDING WITHIN SADRIST MOVEMENT (9 April 2008), https://wikileaks.org/plusd/cables/08BAGHDAD1105_a.html.

69. Ibid.

70. 08BAGHDAD239_a "THE STREET IS STRONGER THAN PARLIAMENT:" SADRIST VOWS OPPOSITION TO LTSR

(27 January 2008), https://wikileaks.org/plusd/cables/08BAGHDAD239_a.html.

71. 08BAGHDAD1027_a DAWA PARTY OFFICIAL ON BASRAH OPERATION AND UIA-SADR NEGOTIATIONS IN IRAN (3 April 2008), https://wikileaks.org/plusd/cables/ 08BAGHDAD1027_a.html.

72. Ibid.

73. 08BAGHDAD2812_a KARBALA: IRAN EXERTS HEAVY INFLU-ENCE THROUGH TOURISM INDUSTRY (2 August 2008), https://wikileaks.org/plusd/cables/08BAGHDAD2812_a.html.

74. Ibid.

75. 08BAGHDAD239_a.

76. Ibid.

77. 10BAGHDAD22_a IRAQI VIEWS ON EVENTS IN IRAN AND IMPACT ON IRAQ (5 January 2010), https://wikileaks.org/plusd/cables/10BAGHDAD22_a.html.

78. Ibid.

79. Ibid.

80. 06HILLAH54_a FORMER NAJAF GOVERNOR ON AL-SADR, IRANIAN INFLUENCE (5 April 2006), https://www.wikileaks.org/plusd/cables/06HILLAH54_a.html.

81. Ibid.

82. 08BAGHDAD3994_a (C) PRT SALAH AD DIN: IRANIAN INVOLVEMENT IN SAMARRA (21 December 2008), https://wikileaks.org/plusd/cables/08BAGHDAD3994_a.html.

83. Ibid.

84. Ibid.

85. 08BAGHADA1416_a SOUTHERN POLITICS AS USUAL: IRAN'S PLAN FOR IRAQI ELECTIONS (6 May 2008), https://wikileaks.org/plusd/cables/08BAGHDAD1416_a.html.

86. Iran faces serious (yet differing) challenges to its territorial integrity, from both secessionist and irredentist groups located predominantly on the periphery of the state, including from Arabs, Azeris, Baluchis, Kurds, Lors and Turkmen.

87. 09BAGHDAD289_a IRAQ-IRAN DIPLOMACY A SIGN OF IRANIAN INFLUENCE OR IRAQI RESOLVE? (4 February 2009), https://www.wikileaks.org/plusd/cables/09BAGHDAD289_a.html.

88. Ibid.

89. 08BAGHDAD3655_a KARBALA, IRAN DUEL OVER PILGRIMS (19 November 2008), https://wikileaks.org/plusd/cables/08BAGH-DAD3655_a.html.

90. Mohamad Bazzi, 'The Sistani factor', *Boston Review* (12 August 2014), accessed 13 August 2015, http://bostonreview.net/world/mohamad-bazzi-sistani-factor-isis-shiism-iraq.

91. The strict Wahhabist ideology that underpinned the actions of the group held Shi'a Muslims to be apostates.

92. Ibid.

Chapter 4   Tribalism and the State

1. Ronald J. Brown, *Humanitarian Operations in Northern Iraq, 1991: With Marines in Operation* (CreateSpace, 1995).

2. Nawzad Mahmoud, 'Kurdish tribe fights IS alone in disputed area', *Rudaw News* (20 September 2014), http://rudaw.net/english/kurdistan/200920141.

3. Abdulaziz Alheis, 'The tribe and democracy: the case of monarchist Iraq (1921–1958)', *Arab Center for Research & Policy Studies* (July 2011), http://english.dohainstitute.org/file/get/6c1fffaa-1a6a-4602-8ddb-1bbc348a394c.pdf, p.16.

4. Amatzia Baram, 'Neo-tribalism in Iraq: Saddam Hussein's tribal policies 1991–96', *International Journal of Middle East Studies*, xxix/1 (1997), p. 4.

5. Following marriage, a female will normally take her husband's family name, thus becoming part of that lineage.

6. See Hussein D. Hassan, 'Iraq: tribal structure, social, and political activities', Congressional Research Service: Report for Congress (US) (15 March 2007), p. 2; and Hosham Dawood, 'The "state-ization" of the tribe and the tribalization of the state: the case of Iraq', in Faleh Jabar and Hosham Dawood (eds), *Tribes and Power: Nationalism and Ethnicity in the Middle East* (London: Saqi Books, 2003), pp. 115–16.

7. For a more detailed breakdown see Hussein, 'Iraq: tribal structure, social, and political activities'.

8. For a more detailed historical overview of Iraq's Shi'a tribes see Yitzhak Nakash, *The Shi'is of Iraq* (Princeton: Princeton University Press, 2003).

9. Ibn Khaldun, *The Muqaddimah: An Introduction to History* (Princeton Classics Abridged, April 2015).

10. Faleh A. Jabar, 'Shaykhs and ideologues: detribalization and retribalization in Iraq, 1968–1998', *Middle East Report*, No. 215 (*Middle East Research and Information Project, Inc.*, Summer 2000).

11. Lawrence E. Cline, 'The prospects of the Shia insurgency movement in Iraq', *Journal of Conflict Studies*, xx/2 (2000), https://journals.lib.unb.ca/index.php/jcs/article/view/4311/4924#a26.

12. Ibid.

13. Judith Yaphe, 'Tribalism in Iraq, the old and the new', *Middle East Policy*, vii/3, pp. 51–8 (June 2000), p. 51.

14. Jabar, 'Shaykhs and ideologues', p. 29.

15. Jabar, 'Shaykhs and ideologues', referred to this in two main patterns: 1. 'Statist' tribalism, where symbols and lineage are integrated into a weaker state to strengthen government; and 2. 'social' tribalism, which normally develops following a reduction in the state's capacity to control urban societal restlessness, leading to the devolving of power to tribal areas via tax collection and judicial powers.

16. Baram, 'Neo-tribalism in Iraq', p. 4.

17. Ibid.

18. Ibid., p. 8.

19. Ibid., pp. 20–1.

20. Jabar 'Shaykhs and ideologues', p. 48.

21. Austin Long, 'The Anbar Awakening', *Survival*, l/2, pp. 67–94, pp. 82–3.

22. David Ucko, 'Militias, tribes and insurgents: the challenge of political reintegration in Iraq', *Conflict, Security & Development*, viii/3, pp. 341–73 (2008), p. 352, DOI: 10.1080/14678800802358171.

23. Ibid.

24. Long, 'The Anbar Awakening', p. 87.

25. For a useful example of this situation, see R. Stewart, *The Prince of the Marshes: And Other Occupational Hazards of a Year in Iraq* (Mariner Books, 2007 reprint). In this book, Stewart lays out his own experience as a governor in the southern province of Maysan.

26. Dahr Jamail and Ali al-Fadhily, 'Southern tribes add to Iraqi resistance', *Inter Service Press* (19 January 2007), https://www.globalpolicy.org/component/content/article/168/37369.html.

27. Information obtained from Control Risks Iraq, Liaison and Analysis, 24 September 2015.

28. John A. McCary, 'The Anbar Awakening: an alliance of incentives', *Washington Quarterly*, 32:1 (2009), pp. 43–59, p. 52.

29. Hala Jaber, 'Sunni leader killed for joining ceasefire talks', *Sunday Times* (6 February 2006), www.thesundaytimes.co.uk/sto/news/world_news/article204068.ece.

30. This was taken from an interview with a senior member of the Albu Fahad tribe in Baghdad, during October 2015.

31. The Albu Fahad tribe also had members in Babil and areas north of Baghdad.

32. See Bill Roggio, 'The Sunni Awakening', *Long War Journal* (3 May 2007), www.longwarjournal.org/archives/2007/05/the_sunni_awakening.php.

33. Joel Wing, 'Anbar before and after the Awakening Pt. IX: Sheikh Sabah Aziz of the Albu Mahal' (23 January 2014), http://musingsoniraq.blogspot.com/2014/01/anbar-before-and-after-awakening-pt-ix.html.

34. The Albu Nimr tribe were supported by former Anbar governor Fasal al-Gaoud of the Albu Nimr tribe.

35. There is some confusion regarding the timeframes for the emergence of Kataib al-Hamza. For Austin Long, 'The Anbar Awakening', p. 78, it was in 2006 after the Desert Protectors, while J.A. McCary, 'The Anbar Awakening', pp. 48, suggests the Desert Protectors were formed after Kataib al-Hamza.

36. For a useful insight into US dealings with Sheikh Sattar al-Rishawi, see William Doyle, *A Soldier's Dream: Captain Travis Patriquin and the Awakening of Iraq* (New York: New American Library, 2012).

37. Daveed Gartenstein-Ross and Sterling Jensen, 'The role of Iraqi tribes after the Islamic state's ascendance', *Military Review* (July–August, 2015), www.defenddemocracy.org/content/uploads/documents/The_Role_of_Iraqi_Tribes_After_the_Islamic_States_Ascendance.pdf.

38. B. Dehghanpisheh and E. Thomas, 'Scions of the surge', *Newsweek* (14 March 2008).

39. This interview was conducted with John Harris in Baghdad on 20 November 2015.

40. Roberto J. González, 'On "tribes" and bribes: "Iraq tribal study", al-Anbar's awakening, and social science', *Focaal: European Journal of Anthropology*, liii (2009), pp. 105–16.

41. Mark Wilbanks and Efraim Karsh, 'How the "Sons of Iraq" stabilized Iraq', *Middle East Quarterly* (Fall 2010), pp. 57–70, p. 68.

42. This interview was conducted with a private contractor within the security sector in Iraq.

43. Liz Sly, 'Iraq plans to cut Sunni fighters' salaries', *Chicago Tribune* (3 November 2008), http://articles.chicagotribune.com/2008-11-03/news/0811020469_1_awakening-leader-sunni-awakening-awakening-members.

44. Wilbanks and Karsh, 'How the sons of Iraq stabilized Iraq', p. 68.

45. Stephen Wicken, 'Iraq's Sunnis in crisis', *Middle East Security Report* 11 (May 2013), www.understandingwar.org/sites/default/files/Wicken-Sunni-In-Iraq.pdf, p. 15.

46. Kirk H. Sowell, 'Iraq's second Sunni insurgency' (9 August 2014), www.hudson.org/research/10505-iraq-s-second-sunni-insurgency.

47. Sheikh Ali Hatem al-Suleimeni was evicted from his offices in Baghdad by soldiers, under orders from al-Maliki in 2011. He even coerced Ali Hatem's uncle, Majid, back from Jordan, in an attempt to undermine Ali Hatem. See Ned Parker and Sulieman al-Khalidi, 'Special Report: The doubt at the heart of Iraq's Sunni revolution' (4 August 2014), www.reuters.com/article/2014/08/04/us-iraq-security-alisuleiman-specialrepo-idUSKBN0G40OP20140804#VYx8KRGOttjQPHXe.97.

48. Adam Schreck and Qassim Abdul-Zahra, 'Iraq: new protests break out in Sunni stronghold', *Associated Press* (26 December 2012), http://news.yahoo.com/iraq-protests-break-sunni-stronghold-184403534.html.

49. Wicken, 'Iraq's Sunnis in crisis', p. 29.

50. 'Iraqi Sunni protest clashes in Hawija leave many dead', *BBC* (23 April 2013), www.bbc.co.uk/news/world-middle-east-22261422.

51. Wicken, 'Iraq's Sunnis in crisis', p. 31.

52. See 'Statement No. 35 on the events in Hawija, Ramadi', YouTube, https://www.youtube.com/watch?v=NxXYi3GCjIA.

53. Ammar Karim and Salam Faraj, 'Maliki's remedy for Iraq sectarian violence: overhaul of security strategy', *Middle East Online* (20 May 2013), www.middle-east-online.com/english/?id = 58868.

54. This was obtained from an interview with a member of the Albu Khalaf tribe, in Baghdad in October 2015.

55. Bashdar Pusho Ismaeel, 'A marriage of convenience: the many faces of Iraq's Sunni insurgency', *Terrorism Monitor*, xii/15 (25 July 2014), p. 5.

56. Kirk H. Sowell, 'Maliki's Anbar blunder', *Foreign Policy* (15 January 2014), http://foreignpolicy.com/2014/01/15/malikis-anbar-blunder/?wp_login_redirect=0.

57. Mohammed Khamis on 30 April 2015 was targeting polling stations set up to support a local political rival to his uncle, the Defence Minister Sadoun al-Dulaymi. See Hawar Berwani, 'Abu Risha's nephew closes electoral center by force in Ramadi', *Iraqi News* (30 April 2014), www.iraqinews.com/iraq-war/abu-risha-s-nephew-closes-electoral-center-by-force-in-ramadi/.

58. Ben Hubbard, 'Sunni tribesmen say ISIS exacts brutal revenge', *New York Times* (30 October 2014), www.nytimes.com/2014/10/31/world/middleeast/sunni-tribesmen-say-isis-exacts-brutal-revenge.html?_r=0.

59. Eli Lake, 'The rise and fall of America's favorite Iraqi sheik', Bloomberg (7 June 2011), www.bloombergview.com/articles/2015-06-11/the-rise-and-fall-of-america-s-favorite-iraqi-sheik.

60. Interview conducted in Baghdad, 24 August 2015.
61. Liz Sly, 'Al-Qaeda disavows any ties with radical Islamist ISIS group in Syria, Iraq', *Washington Post* (3 February 2014), https://www.washington-post.com/world/middle_east/al-qaeda-disavows-any-ties-with-radical-islamist-isis-group-in-syria-iraq/2014/02/03/2c9afc3a-8cef-11e3-98ab-fe5228217bd1_story.html.
62. Interview conducted via translator and mobile telephone, 20 July 2015.
63. This interview was carried out with a senior aid worker of a reputable organisation, in Baghdad, in June 2015.
64. This information was obtained via an intermediary translator, and relative of the police officer in Haditha.
65. This information was the result of a conversation with two members of the Albu Khalaf tribe in Baghdad, 28 November 2015.
66. This interview was conducted in Baghdad, 23 November 2015.

Chapter 5   The Roots of Sunni Militancy and its Enduring Threat in Iraq

1. This interview was conducted with a former senior intelligence officer based in Baghdad, 15 September 2015. His name has been changed to protect his identity.
2. Siobhan Gorman, Nour Malas and Matt Bradley, 'Brutal efficiency: the secret to Islamic State's success', *Wall Street Journal* (3 September 2014), www.wsj.com/articles/the-secret-to-the-success-of-islamic-state-1409 709762.
3. Ahmed Hashim, *Iraq's Sunni Insurgency* (London: Routledge – Adelphi Paper Series, 2009), pp. 30–1.
4. Denise Natali, 'The Islamic State's Baathist roots', *Al-Monitor* (24 April 2015), www.al-monitor.com/pulse/originals/2015/04/baathists-behind-the-islamic-state.html#.
5. See Sonia Alianak, *Middle Eastern Leaders and Islam: A Precarious Equilibrium* (Bern: Peter Lang Publishers, 2007), pp. 119–21.
6. 'Saddam Hussein's speech', *Guardian* (8 August 2002), www.theguardian.com/world/2002/aug/08/iraq3.
7. This interview was conducted in Karrada, Baghdad, on 11 November 2015.
8. Aymenn Jawad Al-Tamimi, 'Violence in Iraq', Rubin Center; Research in International Affairs (14 November 2012), www.rubincenter.org/2012/11/violence-in-iraq/.

9. Anthony Cordesman, 'Iraq's Sunni insurgents: looking beyond Al Qa'ida', Center for Strategic and International Studies (16 July 2007), www.social-sciences-and-humanities.com/PDF/sunni_insurgents.pdf, p. 4.

10. Johnathan Schanzer, 'Ansar al-Islam: back in Iraq', *Middle East Quarterly* (Winter 2004), www.meforum.org/579/ansar-al-islam-back-in-iraq, pp. 41–50.

11. This information was gained from an interview with the two former military officers, in Karrada, Baghdad, on 11 November 2015.

12. Michael Howard, 'Militant Kurds training al-Qaida fighters', *Guardian* (23 August 2002), www.theguardian.com/world/2002/aug/23/alqaida.iraq1.

13. Evan Kohlman, 'Ansar al-Sunnah acknowledges relationship with Ansar al-Islam, reverts to using Ansar al-Islam name', *Counter Terrorism Blog* (16 December 2007), http://counterterrorismblog.org/2007/12/ansar_alsunnah_acknowledges_re.php.

14. Kathryn Gregory, 'Ansar al-Islam (Iraq, Islamists/Kurdish Separatists), Ansar al-Sunnah', *The Council on Foreign Relations* (5 November 2008), accessed 9 December 2015, www.cfr.org/iraq/ansar-al-islam-iraq-islamists-kurdish-separatists-ansar-al-sunnah/p9237.

15. Cordesman, 'Iraq's Sunni insurgents'.

16. See Evan F. Kohlmann, 'State of the Sunni insurgency in Iraq: August 2007', *The NEFA Foundation* (August 2007), p. 16.

17. 'Al Qaeda in Iraq tightening economic grip on Mosul', *Al Bawaba* (3 May 2011), www.albawaba.com/main-headlines/al-qaeda-iraq-tightening-economic-grip-mosul.

18. Huthaifa Azzam fought in Afghanistan and Iraq. He fell out with Zarqawi over the latter's targeting of Jordanian civilians.

19. Anne Weaver, 'The short, violent life of Abu Musab al-Zarqawi', *The Atlantic* (July–August 2006), www.theatlantic.com/magazine/archive/2006/07/the-short-violent-life-of-abu-musab-al-zarqawi/304983/.

20. Kohlman, 'Ansar al-Sunnah acknowledges relationship'.

21. Bill Roggio, 'Islamic Army of Iraq splits from al Qaeda', *Long War Journal* (12 April 2007), www.longwarjournal.org/archives/2007/04/islamic_army_of_iraq.php.

22. Muhammad Rumman, 'The politics of Sunni armed groups in Iraq', *The Carnegie Endowment for International Peace* (18 August 2008), http://carnegieendowment.org/sada/?fa=20836.

23. Taken from Aymenn Jawad al-Tamimi, 'Violence in Iraq', *MERIA Journal*, xvi/03 (14 November 2012), www.rubincenter.org/2012/11/violence-in-iraq/.

24. Anthony Shadid, 'In Iraq, chaos feared as U.S. closes prison, ex-inmates reanimate Sunni, Shiite militias', *Washington Post Foreign Service* (22 March 2009), www.washingtonpost.com/wp-dyn/content/article/2009/03/21/AR2009032102255_pf.html.

25. Siobhan Gorman, Nour Malas and Matt Bradley, 'Brutal efficiency: the secret to Islamic State's success', *Wall Street Journal* (3 September 2014), www.wsj.com/articles/the-secret-to-the-success-of-islamic-state-1409709762.

26. This interview was conducted in Erbil in February 2015. The former intelligence officer was one of 60 former security experts selected by the government of Iraq to help re-establish its intelligence network in 2007.

27. Ibid.

28. Andrew Thompson and Jeremi Surioct, 'How America helped ISIS', *New York Times* (2 October 2014), www.nytimes.com/2014/10/02/opinion/how-america-helped-isis.html?_r=0.

29. Gorman, Malas and Bradley, 'Brutal efficiency'.

30. Former head of Saudi intelligence Prince Bandar provided support to Jaish al-Islam, a group led by Syrian Salafi Zahran Alloush, the son of a Saudi-based cleric. See I. Black, 'Syria crisis: Saudi Arabia to spend millions to train new rebel force', *Guardian* (7 November 2013), www.theguardian.com/world/2013/nov/07/syria-crisis-saudi-arabia-spend-millions-new-rebel-force.

31. Hassan Hassan, 'Isis: a portrait of the menace that is sweeping my homeland', *Guardian* (16 August 2014), www.theguardian.com/world/2014/aug/16/isis-salafi-menace-jihadist-homeland-syria.

32. Liz Sly, 'Al-Qaeda disavows any ties with radical Islamist ISIS group in Syria, Iraq', *Washington Post* (3 February 2014), accessed 28 November 2015, https://www.washingtonpost.com/world/middle_east/al-qaeda-disavows-any-ties-with-radical-islamist-isis-group-in-syria-iraq/2014/02/03/2c9afc3a-8cef-11e3-98ab-fe5228217bd1_story.html.

33. Haian Dukhan and Sinan Hawat, 'The Islamic State and the Arab tribes in Eastern Syria', *E-International Relations* (31 December 2014), www.e-ir.info/2014/12/31/the-islamic-state-and-the-arab-tribes-in-eastern-syria/.

34. This information was obtained through email correspondence with Stephen McGrory on 29 November 2015.

35. 'Islamic State oil trade "worth more than $500m"', *BBC News* (11 December 2015), www.bbc.com/news/world-middle-east-35070204.

184 The Origins of ISIS

36. Erika Solomon, Robin Kwong and Steven Bernard, 'Inside Isis Inc: the journey of a barrel of oil', *Financial Times* (11 December 2015), http://ig. ft.com/sites/2015/isis-oil/.

37. 'Islamic State monthly revenue totals $80 million, IHS says', *IHS Press* (7 December 2015), http://press.ihs.com/press-release/aerospace-defense-security/islamic-state-monthly-revenue-totals-80-million-ihs-says.

38. As noted in Chapter 3, the killing of unarmed protestors in Hawija triggered a reaction from within the Sunni communities. However, following al-Maliki's loss of seats in the local elections, he leaned even further towards the hard-line Shi'a bloc in order to reinforce his own position.

39. 'Bare-faced killer rises to fore of Iraq militancy', Agence France-Presse – *Gulf Times* (28 August 2013), www.gulf-times.com/story/364086/Bare-faced-killer-rises-to-fore-of-Iraq-militancy.

40. This interview was carried out in Baghdad in October 2015 with an associate of Shakir Waheeb's family, who had recently fled the al-Madhaiq area following heavy fighting between ISIS-aligned militants and government-aligned security forces.

41. The establishment of local military councils across Iraq, including Mosul (Ninawah), Dhuluiya and Sharqat (Salahaddin), Abu Ghraib (Anbar), Baghdad and in other towns in Kirkuk and Diyala, provided support for the GMCIR. In Jordan, during July 2014, many of these factions also assembled to discuss the direction of the insurgency.

42. Nicolas A. Heras, 'The tribal component of Iraq's Sunni rebellion: the General Military Council for Iraqi revolutionaries', *Terrorism Monitor*, xii/13 (26 June 2014), www.jamestown.org/uploads/media/Terrorism MonitorVol12Issue13_01.pdf, p. 4.

43. Hassan Hassan, 'Maliki's alienation of Sunni actors is at the heart of ISIS's success in Iraq', *Carnegie Endowment for International Peace* (17 June 2014), http://carnegieendowment.org/sada/?fa=55930.

44. Bashdar Pusho Ismaeel, 'A marriage of convenience: the many faces of Iraq's Sunni insurgency', *Terrorism Monitor*, xii/15 (25 July 2014), www.jamestown.org/uploads/media/TerrorismMonitorVol12Issue15_ 01.pdf, p. 5.

45. Sinan Adnan and Aaron Reese, 'Iraq's Sunni insurgency', *Middle East Security Report* (24 October 2014), www.understandingwar.org/sites/ default/files/Sunni%20Insurgency%20in%20Iraq.pdf, p. 16.

46. Hawar Berwani, 'Gunmen in Fallujah form Military Council, reject Anbar initiative', *Iraq News* (11 February 2014), www.iraqinews.com/iraq-war/ gunmen-in-fallujah-form-military-council-reject-anbar-initiative/.

47. Ruth Sherlock and Carol Malouf, 'Islamic Army of Iraq founder: Isis and Sunni Islamists will march on Baghdad', *Telegraph* (20 June 2015), www.telegraph.co.uk/news/worldnews/middleeast/iraq/10914567/Islamic-Army-of-Iraq-founder-Isis-and-Sunni-Islamists-will-march-on-Baghdad.html.

48. Ibid.

49. Heras, 'The tribal component of Iraq's Sunni rebellion'.

50. Hassan, 'Maliki's alienation of Sunni actors'.

51. Louisa Loveluck, 'Isil releases new video of 2014 Speicher massacre of Shi'a army recruits', *Telegraph* (12 July 2015), www.telegraph.co.uk/news/worldnews/islamic-state/11734606/Isil-releases-new-video-of-2014-Speicher-massacre-of-Shi'a-army-recruits.html.

52. Ben Hubbard, 'Sunni tribesmen say ISIS exacts brutal revenge', *New York Times* (30 October 2014), www.nytimes.com/2014/10/31/world/middleeast/sunni-tribesmen-say-isis-exacts-brutal-revenge.html?_r=0.

53. Adnan and Reese, 'Beyond the Islamic State'.

54. Abdallah Suleiman Ali, 'IS disciplines some emirs to avoid losing base', *Al-Monitor* (2 September 2014), www.al-monitor.com/pulse/security/2014/09/is-takfiri-caliphate.html#ixzz3xlwgdeNZ.

55. 'Ansar al-Islam', Stanford University (2 October 2015), http://web.stanford.edu/group/mappingmilitants/cgi-bin/groups/view/13#note39.

56. '35 abducted from Ansar al-Islam and the Naqshbandi southwest of Kirkuk', *Voice of Iraq* (1 December 2015), www.sotaliraq.com/newsitem.php?id=308852#ixzz3xh7niWYs.

57. This interview was conducted in Erbil in February 2015.

58. Ned Parker, 'Divided Iraq has two spy agencies', *Los Angeles Times* (15 April 2007), http://articles.latimes.com/2007/apr/15/world/fg-intel15. For more detail on Shahwani, see Global Security, Iraqi National Intelligence Service, www.globalsecurity.org/intell/world/iraq/inis.htm.

59. Sherwan Waili, a Shi'a and a former Iraqi army brigadier arrested by Saddam's forces following the 1991 uprising, led the MSNS in the beginning. The network consists mainly of Shi'a pro-Iranian members.

60. 'An uncertain future for Iraq's intelligence services', *Stratfor* (11 January 2012), https://www.stratfor.com/sample/analysis/uncertain-future-iraqs-intelligence-services.

61. Mustafa Al-Kadhimi, 'Overhauling Iraq's intelligence services', *Al-Monitor* (15 June 2015), www.al-monitor.com/pulse/originals/2015/06/iraq-security-intelligence-services-quota-terrorists.html#.

62. Andreas Kreig, 'ISIS success in Iraq: a testamony to failed security sector reform', Centre for Security Governance: Security Sector Reform Resource Centre (22 July 2014), www.ssrresourcecentre.org/2014/07/22/isis-success-in-iraq-a-testimony-to-failed-security-sector-reform/.

63. 'Learning from Iraq: A final report from the special inspector general for Iraq reconstruction', SIGIR (March 2013), www.globalsecurity.org/military/library/report/2013/sigir-learning-from-iraq.pdf, p. 93.

64. SIGIR, Quarterly report to the United States Congress (30 April 2008), p. 99.

65. Interview conducted in Baghdad, 11 December 2015.

66. 'Abadi to purge Iraq's interior ministry of Maliki supporters', *Al-Araby al-Jadeed* (17 November 2014), www.alaraby.co.uk/english/news/2014/11/17/abadi-to-purge-iraqs-interior-ministry-of-maliki-supporters.

67. Suadad Al-Salhy, 'How Iraq's "ghost soldiers" helped ISIL: discovering 50,000 ghost soldiers in the army forced Iraq to rebuild their troops to face ISIL', Al Jazeera (11 December 2014), www.aljazeera.com/news/middleeast/2014/12/how-iraq-ghost-soldiers-helped-isil-201412107 2749979252.html.

68. Ibid.

69. Interview carried out in Baghdad, 7 November 2015.

70. Benjamin Bahney, Patrick. B. Johnston and Patrick Ryan, 'The enemy you know and the ally you don't', *Foreign Policy* (23 June 2015), http://foreignpolicy.com/2015/06/23/the-enemy-you-know-and-the-ally-you-dont-arm-sunni-militias-iraq/.

71. Al-Nujaifi's political manoeuvrings and accusations of his corruption led to his dismissal as Ninawa governor in May 2015. Exiled, Nujaifi has since sought refuge in the Kurdistan region under the protection of President Masoud Barzani.

72. Ruth Sherlock and Carol Malouf, 'Mosul governor calls for fragmentation of Iraq', *Telegraph* (12 June 2014), accessed 16 November 2015, www.telegraph.co.uk/news/worldnews/middleeast/iraq/10895792/Mosul-governor-calls-for-fragmentation-of-Iraq.html.

73. This information was obtained via a family source of the security force members, in Baghdad on 28 October 2015.

74. AAH split from Moqtada al-Sadr's Jaish al-Mahdi (JAM) in 2006.

75. 'Absolute impunity: militia rule in Iraq', Amnesty International (2014), https://www.amnesty.org.uk/sites/default/files/absolute_impunity_iraq_report.pdf.

76. This became something of a normal process for the families of the fallen, particularly observed in Basra province.

77. Data obtained from Control Risks Group, Iraq, 15 March 2015, information processed by A. Atkinson, S. Royle and J. Harris. The graph indicates the number of incidents in Babil province between July 2014 and February 2015. The thickness of the line denotes the actual number of a particular type of attack relative to the number of incidents in total.

78. It is important to note that since the end of Shi'a militia activity against the occupation, IEDs have become associated with Sunni militancy and account for the majority of attacks in the country, with civilians being the primary target.

79. Although we cannot ascertain the exact religion of the victims, we do know that a majority of Sunni militant attacks target civilians in Shi'a, mixed and densely populated areas.

80. Data obtained from Control Risks Group, Iraq, 22 March 2015, information processed by A. Atkinson, S. Royle and J. Harris. Using open sources and Control Risks' sources, Graph 2 shows the data for attack targets and estimated casualty numbers during the period July 2014 to February 2015. The thickness of the line denotes the number of a particular target casualty relative to the number of attacks in total. Casualty numbers are based on open source reports, and although their accuracy is difficult to verify, it is likely that there are many more casualties and incidents that have not been reported or accounted for. There are also likely to be cases where civilians have been recorded as militants and vice versa. Nevertheless, the data offers an indication of continued violence against civilians in Babil.

81. From the end of 2014, the city was officially renamed Jurf al-Nasr, translated as 'Victory Banks', following government-militia security operations. For the purpose of consistency, this book will refer to it as Jurf al-Sakhar (Rocky Bank).

82. Ahmed Rasheed and Ned Parker, 'Shi'ite militias expand influence, redraw map in central Iraq', Reuters (31 December 2014), www.reuters.com/article/2014/12/31/us-mideast-crisis-iraq-idUSKBN0K909K20141231.

83. W.G. Dunlop, 'Iraq area retaken, but destruction and anger remain', Associated Free Press (9 November 2014), http://news.yahoo.com/iraq-area-retaken-destruction-anger-remain-113132316.html.

84. Kashmira Gander, 'Isis car bomb kills more than 100 including children during Eid celebrations in the Iraqi town of Khan Bani Saad', *Independent* (17 July 2015), www.independent.co.uk/news/uk/home-news/car-bomb-kills-at-least-80-including-children-in-iraqi-town-of-khan-bani-saad-10398064.html.

85. Data obtained from Control Risks Group, Iraq, 15 March 2015, information processed by S. Royle. The graph indicates the number of incidents in Babil province between August 2014 and June 2015. The thickness of the line denotes the actual number of a particular type of attack relative to the number of incidents in total.

86. 'Iraq: militias escalate abuses, possibly war crimes killings, kidnappings, forced evictions', *Human Rights Watch* (15 February 2015), https://www.hrw.org/news/2015/02/15/iraq-militias-escalate-abuses-possibly-war-crimes.

87. This interview was conducted on mobile telephone via a translator. The interviewee was with family in Salahaddin province at the time.

88. This information was provided by a local police officer in Diyala, on a mobile telephone via a translator.

89. Erin Cunningham, 'Sectarian violence besets key province in Iraq after an Islamic State attack', *Washington Post* (18 January 2016), https://www.washingtonpost.com/world/sectarian-violence-hits-key-iraqi-province-after-islamic-state-attack/2016/01/18/b2e674e6-bd7a-11e5-98c8-7fab78677d51_story.html?tid=ss_tw.

90. This information was obtained from a police officer working in Amiriyat al-Fallujah in Anbar province, via translator and mobile phone on 12 April 2015.

91. This interview was conducted with a journalist of Sunni Arab origin in Baghdad, on 4 December 2015. At the time of publication, the journalist wished to remain anonymous.

92. Kurdish forces are primarily made up of Peshmerga soldiers from both KDP and PUK factions, and other Kurdish militia, which in several cases such as Sinjar included the more extremist PKK.

93. 'Iraqi Kurdistan: Arabs displaced, cordoned off, detained', *Human Rights Watch* (25 February 2015), accessed 6 November 2015, https://www.hrw.org/news/2015/02/25/iraqi-kurdistan-arabs-displaced-cordoned-detained.

94. 'Iraq: banished and dispossessed: forced displacement and deliberate destruction in Northern Iraq', *Amnesty International* (20 January 2016), https://www.amnesty.org/en/documents/mde14/3229/2016/en/.

95. Yazidis are of monotheistic faith and while they have been referred to as Christian in the media, they are of a stand-alone faith particular to the region and Ninawa province.

96. Mohammed A. Salih, 'With the Islamic State gone from Sinjar, Kurdish groups battle for control', *Al-Monitor* (10 December 2015), www.al-monitor.com/pulse/originals/2015/12/iraq-kurdistan-sinjar-liberated-isis-hegemony.html#ixzz3yRNmvwGi.

97. Ben Kesling and Ali A. Nabhan, 'Recaptured Iraqi city of Sinjar offers window on Islamic State's destruction', *Wall Street Journal* (15 November 2015), www.wsj.com/articles/recaptured-iraqi-city-of-sinjar-offers-window-on-islamic-states-destruction-1447621010.

98. Amnesty International (20 January 2016), p. 44, https://www.amnesty.org/en/documents/mde14/3229/2016/en/.

99. Kesling and Nabhan, 'Recaptured Iraqi city of Sinjar offers window on Islamic State's destruction'.

100. Adnan Abu Zeed, 'Arab–Kurd conflict heats up after Tuz Khormato incidents', *Al-Monitor* (8 December 2015), www.al-monitor.com/pulse/originals/2015/12/iraq-kurdistan-region-tuz-khormato-arabs-kurds-conflict.html#ixzz3yGHJz18s.

Chapter 6   The Human Tragedy

1. Ibn Khaldoun, *The Muqaddimah: An Introduction to History* (Princeton: Princeton University Press, 2005), p. 39.

2. This raises serious questions about the extent to which Iraq can be viewed as a functioning sovereign state, a question that this book has been engaging with.

3. The structural theme is holistic in nature, encompassing political, judicial and security. It builds upon a definition of structural violence provided by Johan Galtung, who defines it as the 'avoidable impairment of fundamental human needs', ranging across social, economic and political spheres. Victims of structural violence become increasingly marginalised from political life, resulting, in the case of many across Iraq, in what Georgio Agamben has termed 'bare life'.

4. The names of all interviewees have been changed to protect them.

5. Human Rights Watch, 'World Report: Events of 2004' (2005), https://www.hrw.org/legacy/wr2k5/wr2005.pdf.

6. Ibid.

7. Ibid.

8. Ibid.

9. The use of torture in extracting confessions became a common theme across the following decade.

10. UN Assistance Mission for Iraq (UNAMI), 'Human Rights Report (1 November–31 December 2005)', www.ohchr.org/Documents/Countries/Nov-Dec05_en.pdf.

11. US Department of State, 'Iraq: Bureau of Democracy, Human Rights, and Labor' (2006), www.state.gov/j/drl/rls/hrrpt/2005/61689.htm.

12. UNAMI, 'Human Rights Report 1'.

13. Human Rights Watch, 'World Report: Events of 2005 (2006)', www.hrw.org/legacy/wr2k6/wr2006.pdf.

14. UNAMI, 'Human Rights Report' (1 November–31 December 2005)'.

15. Human Rights Watch, 'World Report: Events of 2005'.

16. Ibid.

17. UN Assistance Mission for Iraq (UNAMI), 'Human Rights Report (1 July–31 August 2005)', www.ohchr.org/Documents/Countries/Jul-Aug05_en.pdf.

18. Human Rights Watch, 'World Report: Events of 2005'.

19. UNAMI, 'Human Rights Report (1 November–31 December 2005)'.

20. UN Assistance Mission for Iraq (UNAMI), 'Human Rights Report (1 September–31 October 2005)', www.ohchr.org/Documents/Countries/Sep-Oct05_en.pdf.

21. Ibid.

22. Human Rights Watch, 'World Report: Events of 2005'.

23. Human Rights Watch, 'World Report: Events of 2006 (2007)', www.hrw.org/legacy/wr2k7/wr2007master.pdf.

24. UN Assistance Mission for Iraq (UNAMI), 'Human Rights Report (1 November–31 December 2006)', www.ohchr.org/Documents/Countries/sept-october06.pdf.

25. Ibid.

26. UN Assistance Mission for Iraq (UNAMI), 'Human Rights Report (1 September–31 October 2005)', www.ohchr.org/Documents/Countries/Sep-Oct05_en.pdf.

27. Human Rights Watch, 'World Report: Events of 2006'.

28. UN Assistance Mission for Iraq (UNAMI), 'Human Rights Report (1 January–28 February 2006)', www.ohchr.org/Documents/Countries/Jan-Feb06_en.pdf.

29. UN Assistance Mission for Iraq (UNAMI), 'Human Rights Report (1 May–30 June 2006)', www.ohchr.org/Documents/Countries/May-June06-new_en.pdf.

30. UN Assistance Mission for Iraq (UNAMI), 'Human Rights Report (1 March–30 April 2006)', www.ohchr.org/Documents/Countries/Mar-Apr06_en.pdf.

31. UNAMI, 'Human Rights Report (1 May–30 June 2006)'.

32. Human Rights Watch, 'World Report: Events of 2007 (2008)', https://www.hrw.org/legacy/wr2k8/pdfs/wr2k8_web.pdf.

33. Ibid.

34. For more information see UN Assistance Mission for Iraq (UNAMI), 'Human Rights Report (1 April–30 June 2007)', www.ohchr.org/Documents/Countries/IQ/HRReportAprJun2007EN.pdf p. 18.

35. For more information on the restrictions see ibid., p. 17.

36. UNAMI, 'Human Rights Report (1 January–28 February 2006)'.

37. Which are reported as being increasingly corrupted.

38. UNAMI, 'Human Rights Report (1 January–28 February 2006)'.

39. Ibid. Most Shi'a Arabs fled central governorates such as Baghdad, Anbar and Salah Al-Din towards the southern governorates of Najaf, Qadissya, Wasit and Karbala, while Sunnis moved towards Baghdad, Diyala and Anbar. For more information, UNAMI, 'Human Rights Report (1 May–30 June 2006)', pp. 12–13.

40. The Sabean-Mandeans community received increasing threats to convert to Islam or be killed, and they decreased from 13,500 people in 2001 to approximately 4,000 people in 2006. For more information, see UNAMI, 'Human Rights Report (1 September–30 October 2006)', pp. 13–14. Christians were targeted after Pope Benedict XVI's controversial remarks on Islam of 12 September. For more information see ibid., pp. 12–13.

41. UNAMI, 'Human Rights Report (1 March–30 April 2006)'.

42. Ibid.

43. Ibid.

44. According to the Iraqi Penal Code, 'honour' constitutes an attenuating factor, and even if men are found guilty of 'honour killing' their jail time is restricted to a period of three years. These crimes are infrequently reported and judges often sympathize with the accused. For more information see UNAMI, 'Human Rights Report (1 July–31 August 2006)', pp. 10–11.

45. UNAMI, 'Human Rights Report (1 January–28 February 2006)'.

46. Ibid., pp. 2–3.

47. Ibid. This was done predominantly as a consequence of the rising number of extra-judicial executions targeting people on the basis of their name, stressing the rising sectarian violence across the state and the failure of the state to protect its citizens. For more information, see Edward Wong, 'To stay alive, Iraqis change their names', *New York Times* (6 September 2006), www.nytimes.com/2006/09/06/world/middleeast/06identity.html?ref=familiesandfamilylife&_r=0 and Peter Beaumont, 'Sunnis change names to avoid Shia death squads', *Guardian* (10 October 2006), www.theguardian.com/world/2006/oct/10/iraq.peterbeaumont. This will be a recurring theme over the coming years. Examples of this can be found here: Wassim Bassem, 'From Omar to

Hussain: Why Iraqis are changing their names', *Al Monitor* (17 June 2015), www.al-monitor.com/pulse/originals/2015/06/iraq-sectarian-killing-name-changing.html#; and Amir al-Obaidi, 'Surrendering to sectarianism: Iraq's Sunnis change their names', *Al-Araby* (8 May 2015), www.alaraby.co.uk/english/features/2015/5/8/surrendering-to-sectarianism-iraqs-sunnis-change-their-names.

48. UNAMI, 'Human Rights Report (1 April–30 June 2007)'.
49. For the specifics of each attack, see UNAMI, 'Human Rights Report (1 July–31 December 2007)', www.ohchr.org/Documents/Countries/IQ/double_quarterly_1july-31dec2007_engl.pdf, pp. 8–9.
50. Ibid. UNHCR estimates that 525 houses were destroyed and more than 2,000 houses were damaged, leaving hundreds homeless, 400 orphaned and 100 widowed.
51. Ibid.
52. UNAMI, 'Human Rights Report (1 April–30 June 2007)'.
53. UNAMI, 'Human Rights Report (1 July–31 December 2006)'.
54. UN Assistance Mission for Iraq (UNAMI), 'Human Rights Report (1 January–30 June 2008)', www.ohchr.org/Documents/Countries/IQ/UNAMI_Human_Rights_Report_January_June_2008_EN.pdf.
55. Human Rights Watch, 'World Report: Events of 2008 (2009)', www.hrw.org/sites/default/files/reports/wr2009_web.pdf.
56. UNAMI, 'Human Rights Report (1 January–30 June 2008)'.
57. National Legislative Bodies National Authorities, 'Iraq: Prime Minister's Order 101/S of 2008 (property)' (3 August 2008), www.refworld.org/docid/49da18482.html.
58. Human Rights Watch, 'World Report: Events of 2008'.
59. UN Assistance Mission for Iraq, January–June 2008.
60. Ibid.
61. Eli Lake, 'The rise and fall of America's favorite Iraqi sheik', Bloomberg (11 June 2015), www.bloombergview.com/articles/2015-06-11/the-rise-and-fall-of-america-s-favorite-iraqi-sheik.
62. UN Assistance Mission for Iraq (UNAMI), 'Human Rights Report (1 July–31 December 2009)', www.ohchr.org/Documents/Countries/IQ/UNAMI_Human_Rights_Report16_July_December_2009_EN.pdf.
63. Human Rights Watch, 'World Report: Events of 2009 (2010)', www.hrw.org/sites/default/files/reports/wr2010.pdf.
64. Human Rights Watch, 'World Report: Events of 2010 (2011)', www.hrw.org/sites/default/files/related_material/wr2011_book_complete.pdf. For more information on the banning of the candidates see: BBC, 'Iraqi

election commission bans 500 candidates' (15 January 2010), http://news.bbc.co.uk/1/hi/world/middle_east/8461275.stm. An analysis of the elections can be found here: Human Rights Watch, 'Iraq's 2010 National Elections: A Human Rights Platform for Candidates' (25 February 2010), https://www.hrw.org/news/2010/02/25/iraqs-2010-national-elections.

65. Human Rights Watch, 'World Report: Events of 2010'.
66. Ibid.
67. UN Assistance Mission for Iraq, 'Human Rights Report (1 January–31 December 2010)', www.ohchr.org/Documents/Countries/IQ/UNAMI_HR%20Report_1Aug11_en.pdf.
68. Ibid.
69. Ibid. For more information see: 'Al Qaeda claims responsibility for Iraq's Tikrit attack', Reuters (2 September 2011), www.reuters.com/article/2011/04/02/us-iraq-violence-qaeda-idUSTRE7310R520110402.
70. UN Assistance Mission for Iraq (UNAMI), 'Human Rights Report (1 January–31 December 2011)', www.ohchr.org/Documents/Countries/IQ/IraqUNAMI-OHCHR_HR_Report2011_en.pdf. On the same day, 17 armed groups (predominantly Sunni) announced they were resuming their jihad against the Government of Iraq.
71. Ibid.
72. Ibid. This included the targeting of individual clerics; see p. 23.
73. Ibid.
74. UN Assistance Mission for Iraq (UNAMI), 'Human Rights Report (1 July–31 December 2011)', www.ohchr.org/Documents/Countries/IQ/HRO_July-December2013Report_en.pdf.
75. See Charles R. Lister, *The Syrian Jihad: Al-Qaeda, the Islamic State and the Evolution of an Insurgency* (London: Hurst: 2015).
76. Human Rights Watch, 'World Report: Events of 2013 (2014)', https://www.hrw.org/sites/default/files/wr2014_web_0.pdf.
77. Details of the attacks targeting civilians in the last six months of the year can be found at UNAMI, 'Human Rights Report (1 July–31 December 2013)', pp. 20–1.
78. Ibid.
79. UN Assistance Mission for Iraq (UNAMI), 'Human Rights Report (1 January–30 June 2013)', http://reliefweb.int/sites/reliefweb.int/files/resources/HRO_Human%20Rights%20Report%20January%20-%20June%202013_FINAL_ENG_15Dec2013%20%282%29.pdf.
80. Ibid. The majority of the attacks targeted candidates of the al-Iraqiya bloc or its affiliates, but Shi'a political parties were targeted as well.

81. Ibid.

82. Martin Chulov, 'Iraq "doomed" if new prime minister Abadi fails to bridge sectarian divide', *Guardian* (15 August 2014), www.theguardian.com/world/2014/aug/15/iraq-doomed-if-prime-minister-fails-unite-factions-haidar-al-abadi.

83. BBC News, 'Iraq reforms: parliament backs PM Haider al-Abadi's plan' (11 August 2015), www.bbc.co.uk/news/world-middle-east-33861080. See also Omar Al-Jawoshy and Tim Arango, 'Premier Haider al-Abadi, facing protests, proposes Iraqi government overhaul', *New York Times* (9 August 2015), www.nytimes.com/2015/08/10/world/middleeast/iraqs-premier-facing-protests-proposes-government-overhaul.html; and Nour Malas and Safa Majeed, 'Iraq cabinet approves sweeping overhaul to political system', *Wall Street Journal* (9 September 2015), www.wsj.com/articles/iraq-cabinet-approves-sweeping-reforms-to-political-system-1439133137.

84. *Dabiq* 1.

85. For a month-by-month breakdown of casualty figures, see United Nations Iraq, Civilian Casualties, www.uniraq.org/index.php?option=com_k2&view=itemlist&layout=category&task=category&id=159&Itemid=633&lang=en.

86. It is important to note the problems with using the term supporter. Following the declaration of the caliphate, al-Baghdadi sought to portray unity and coherence amongst those living in the territory. Yet while many may agree with – and support – the ISIS ideology and use of violence, in a form of active support, others may be more passive in their support. Moreover, we cannot remove the threat of violence from such calculations. Clearly, gauging the nature of this support is problematic, methodologically, but we need to avoid a homogenised view of those living in ISIS-controlled territory. As Brandon M. Boylan argues, we must consider the interaction of the 'behavioural (active and passive) and induced (enticed and coerced) continuums of support'. See Brandon M. Boylan, 'Sponsoring violence: a typology of constituent support for terrorist organisations', *Studies in Conflict & Terrorism*, xxxviii/8 (2015), p. 653.

87. United Nations Assistance Mission for Iraq (UNAMI), 'Report on the Protection of Civilians in the Armed Conflict in Iraq: 11 December 2014–30 April 2015', www.ohchr.org/Documents/Countries/IQ/UNAMI_OHCHR_4th_POCReport-11Dec2014-30April2015.pdf.

88. For a comprehensive overview of broken laws, see chapters 1–4 of Jean-Marie Henckaerts and Louise Doswald-Beck, *Customary International*

Humanitarian Law: Volume 1 (Cambridge: Cambridge University Press, 2009), https://www.icrc.org/eng/assets/files/other/customary-international-humanitarian-law-i-icrc-eng.pdf.

89. Wherein actors are in breach of Rule 83. At the end of active hostilities, a party to the conflict which has used landmines must remove or otherwise render them harmless to civilians, or facilitate their removal (Volume II, Chapter 29, Section C). See International Committee of the Red Cross, *Customary IHL*, https://www.icrc.org/customary-ihl/eng/docs/v1_rul_rule83.

90. United Nations Iraq, 'Iraq displacement passes 3.1 Million' (21 August 2015), www.uniraq.org/index.php?option=com_k2&view=item&id=4082:iraq-displacement-passes-3-1-million&Itemid=605&lang=en.

91. Predominantly in rented housing, with host families and in hotels.

92. Unfinished buildings, religious buildings and schools. Of course, much like the above, questions emerge about the financing of such projects.

93. United Nations General Assembly Human Rights Council, 'Report of the Office of the United Nations High Commissioner for Human Rights on the human rights situation in Iraq in the light of abuses committed by the so-called Islamic State in Iraq and the Levant and associated groups', *Security Council Report* (27 March 2015), www.securitycouncilreport.org/atf/cf/%7B65BFCF9B-6D27-4E9C-8CD3-CF6E4FF96FF9%7D/a_hrc_28_18.pdf.

94. Nick Cumming-Bruce, 'United Nations investigators accuse ISIS of genocide over attacks on Yazidis', *New York Times* (19 March 2015), www.nytimes.com/2015/03/20/world/middleeast/isis-genocide-yazidis-iraq-un-panel.html.

95. UNAMI, 'Report on the Protection of Civilians in the Armed Conflict in Iraq: 11 December 2014–30 April 2015'.

96. Cumming-Bruce, 'United Nations investigators'.

97. Colum Lynch, 'Women and children for sale', *Foreign Policy* (2 October 2014), http://foreignpolicy.com/2014/10/02/women-and-children-for-sale/?wp_login_redirect=0.

98. United Nations General Assembly Human Rights Council, Security Council Report.

99. Ibid.

100. Ibid.

101. UNAMI, 'Report on the Protection of Civilians in the Armed Conflict in Iraq: 11 December 2014–30 April 2015'.

102. Ibid.

103. UN Assistance Mission for Iraq (UNAMI), 'Report on the Protection of Civilians in the Armed Conflict in Iraq: 11 September–10 December 2014', www.ohchr.org/Documents/Countries/IQ/UNAMI_OHCHR_Sep_Dec_2014.pdf, p. 6.

104. Ibid.

105. UNAMI, 'Human Rights Report (1 September–31 December 2014)'.

106. Patrick Cockburn, *The Rise of Islamic State: ISIS and the New Sunni Revolution* (London: Verso, 2014).

107. While evidence has emerged suggesting that ISIS membership includes former Baathists from the military, this desire to capture former party members is both symbolic and an attempt to further destabilise the current government.

108. Here, Omar chose to use the derogatory Arabic slang-term for ISIS.

109. Again, Omar chose his words carefully, reflecting the perceived parallels with the religion of Saudi Arabia and its influence in Iraq.

110. UN Assistance Mission for Iraq, 'Report on the Protection of Civilians in the Armed Conflict in Iraq: 11 December 2014–30 April 2015'. See also Robert Fisk, 'ISIS profits from destruction of antiquities by selling relics to dealers – and then blowing up the buildings they come from to conceal the evidence of looting', *Independent* (20 September 2015), www.independent.co.uk/voices/isis-profits-from-destruction-of-antiquities-by-selling-relics-to-dealers-and-then-blowing-up-the-10483421.html.

111. See *Mosul Eye*, https://mosuleye.wordpress.com and https://www.facebook.com/Mosul-Eye-552514844870022/?fref=ts.

112. A *wilayat* is an administrative division or province; in this context, they are areas that have pledged allegiance to ISIS.

113. Aaron Y. Zelin, 'The Islamic State's Saudi chess match', *Washington Institute* (2 June 2015), www.washingtoninstitute.org/policy-analysis/view/the-islamic-states-saudi-chess-match.

114. For instance, the 7/7 bombers in London.

115. Peter R. Neumann, 'Foreign fighter total in Syria/Iraq now exceeds 20,000; surpasses Afghanistan conflict in the 1980s', ICSR (26 January 2015), http://icsr.info/2015/01/foreign-fighter-total-syriairaq-now-exceeds-20000-surpasses-afghanistan-conflict-1980s/.

116. Erin Marie Saltman and Melanie Smith, '"Till martyrdom do us part": gender and the ISIS phenomenon', *The Institute for Strategic Dialogue* (2015), http://icsr.info/wpcontent/uploads/2015/06/Till_Martyrdom_Do_Us_Part_Gender_and_the_ISIS_Phenomenon.pdf.

117. Ibid.

118. UNAMI, 'Human Rights Report (1 September–31 December 2014)'.

Conclusions

1. Patrick Wintour and Ewen MacAskill, 'UK foreign secretary: US decision on Iraqi army led to rise of ISIS', *Guardian* (7 July 2016), https://www.theguardian.com/world/2016/jul/07/uk-foreign-secretary-us-decision-iraqi-army-rise-isis-philip-hammond.
2. Ibid.
3. Nicholas Watt, 'Tony Blair makes qualified apology for Iraq war ahead of Chilcot report', *Guardian* (25 October 2015), www.theguardian.com/uk-news/2015/oct/25/tony-blair-sorry-iraq-war-mistakes-admits-conflict-role-in-rise-of-isis.
4. Ibid.
5. Wassim Bassem, 'When conflict arises, these Iraqis go to the madeef', *Al-Monitor* (30 October 2015), www.al-monitor.com/pulse/originals/2015/10/iraq-madeef-tribes-host-disputes-politicans.html#ixzz3q5TJkME8.
6. *Dabiq* 1.
7. Baiji oil refinery in the north of Salahaddin province (and north of Tikrit) draws oil from the fields in its surrounding areas. However, control of the facility has exchanged hands between ISIS and the government on several occasions, and now it lies in a dilapidated state.
8. The gas field is situated close to Qaim, near the Syrian border, an area of particular insecurity.
9. The World Bank, 'US$1.2 billion to support Iraq amid challenging economic situation' (17 December 2015), www.worldbank.org/en/news/press-release/2015/12/17/support-iraq-amid-challenging-economic-situation.
10. For further understanding of chaos theory or chaotic systems, see Boris Hasselblatt and Anatole Katok, *A First Course in Dynamics: With a Panorama of Recent Developments* (Cambridge: Cambridge University Press, 2003).
11. Russia Today, 'Evidence reveals Turkish regime affair with ISIS as global threat – Iraqi militia to RT' (25 December 2015), https://www.rt.com/news/327052-iraqi-militia-isis-turkey/.
12. Agence France Presse in the *Guardian*, 'Turkish troops move out of northern Iraq after Obama appeal for calm' (20 December 2015), www.theguardian.com/world/2015/dec/20/turkish-troops-move-out-of-northern-iraq-after-obama-appeal-for-calm.
13. Ahmed Rasheed and Stephen Kalin, 'Iraq blames Iran after thousands of pilgrims storm border crossing', Reuters (30 November 2015), www.reuters.com/article/us-iraq-iran-pilgrims-idUSKBN0TJ2RQ20151130.

14. See Ali Khedery, 'Iran's Shiite militias Are running amok in Iraq', *Foreign Policy* (19 February 2015), http://foreignpolicy.com/2015/02/19/irans-shiite-militias-are-running-amok-in-iraq/.

15. Guy Taylor, 'Nouri al-Maliki undermines U.S. interests in Iraq, plots return to power', *Washington Times* (15 June 2015), www.washingtontimes.com/news/2015/jun/15/nouri-al-maliki-undermines-us-interests-in-iraq-pl/?page=all.

16. See Renad Mansour, 'The popularity of the Hashd in Iraq', *Carnegie Endowment for International Peace* (1 February 2016), http://carnegieendowment.org/syriaincrisis/?fa = 62638.

17. Militia involvement in criminal activity across Iraq is an ongoing issue that is gaining attention. Both Sunni and Shi'a communities are targeted, particularly in Baghdad where focus on the war with ISIS has reduced local security levels. For example, see Omar al-Jaffal, 'Who's to blame for recent kidnappings in Iraq?', *Al-Monitor* (29 January 2016), www.al-monitor.com/pulse/originals/2016/01/iraq-wave-abductions-foreigners-accusations.html#ixzz3z6R3KGgZ.

18. For a more detailed understanding of management and complexity theory, see R.J. Stacey, *Managing the Unknowable: The Strategic Boundaries Between Order and Chaos* (San Francisco: Jossey Bass, 1992).

Bibliography

Books

Agamben, Georgio, *Homer Sacer: Sovereign Power and Bare Life* (Stanford: Stanford University Press, 1998).

Alianak, Sonia, *Middle Eastern Leaders and Islam: A Precarious Equilibrium* (Bern: Peter Lang Publishers, 2007).

Anderson, Benedict, *Imagined Communities* (London: Verso, 1983).

Anderson, Liam and Gareth Stansfield, *The Future of Iraq: Dictatorship, Democracy, or Division* (New York: Palgrave Macmillan, 2004).

Baker, James A. and Lee H. Hamilton (co-chairs), *Iraq Study Group Report* (New York: Vintage Books, 2006).

Barnett, Michael N., *Dialogues in Arab Politics* (New York: Columbia University Press, 1998).

Barr, James, *A Line in the Sand: Britain, France and the Struggle that Shaped the Middle East* (London: Simon & Schuster, 2011).

Batatu, Hanna, *The Old Social Classes and the Revolutionary Movements in Iraq* (Princeton: Princeton University Press, 1978).

Brown, L. Carl, *Religion and State: The Muslim Approach to Politics* (New York: Columbia University Press, 2001).

Brown, Ronald J., *Humanitarian Operations in Northern Iraq, 1991: With Marines in Operation* (CreateSpace Independent Publishing Platform, 1995)

Bruce, Steve, *Politics and Religion* (Cambridge: Polity Press, 2003).

Burke, Jason, *The New Threat from Islamic Militancy* (London: Bodley Head, 2015).

Byrne, David, *Complexity Theory and the Social Sciences: An Introduction* (London; New York: Routledge, 1998).

Champion, Darryl, *The Paradoxical Kingdom: Saudi Arabia and the Momentum of Reform* (London: C. Hurst & Co., 2003).

Chubin, Shahram and Charles Tripp, *Iran–Saudi Arabia Relations and Regional Order* (London: Oxford University Press for IISS, 1996).

Cockburn, Patrick, *Muqtada al-Sadr and the Fall of Iraq* (London: Faber and Faber, 2005).

————, *The Rise of Islamic State: ISIS and the New Sunni Revolution* (London: Verso, 2014).

Coughlin, Con, *Khomeini's Ghost: The Iranian Revolution and the Rise of Militant Islam* (London: Macmillan, 2009).

Dawisha, Adeed, *Iraq: A Political History from Independence to Occupation* (Princeton: Princeton University Press, 2009).

Dodge, Toby, *Inventing Iraq* (New York: Columbia University Press, 2005).

Doyle, William, *A Soldier's Dream: Captain Travis Patriquin and the Awakening of Iraq* (New York: New American Library, 2012).

Grotius, *De Jure Belli ac Pacis* (1625), trans. Kelsey, F. (1925).

Haldane, Aylmer, *The Insurrection in Mesopotamia, 1920* (Edinburgh: Blackwood, 1922).

Hashim, A., *Iraq's Sunni Insurgency* (London: Routledge – Adelphi Paper Series, 2009).

Hasselblatt, Boris and Anatole Katok, *A First Course in Dynamics: With a Panorama of Recent Developments* (Cambridge: Cambridge University Press, 2003).

Henckaerts, Jean-Marie and Louise Doswald-Beck, *Customary International Humanitarian Law: Volume 1* (Cambridge: Cambridge University Press, 2009).

Hilterman, Joost R., *A Poisonous Affair: America, Iraq, and the Gassing of Halabja* (Cambridge: Cambridge University Press, 2007).

Holt, Peter M., *Egypt and the Fertile Crescent, 1516–1922: A Political History* (Cornell University Press, 1996).

Issawi, Charles and Muhammed Yeganeh, *The Economies of Middle Eastern Oil* (New York: Praeger, 1962).

Khaldun, Ibn, *The Muqaddimah: An Introduction to History* (Princeton: Princeton University Press, 2005).

Lister, Charles R., *The Syrian Jihad: Al-Qaeda, the Islamic State and the Evolution of an Insurgency* (London: Hurst, 2015).

Luttwak, Edward, *Coup d'Etat: A Practical Handbook* (Cambridge, MA: Harvard University Press, 1979).

Mabon, Simon, *Saudi Arabia and Iran: Soft Power Rivalry in the Middle East* (London: I.B.Tauris, 2013).

Moubayed, Sami, *Under the Black Flag* (London: I.B.Tauris, 2016).

Nakash, Yitzhak, *The Shi'is of Iraq* (Princeton: Princeton University Press, 2003).

Osman, Khalil, *Sectarianism in Iraq: The Making of State and Nation since 1920* (Abingdon: Routledge, 2014).

Potter, Lawrence, *Sectarian Politics in the Persian Gulf* (London: C. Hurst & Co., 2013).

Rosen, Nir, *Aftermath: Following the Bloodshed of America's Wars in the Muslim World* (New York: Perseus Books, 2010).

Stacey, R.J., *Managing the Unknowable: The Strategic Boundaries Between Order and Chaos* (San Francisco: Jossey Bass, 1992).

Stewart, Rory, *The Prince of the Marshes: And Other Occupational Hazards of a Year in Iraq* (New York: Mariner Books, 2007).

Tripp, Charles, *A History of Iraq* (Cambridge: Cambridge University Press, 2007).

Wallis, Roy (ed.), *Sectarianism: Analyses of Religious and Non-religious Sects* (London: Peter Owen, 1975).

Weber, Max, *The Theory of Social and Economic Organization* (New York: The Free Press, 1947).

Weiss, Michaek and Hassan Hassan, *ISIS: Inside the Army of Terror* (New York: Raegan, 2016).

Wilson, Arnold T., *Mesopotamia, 1917–1920: A Clash of Loyalties* (London: H. Milford, 1931).

Journal Articles

Alhasan, Hasan T., 'The role of Iran in the failed coup of 1981: The IFLB in Bahrain', *Middle East Journal*, lxv/4 (2011), pp. 603–17.

Alheis, Abdulaziz, 'The tribe and democracy: the case of monarchist Iraq (1921–1958)', *Arab Center for Research & Policy Studies* (July 2011), http://english.dohainstitute.org/file/get/6c1fffaa-1a6a-4602-8ddb-1bbc348a394c.pdf.

Anderson, Lisa, 'The state in the Middle East and North Africa', *Comparative Politics*, xx/1 (1987).

Baram, Amatzia, 'Neo-tribalism in Iraq: Saddam Hussein's tribal policies 1991–96', *International Journal of Middle East Studies*, xxix/1 (1997), pp. 1–31.

Batatu, Hanna, 'Iraq's underground Shi'i movements' (MER102, 1981), www.merip.org/mer/mer102/iraqs-underground-shii-movements.

Boylan, Brandon M., 'Sponsoring violence: a typology of constituent support for terrorist organisations', *Studies in Conflict & Terrorism*, xxxviii/8 (2015), pp. 652–70.

Caporaso, James, 'Changes in the Westphalian order: territory, public authority, and sovereignty', *International Studies Review*, ii/2.

Cline, Lawrence, 'The prospects of the Shia insurgency movement in Iraq', *Journal of Conflict Studies*, xx/2 (2000).

Coates-Ulrichsen, Kristian, 'The British occupation of Mesopotamia, 1914–1922', *Journal of Strategic Studies*, xxx/2 (2007), pp. 349–77.

Cordesman, Anthony, 'Iraq's Sunni insurgents: looking beyond Al Qa'ida', *Center for Strategic and International Studies* (16 July 2007), www.social-sciences-and-humanities.com/PDF/sunni_insurgents.pdf.

Croxton, Derek, 'The Peace of Westphalia of 1648 and the origins of sovereignty', *The International History Review*, xxi/3.

Cunningham, Erin, 'Sectarian violence besets key province in Iraq after an Islamic State attack' *Washington Post* (18 January 2016), www.washington post.com/world/sectarian-violence-hits-key-iraqi-province-after-islamic-state-attack/2016/01/18/b2e674e6-bd7a-11e5-98c8-7fab78677d51_story. html?tid=ss_tw.

Dawisha, Adeed, 'Identity and political survival in Saddam's Iraq', *Middle East Journal*, liii/4 (1999), pp. 553–67.

———, 'National identity and sub-state sectarian loyalties in Iraq', *International Journal of Contemporary Iraqi Studies*, iv/3 (2010).

Dodge, Toby, 'Can Iraq be saved?', *Survival: Global Politics and Strategy*, lvi/5 (2014), pp. 7–20.

González, Roberto, 'On "tribes" and bribes: Iraq tribal study, al-Anbar's awakening, and social science', *Focaal: European Journal of Anthropology*, liii (2009), pp. 105–16.

Gorman, Siobhan, Nour Malas and Matt Bradley, 'Brutal efficiency: the secret to Islamic State's success', *Wall Street Journal* (3 September 2014), www.wsj. com/articles/the-secret-to-the-success-of-islamic-state-1409709762.

Gregory, Kathryn, 'Ansar al-Islam (Iraq, Islamists/Kurdish Separatists), Ansar al-Sunnah', *The Council on Foreign Relations* (5 November 2008), www.cfr. org/iraq/ansar-al-islam-iraq-islamistskurdish-separatists-ansar-al-sunnah/ p9237.

Haddad, Fanar, 'Sectarian relations in Arab Iraq: contextualising the civil war of 2006–2007', *British Journal of Middle Eastern Studies*, xl/2 (2013), pp. 115–38.

Hashim, Ahmed, 'Military power and state formation in modern Iraq', *Middle East Policy*, x/4 (2003).

Heras, Nicolas, 'The tribal component of Iraq's Sunni Rebellion: the General Military Council for Iraqi Revolutionaries', *Terrorism Monitor*, xii/13, (26 June 2014) www.jamestown.org/uploads/media/TerrorismMonitor Vol12Issue13_01.pdf.

Ismaeel, B.P., 'A marriage of convenience: the many faces of Iraq's Sunni Insurgency', *Terrorism Monitor*, xii/15, (25 July 2014), www.jamestown. org/uploads/media/TerrorismMonitorVol12Issue15_01.pdf.

Ismael, Tareq and Jacqueline Ismael, 'The sectarian state in Iraq and the new political class', *International Journal of Contemporary Iraqi Studies*, iv/3 (2010), pp. 339–56.

Kedouri, Elie, 'Réflexions sur l'histoire du Royaume d'Irak (1921–1958)', *Orient*, xi/3 (1959), pp. 55–79.

Kesling, B. and A. Nabhan, 'Recaptured Iraqi city of Sinjar offers window on Islamic State's destruction', *Wall Street Journal* (15 November 2015), www.wsj.com/articles/recaptured-iraqi-city-of-sinjar-offers-window-on-islamic-states-destruction-1447621010.

Krasner, S., 'Compromising Westphalia', *International Security*, xx/3 (1995–6), pp. 115–51.

——, 'Sharing sovereignty: new institutions for collapsed and failing states', *International Security*, xxix/2.

Kreig, A., 'ISIS success in Iraq: a testimony to failed security sector reform', Centre for Security Governance: Security Sector Reform Resource Centre (22 July 2014), www.ssrresourcecentre.org/2014/07/22/isis-success-in-iraq-a-testimony-to-failed-security-sector-reform/.

Krohley, N., 'Opportunity in chaos: how Iraq's Medhi Army almost succeeded – and why it matters', *Foreign Affairs* (26 August 2015), www.foreignaffairs.com/articles/iraq/2015-08-26/opportunity-chaos.

Long, Austin, 'The Anbar Awakening', *Survival*, l/2 (2008), pp. 67–94.

Mabon, Simon, 'The battle for Bahrain', *Middle East Policy*, xix/2 (2012), pp. 84–97.

——, 'Kingdom in Crisis', *Contemporary Security Policy*, xxxiii/3 (2012), pp. 530–3.

McCary, John, 'The Anbar Awakening: an alliance of incentives', *The Washington Quarterly*, xxxii/1 (2009), pp. 43–59.

Quinlivan, James, 'Coup-proofing: its practice and consequences in the Middle East', *International Security*, xxiv/2 (1999), pp. 131–65.

Roggio, Bill, 'Islamic Army of Iraq splits from al Qaeda', *Long War Journal* (12 April 2007), www.longwarjournal.org/archives/2007/04/islamic_army_of_iraq.php.

——, 'The Sunni Awakening', *Long War Journal* (3 May 2007), www.longwarjournal.org/archives/2007/05/the_sunni_awakening.php.

Schanzer, Jonathan, 'Ansar al-Islam: back in Iraq', *Middle East Quarterly* (Winter 2004), pp. 41–50, www.meforum.org/579/ansar-al-islam-back-in-iraq.

Schmidt, Soren, 'The role of religion in politics. The case of Shia-Islamism in Iraq', *Nordic Journal of Religion and Society*, xxii/2 (2009), pp. 123–43.

Al-Tamimi, Aymenn, 'Violence in Iraq', *MERIA Journal*, xvi/3 (14 November 2012), www.rubincenter.org/2012/11/violence-in-iraq/.

Ucko, David, 'Militias, tribes and insurgents: the challenge of political reintegration in Iraq', *Conflict, Security & Development*, viii/3 (2008), pp. 341–73.

Vinogradov, Amal, 'The 1920 revolt in Iraq reconsidered: the role of tribes in national politics', *International Journal of Middle East Studies*, iii/2 (1972), pp. 123–39.

Wilbanks, Mark and Efriam Karsh, 'How the "Sons of Iraq" stabilized Iraq', *Middle East Quarterly* (Fall 2010), pp. 57–70.

Yaphe, Judith, 'Tribalism in Iraq, the old and the new', *Middle East Policy* vii/3 (2000), pp. 51–8.

Chapters in edited books

Baram, Amatzia, 'The radical Shi'ite opposition movements in Iraq', in Emmanuel Sivan and Menachem Friedman (eds), *Religious Radicalism and Politics in the Middle East* (Albany: State University of New York Press, 1990).

Dawood, H., 'The "state-ization" of the tribe and the tribalization of the state: the case of Iraq', in Faleh Jabar and Hosham Dawood (eds), *Tribes and Power: Nationalism and Ethnicity in the Middle East* (London: Saqi Books, 2003).

Reports and Official Documents

Adnan, Sinan and Aaron Reese, 'Iraq's Sunni Insurgency', 'Middle East Security Report', 24 (October 2014), www.understandingwar.org/sites/default/files/Sunni%20Insurgency%20in%20Iraq.pdf.

Amnesty International, 'Absolute Impunity: Militia Rule in Iraq' (2014), www.amnesty.org.uk/sites/default/files/absolute_impunity_iraq_report.pdf.

———, 'Iraq: Banished and Dispossessed: Forced Displacement and Deliberate Destruction in Northern Iraq' (20 January 2016), https://www.amnesty.org/en/documents/mde14/3229/2016/en/

Blanchard, Christopher M., 'Al Qaeda: Statements and Evolving Ideology' (Congressional Research Service Report, 2007), www.fas.org/sgp/crs/terror/RL32759.pdf.

'Charter of the United Nations', www.un.org/en/documents/charter/chapter1.shtml.

Chilcot, John, 'The Iraq Inquiry' (2016), www.iraqinquiry.org.uk/the-report/.

'Coalition Provisional Authority Order Number 1: De-Ba'athification of Iraqi Society' (2003), http://nsarchive.gwu.edu/NSAEBB/NSAEBB418/docs/9a%20-%20Coalition%20Provisional%20Authority%20Order%20No%201%20-%205-16-03.pdf.

'Coalition Provisional Authority Order Number 2: Dissolution of Entities' (2003), www.iraqcoalition.org/regulations/20030823_CPAORD_2_Dissolution_of_Entities_with_Annex_A.pdf.

'Coalition Provisional Authority Order Number 91: Regulation of Armed Forces and Militias within Iraq' (2004), www.iraqcoalition.org/regulations/20040607_CPAORD91_Regulation_of_Armed_Forces_and_Militias_within_Iraq.pdf.

Hassan, H.D., 'Iraq: Tribal Structure, Social, and Political Activities' (CRS Report for Congress, 2007), http://fpc.state.gov/documents/organization/81928.pdf.

Human Rights Watch, 'Endless Torment: The 1991 Uprising in Iraq and Its Aftermath' (1992), www.hrw.org/reports/1992/Iraq926.htm.

——, 'World Report: Events of 2004' (2005), www.hrw.org/legacy/wr2k5/wr2005.pdf.

——, 'World Report: Events of 2005' (2006),www.hrw.org/legacy/wr2k6/wr2006.pdf.

——, 'World Report: Events of 2006' (2007), www.hrw.org/legacy/wr2k7/wr2007master.pdf.

——, 'World Report: Events of 2007' (2008),www.hrw.org/legacy/wr2k8/pdfs/wr2k8_web.pdf.

——, 'World Report: Events of 2008' (2009), www.hrw.org/sites/default/files/reports/wr2009_web.pdf.

——, 'World Report: Events of 2009' (2010), www.hrw.org/sites/default/files/reports/wr2010.pdf.

——, 'World Report: Events of 2010' (2011), www.hrw.org/sites/default/files/related_material/wr2011_book_complete.pdf.

——, 'Iraq's 2010 National Elections: A Human Rights Platform for Candidates' (25 February 2010), www.hrw.org/news/2010/02/25/iraqs-2010-national-elections.

——, 'World Report: Events of 2013' (2014), www.hrw.org/sites/default/files/wr2014_web_0.pdf.

——, 'Iraq: Militias Escalate Abuses, Possibly War Crimes Killings, Kidnappings, Forced Evictions' (15 February 2015), www.hrw.org/news/2015/02/15/iraq-militias-escalate-abuses-possibly-war-crimes.

——, 'Iraqi Kurdistan: Arabs Displaced, Cordoned Off, Detained' (25 February 2015), www.hrw.org/news/2015/02/25/iraqi-kurdistan-arabs-displaced-cordoned-detained

International Crisis Group, 'The Next Iraq War? Sectarianism and Civil Conflict, Middle East Report', No. 52 (2006), www.crisisgroup.org/~/media/Files/Middle%20East%20North%20Africa/Iraq%20Syria%

20Lebanon/Iraq/52_the_next_iraqi_war_sectarianism_and_civil_conflict.
pdf.

———, 'Make or Break: Iraq's Sunnis and the State, Middle East Report',
No. 144 (2013), www.crisisgroup.org/~/media/Files/Middle%20East%
20North%20Africa/Iraq%20Syria%20Lebanon/Iraq/144-make-or-break-
iraq-s-sunnis-and-the-state.pdf.

Jabar, F., 'Shaykhs and Ideologues: Detribalization and Retribalization in Iraq,
1968–1998, Middle East Report', No. 215 (Middle East Research and
Information Project, Inc., Summer 2000).

National Legislative Bodies/National Authorities, 'Iraq: Prime Minister's
Order 101/S of 2008 (property)' (3 August 2008), www.refworld.org/docid/
49da18482.html.

Saltman, Erin Marie, and Melanie Smith, 'Till Martyrdom Do Us Part:
Gender and the ISIS Phenomenon' (The Institute for Strategic Dialogue,
2015), http://icsr.info/wpcontent/uploads/2015/06/Till_Martyrdom_Do_Us_
Part_Gender_and_the_ISIS_Phenomenon.pdf.

Sharp, Jeremy M., 'The Iraqi Security Forces: The Challenge of Sectarian and
Ethnic Influences' (Congressional Research Service Report, 2005), www.
fas.org/sgp/crs/mideast/RS22093.pdf.

SIGIR, 'Learning from Iraq: A Final Report from the Special Inspector
General for Iraq Reconstruction' (March 2013), ppwww.globalsecurity.org/
military/library/report/2013/sigir-learning-from-iraq.pdf.

UN Assistance Mission for Iraq (UNAMI), 'Human Rights Report 1 July–
31 August 2005', www.ohchr.org/Documents/Countries/Jul-Aug05_en.pdf.

———, 'Human Rights Report 1 September–31 October 2005', www.ohchr.
org/Documents/Countries/Sep-Oct05_en.pdf.

———, 'Human Rights Report 1 November–31 December 2005', www.ohchr.
org/Documents/Countries/Nov-Dec05_en.pdf.

———, 'Human Rights Report 1 January–28 February 2006', www.ohchr.org/
Documents/Countries/Jan-Feb06_en.pdf.

———, 'Human Rights Report 1 March–30 April 2006', www.ohchr.org/
Documents/Countries/Mar-Apr06_en.pdf.

———, 'Human Rights Report 1 May–30 June 2006', www.ohchr.org/
Documents/Countries/May-June06-new_en.pdf.

———, 'Human Rights Report 1 November–31 December 2006', www.
ohchr.org/Documents/Countries/sept-october06.pdf.

———, 'Human Rights Report 1 April–30 June 2007', www.ohchr.org/
Documents/Countries/IQ/HRReportAprJun2007EN.pdf.

———, 'Human Rights Report 1 July–31 December 2007', www.ohchr.org/
Documents/Countries/IQ/double_quarterly_1july-31dec2007_engl.pdf.

────, 'Human Rights Report 1 January–30 June 2008', www.ohchr.org/Documents/Countries/IQ/UNAMI_Human_Rights_Report_January_June_2008_EN.pdf.

────, 'Human Rights Report 1 July–31 December 2009', www.ohchr.org/Documents/Countries/IQ/UNAMI_Human_Rights_Report16_July_December_2009_EN.pdf.

────, 'Human Rights Report 1 January–31 December 2010', www.ohchr.org/Documents/Countries/IQ/UNAMI_HR%20Report_1Aug11_en.pdf.

────, 'Human Rights Report 1 January–31 December 2011', www.ohchr.org/Documents/Countries/IQ/IraqUNAMI-OHCHR_HR_Report2011_en.pdf.

────, 'Report on Human Rights in Iraq: January – June 2013', http://reliefweb.int/sites/reliefweb.int/files/resources/HRO_Human%20Rights%20Report%20January%20-%20June%202013_FINAL_ENG_15Dec2013%20%282%29.pdf.

────, 'Report on the Protection of Civilians in the Armed Conflict in Iraq: 11 September–10 December 2014', www.ohchr.org/Documents/Countries/IQ/UNAMI_OHCHR_Sep_Dec_2014.pdf.

────, 'Report on the Protection of Civilians in the Armed Conflict in Iraq: 11 December 2014–30 April 2015', www.ohchr.org/Documents/Countries/IQ/UNAMI_OHCHR_4th_POCReport-11Dec2014-30April2015.pdf.

United Nations General Assembly Human Rights Council, 'Report of the Office of the United Nations High Commissioner for Human Rights on the human rights situation in Iraq in the light of abuses committed by the so-called Islamic State in Iraq and the Levant and associated groups' (27 March 2015), www.securitycouncilreport.org/atf/cf/%7B65BFCF9B-6D27-4E9C-8CD3-CF6E4FF96FF9%7D/a_hrc_28_18.pdf.

United Nations Iraq, 'Civilian Casualties', www.uniraq.org/index.php?option=com_k2&view=itemlist&layout=category&task=category&id=159&Itemid=633&lang=en.

────, 'Iraq Displacement Passes 3.1 Million' (21 July 2015), www.uniraq.org/index.php?option=com_k2&view=item&id=4082:iraq-displacement-passes-3-1-million&Itemid=605&lang=en.

United Nations Security Council, 'Resolution 1511' (2003), www.iaea.org/OurWork/SV/Invo/resolutions/res1511.pdf.

US Department of State, 'Iraq: Bureau of Democracy, Human Rights, and Labor' (2006), www.state.gov/j/drl/rls/hrrpt/2005/61689.htm.

Wehrey, Frederick, Theodore W. Karasik, Alireza Nader, Jeremy J. Ghez, Lydia Hansell and Robert A. Guffey, 'Saudi–Iranian Relations since the Fall of Saddam: Rivalry, Cooperation, and Implications for U.S. Policy' (Santa Monica, CA: RAND Corporation, 2009).

The White House, Office of the Press Secretary, 'Remarks by the President and First Lady on the End of the War in Iraq' (14 December 2011), www.whitehouse.gov/the-press-office/2011/12/14/remarks-president-and-first-lady-end-war-iraq.

Wicken, 'Iraq's Sunnis in Crisis', 'Middle East Security Report', 11 (May 2013), www.understandingwar.org/sites/default/files/Wicken-Sunni-In-Iraq.pdf.

The World Bank, 'US$1.2 Billion to Support Iraq amid Challenging Economic Situation' (17 December 2015), www.worldbank.org/en/news/press-release/2015/12/17/support-iraq-amid-challenging-economic-situation.

Zelin, A.Y., 'The Islamic State's Saudi Chess Match', The Washington Institute (2 June 2015), www.washingtoninstitute.org/policy-analysis/view/the-islamic-states-saudi-chess-match.

Diplomatic Cables

09RIYADH447_a COUNTERTERRORISM ADVISER BRENNAN'S MEETING WITH SAUDI KING ABDULLAH (22 March 2014), https://wikileaks.org/plusd/cables/09RIYADH447_a.html.

06RIYADH9175_a SAUDI MOI HEAD SAYS IF U.S. LEAVES IRAQ, SAUDI ARABIA WILL STAND WITH SUNNIS (26 December 2006), https://wikileaks.org/plusd/cables/06RIYADH9175_a.html.

05BAGHDAD2547 ISLAMIC HUMAN RIGHTS ORGANIZATION ALLEGES IRAQI FORCES DETAINEE ABUSE IN NINEWA (16 May 2005), https://wikileaks.org/plusd/cables/05BAGHDAD2547_a.html.

05BAGHDAD3015_a BUILDING A HOUSE ON SHIFTING SANDS – IRAN'S INFLUENCE IN IRAQ'S CENTER-SOUTH (20 July 2005), www.wikileaks.org/plusd/cables/05BAGHDAD3015_a.html.

08BAGHDAD239_a 'THE STREET IS STRONGER THAN PARLIAMENT': SADRIST VOWS OPPOSITION TO LTSR (27 January 2008), https://wikileaks.org/plusd/cables/08BAGHDAD239_a.html.

08BAGHDAD1105_a SADRIST CONFIDANTE WARNS OF BAD PRESSURE BUILDING WITHIN SADRIST MOVEMENT (9 April 2008), https://wikileaks.org/plusd/cables/08BAGHDAD1105_a.html.

08BAGHDAD239_a 'THE STREET IS STRONGER THAN PARLIA-MENT:' SADRIST VOWS OPPOSITION TO LTSR (27 January 2008), https://wikileaks.org/plusd/cables/08BAGHDAD239_a.html.

08BAGHDAD1027_a DAWA PARTY OFFICIAL ON BASRAH OPER-ATION AND UIA-SADR NEGOTIATIONS IN IRAN (3 April 2008), https://wikileaks.org/plusd/cables/08BAGHDAD1027_a.html.

08BAGHDAD2812_a KARBALA: IRAN EXERTS HEAVY INFLUENCE THROUGH TOURISM INDUSTRY (2 August 2008), https://wikileaks. org/plusd/cables/08BAGHDAD2812_a.html.

10BAGHDAD22_a IRAQI VIEWS ON EVENTS IN IRAN AND IMPACT ON IRAQ (5 January 2010), https://wikileaks.org/plusd/cables/10BAGH-DAD22_a.html.

06HILLAH54_a FORMER NAJAF GOVERNOR ON AL-SADR, IRANIAN INFLUENCE (5 April 2006), www.wikileaks.org/plusd/ cables/06HILLAH54_a.html.

08BAGHDAD3994_a (C) PRT SALAH AD DIN: IRANIAN INVOLVE-MENT IN SAMARRA (21 December 2008), https://wikileaks.org/plusd/ cables/08BAGHDAD3994_a.html.

08BAGHADA1416_a SOUTHERN POLITICS AS USUAL: IRAN'S PLAN FOR IRAQI ELECTIONS (6 May 2008), https://wikileaks.org/ plusd/cables/08BAGHDAD1416_a.html.

09BAGHDAD289_a IRAQ-IRAN DIPLOMACY A SIGN OF IRANIAN INFLUENCE OR IRAQI RESOLVE? (4 February 2009), www.wikileaks. org/plusd/cables/09BAGHDAD289_a.html.

08BAGHDAD3655_a KARBALA, IRAN DUEL OVER PILGRIMS (19 November 2008), https://wikileaks.org/plusd/cables/08BAGH-DAD3655_a.html.

Online Sources

Al-Abadi, Haider, 'We have heard the Iraqi people', *Wall Street Journal* (8 September 2015), www.wsj.com/articles/we-have-heard-the-iraqi-people-1441754816.

Abu Zeed, A., 'Arab-Kurd conflict heats up after Tuz Khormato incidents', *Al-Monitor* (8 December 2015), www.al-monitor.com/pulse/originals/ 2015/12/iraq-kurdistan-region-tuz-khormato-arabs-kurds-conflict.html# ixzz3yGHJz18s.

Agence France-Presse – *Gulf Times*, 'Bare-faced killer rises to fore of Iraq militancy' (28 August 2013), www.gulf-times.com/story/364086/Bare-faced-killer-rises-to-fore-of-Iraq-militancy.

Al Arabiya News, 'Saudi refutes UK media claims of 'ISIS support' (10 July 2014), http://english.alarabiya.net/en/News/world/2014/07/09/Saudi-Arabia-refutes-UK-media-allegations-of-supporting-ISIS-.html.

Al-Araby al-Jadeed, 'Abadi to purge Iraq's interior ministry of Maliki supporters' (17 November 2014), www.alaraby.co.uk/english/news/2014/ 11/17/abadi-to-purge-iraqs-interior-ministry-of-maliki-supporters.

Arutz Sheva, quoting Channel 2 News in Israel, 'ISIS: Fighting "Infidels" Takes Precedence Over Fighting Israel' (8 July 2014), www.israelnationalnews.com/News/News.aspx/182632#.U7uLApSSw00.

Bahney, B., P. Johnston and P. Ryan, 'The enemy you know and the ally you don't', *Foreign Policy* (23 June 2015), foreignpolicy.com/2015/06/23/the-enemy-you-know-and-the-ally-you-dont-arm-sunni-militias-iraq/.

Bassem, Wassim, 'From Omar to Hussain: why Iraqis are changing their names', *Al-Monitor* (17 June 2015), www.al-monitor.com/pulse/originals/2015/06/iraq-sectarian-killing-name-changing.html#.

——— 'When conflict arises, these Iraqis go to the madeef', *Al-Monitor* (30 October 2015), www.al-monitor.com/pulse/originals/2015/10/iraq-madeef-tribes-host-disputes-politicans.html#ixzz3q5TJkME8.

Al Bawaba, 'Al Qaeda in Iraq tightening economic grip on Mosul' (3 May 2011), www.albawaba.com/main-headlines/al-qaeda-iraq-tightening-economic-grip-mosul.

Bazzi, Mohamad, 'The Sistani factor', *Boston Review* (12 August 2014), http://bostonreview.net/world/mohamad-bazzi-sistani-factor-isis-shiism-iraq.

BBC News, *Full text: State of the Union address* (30 January 2002), http://news.bbc.co.uk/1/hi/world/americas/1790537.stm.

———, 'Iraqi Sunni protest clashes in Hawija leave many dead' (23 April 2013), www.bbc.co.uk/news/world-middle-east-22261422.

———, 'Profile: Islamic State in Iraq and the Levant (ISIS)' (16 June 2014), www.bbc.com/news/world-middle-east-24179084.

———, 'Syria Iraq: The Islamic State Militant Group' (2 August 2014), www.bbc.com/news/world-middle-east-24179084.

———, 'Iraq reforms: Parliament backs PM Haider al-Abadi's plan' (11 August 2015), www.bbc.co.uk/news/world-middle-east-33861080.

———, 'Islamic State oil trade "worth more than $500m"' (11 December 2015), www.bbc.com/news/world-middle-east-35070204.

Beaumont, Peter, 'Sunnis change names to avoid Shia death squads,' *Guardian* (10 October 2006), www.theguardian.com/world/2006/oct/10/iraq.peterbeaumont.

Benari, Elad, 'ISIS: fighting 'Infidels' takes precedence over fighting Israel', Israel National News (8 July 2014), www.israelnationalnews.com/News/News.aspx/182632#.U7uLApSSw00.

Berwani, H., 'Gunmen in Fallujah form Military Council, reject Anbar initiative', *Iraq News* (11 February 2014), www.iraqinews.com/iraq-war/gunmen-in-fallujah-form-military-council-reject-anbar-initiative/.

Black, I., 'Syria crisis: Saudi Arabia to spend millions to train new rebel force', *Guardian* (7 November 2013), www.theguardian.com/world/2013/nov/07/syria-crisis-saudi-arabia-spend-millions-new-rebel-force.

Bruno, Greg, 'Badr vs. Sadr in Iraq', Council on Foreign Relations (31 March 2008), www.cfr.org/iraq/badr-vs-sadr-iraq/p15839.

Chulov, Martin, 'Iraq "doomed" if new prime minister Abadi fails to bridge sectarian divide', *Guardian* (15 August 2014), www.theguardian.com/world/2014/aug/15/iraq-doomed-if-prime-minister-fails-unite-factions-haidar-al-abadi.

———, 'Isis: the inside story', *Guardian* (11 December 2014), www.theguardian.com/world/2014/dec/11/-sp-isis-the-inside-story.

CIA: World Fact Book, Iraq (20 July 2014), www.cia.gov/library/publications/the-worldfactbook/geos/iz.html.

CIA: World Fact Book: Syria (21 July 2014), www.cia.gov/library/publications/the-world-factbook/geos/sy.html.

Cline, Lawrence E., 'The prospects of the Shia insurgency movement in Iraq', *Journal of Conflict Studies*, 20:1 (2000), https://journals.lib.unb.ca/index.php/jcs/article/view/4311/4924.

Cockburn, Patrick, 'Iraq crisis: how Saudi Arabia helped Isis take over the north of the country', *Independent* (21 July 2014), www.independent.co.uk/voices/comment/iraq-crisis-how-saudi-arabia-helped-isis-take-over-the-north-of-the-country-9602312.html.

Crompton, P., 'Can ISIS maintain its self-declared caliphate?', *Al-Arabiya News* (16 July 2014), http://english.alarabiya.net/en/perspective/analysis/2014/07/16/Can-ISIS-maintain-its-self-declared-caliphate-.html.

Cumming-Bruce, Nick, 'United Nations investigators accuse ISIS of genocide over attacks on Yazidis', *New York Times* (19 April 2015), www.nytimes.com/2015/03/20/world/middleeast/isis-genocide-yazidis-iraq-un-panel.html.

Dabiq, 'The return of Khalifah' (5 July 2014).

Dehghanpisheh, B. and E. Thomas, 'Scions of the surge', *Newsweek* (14 March 2008).

Dombey, Daniel, 'Iraq crisis: Turkey's Erdogan warns on air strikes against Isis', *Financial Times* (19 July 2014), www.ft.com/intl/cms/s/0/ae101292-f7b0-11e3-90fa-00144feabdc0.html #axzz38Yh5ieU7.

Dukhan, Haian and Hawat, Sinan, 'The Islamic State and the Arab tribes in Eastern Syria', *E-International Relations* (31 December 2014), www.e-ir.info/2014/12/31/the-islamic-state-and-the-arab-tribes-in-eastern-syria/.

Dunlop, W., 'Iraq area retaken, but destruction and anger remain', Associated Free Press (9 November 2014), http://news.yahoo.com/iraq-area-retaken-destruction-anger-remain-113132316.html.

Fam, Mariam, 'Militias growing in power in Iraq', Associated Press (7 November 2005), www.washingtonpost.com/wp-dyn/content/article/2005/11/07/AR2005110700977_pf.html.

Fisk, Robert, 'ISIS profits from destruction of antiquities by selling relics to dealers – and then blowing up the buildings they come from to conceal the evidence of looting', *Independent* (20 September 2015), www.independent.co.uk/voices/isis-profits-from-destruction-of-antiquities-by-selling-relics-to-dealers-and-then-blowing-up-the-10483421.html.

Gander, K., 'Isis car bomb kills more than 100 including children during Eid celebrations in the Iraqi town of Khan Bani Saad', *Independent* (17 July 2015), www.independent.co.uk/news/uk/home-news/car-bomb-kills-at-least-80-including-children-in-iraqi-town-of-khan-bani-saad-10398064.html.

Gartenstein-Ross, Daveed, and Sterling Jensen, 'The Role of Iraqi Tribes after the Islamic State's Ascendance', *Military Review* (July–August, 2015), www.defenddemocracy.org/content/uploads/documents/The_Role_of_Iraqi_Tribes_After_the_Islamic_States_Ascendance.pdf.

Al-Ghoul, Asmaa, 'Gaza Salafist jihadists pledge allegiance to ISIS', *Al-Monitor* (27 February 2014), www.al-monitor.com/pulse/originals/2014/02/isis-gaza-salafist-jihadist-qaeda-hamas.html##ixzz36aAvHY9I.

Guardian, 'Saddam Hussein's speech' (8 August 2002), www.theguardian.com/world/2002/aug/08/iraq3.

Agence France-Presse in *Guardian*, 'Turkish troops move out of northern Iraq after Obama appeal for calm' (20 December 2015), www.theguardian.com/world/2015/dec/20/turkish-troops-move-out-of-northern-iraq-after-obama-appeal-for-calm.

Harding, Luke, Fazel Hawramy and Mohammad Moslawi, 'New militant group replacing Isis in Mosul, says city governor', *Guardian* (18 July 2014), www.theguardian.com/world/2014/jul/18/new-militant-group-replaces-isis-mosul.

Harvey, D. and M. Pregent, 'Who's to blame for Iraq crisis?', CNN (12 June 2014), http://edition.cnn.com/2014/06/12/opinion/pregent-harvey-northern-iraq-collapse/?c=&page=0.

Hassan, H.,'Maliki's alienation of Sunni actors is at the heart of ISIS's success in Iraq', *Carnegie Endowment for International Peace* (17 June 2014), http://carnegieendowment.org/sada/?fa=55930.

———, 'Isis: a portrait of the menace that is sweeping my homeland', *Guardian* (16 August 2014), www.theguardian.com/world/2014/aug/16/isis-salafi-menace-jihadist-homeland-syria.

Howard, M., 'Militant Kurds training al-Qaida fighters', *Guardian* (23 August 2002), www.theguardian.com/world/2002/aug/23/alqaida.iraq1.

Hubbard, B., 'Sunni tribesmen say ISIS exacts brutal revenge', *New York Times* (30 October 2014), www.nytimes.com/2014/10/31/world/middleeast/sunni-tribesmen-say-isis-exacts-brutal-revenge.html?_r=0.

IHS Press, 'Islamic State monthly revenue totals $80 million, IHS says' (7 December 2015), http://press.ihs.com/press-release/aerospace-defense-security/islamic-state-monthly-revenue-totals-80-million-ihs-says.

International Committee of the Red Cross, *Customary IHL*, www.icrc.org/customary-ihl/eng/docs/v1_rul_rule83.

Izzat Ibrahim Al-Douri/Izzat Ibrahim al-Duri, 'Globalsecurity' (2014), www.globalsecurity.org/military/world/iraq/al-douri.htm.

Jaber, H., 'Sunni leader killed for joining ceasefire talks', *Sunday Times* (6 February 2006), www.thesundaytimes.co.uk/sto/news/world_news/article204068.ece.

Al-Jaffal, Omar, 'Who's to blame for recent kidnappings in Iraq?', *Al-Monitor* (29 January 2016), www.al-monitor.com/pulse/originals/2016/01/iraq-wave-abductions-foreigners-accusations.html#ixzz3z6R3KGgZ.

Jamail, D. and Ali al-Fadhily, 'Southern tribes add to Iraqi resistance', *Inter Service Press* (19 January 2007), www.globalpolicy.org/component/content/article/168/37369.html.

Al-Jawoshy, Omar, and Tim Arango, *Premier Haider al-Abadi, Facing Protests, Proposes Iraqi Government Overhaul* (9 August 2015), www.nytimes.com/2015/08/10/world/middleeast/iraqs-premier-facing-protests-proposes-government-overhaul.html.

Al-Kadhimi, M., 'Overhauling Iraq's intelligence services', *Al-Monitor* (15 June 2015), www.al-monitor.com/pulse/originals/2015/06/iraq-security-intelligence-services-quota-terrorists.html#.

Karim, A. and Faraj, S., 'Maliki's remedy for Iraq sectarian violence: overhaul of security strategy', *Middle East Online* (20 May 2013), www.middle-east-online.com/english/?id=58868.

Keinon, Herb, 'In face of ISIS threat, Lieberman terms Jordan's stability a vital Israeli national interest', *Jerusalem Post* (30 June 2014), www.jpost.com/Diplomacy-and-Politics/In-face-of-ISIS-threat-Liberman-terms-Jordans-stability-a-vital-Israeli-national-interest-361028.

Khalaf, Roula, 'Abu Bakr al-Baghdadi, Isis leader', *Financial Times* (4 July 2014), www.ft.com/cms/s/0/ec63d94c-02b0-11e4-a68d-00144feab7de.html#axzz36WPWiRgC.

Khedery, Ali, 'Iran's Shiite Militias Are Running Amok in Iraq', *Foreign Policy* (19 February 2015), http://foreignpolicy.com/2015/02/19/irans-shiite-militias-are-running-amok-in-iraq/.

Kohlmann, Evan F., 'State of the Sunni insurgency in Iraq: August 2007', *The NEFA Foundation* (August 2007), p. 16.

———, 'Ansar al-Sunnah acknowledges relationship with Ansar al-Islam, reverts to using Ansar al-Islam name', *Counter Terrorism Blog* (16 December 2007), http://counterterrorismblog.org/2007/12/ansar_alsunnah_acknowledges_re.php.

Lake, Eli, 'The Rise and Fall of America's Favorite Iraqi Sheik', *Bloomberg* (11 June 2015), www.bloombergview.com/articles/2015-06-11/the-rise-and-fall-of-america-s-favorite-iraqi-sheik.

Lamb, Franklin, 'ISIS (Daesh) Now Recruiting in Palestinian Camps in Lebanon,' *Al Manar* (1 July 2014), www.almanar.com.lb/english/adetails.php?eid=159179&cid=41&fromval=1.

———, 'ISIS now recruiting in Palestinian camps in Lebanon', *Foreign Policy Journal* (30 June 2014), www.foreignpolicyjournal.com/2014/06/30/isis-now-recruiting-in-palestinian-camps-in-lebanon/.

Loveluck, Louisa, 'Isil releases new video of 2014 Speicher massacre of Shi'a army recruits', *Telegraph* (12 July 2015), www.telegraph.co.uk/news/worldnews/islamic-state/11734606/Isil-releases-new-video-of-2014-Speicher-massacre-of-Shi'a-army-recruits.htm.

Lynch, Colum, 'Women and children for sale', *Foreign Policy* (2 October 2014), http://foreignpolicy.com/2014/10/02/women-and-children-for-sale/?wp_login_redirect=0.

Mabon, Simon, 'FPC briefing: constructing sectarianisms' (2014), http://fpc.org.uk/fsblob/1614.pdf.

Mahmoud, N., 'Kurdish tribe fights IS alone in disputed area', *Rudaw News* (20 September 2014), http://rudaw.net/english/kurdistan/200920141.

Malas, Nour and Safa Majeed, 'Iraq cabinet approves sweeping overhaul to political system' (9 August 2015), www.wsj.com/articles/iraq-cabinet-approves-sweeping-reforms-to-political-system-1439133137.

Mansour, Renad, 'The popularity of the Hashd in Iraq', Carnegie Endowment for International Peace (1 February 2016), http://carnegieendowment.org/syriaincrisis/?fa=62638.

'Mapping the Global Muslim Population', *Pew Research* (7 October 2009), www.pewforum.org/2009/10/07/mapping-the-global-muslim-population/.

McNeice, Angus, 'Police launch investigation into Chilean–Norwegian jihadist in Syria', *Santiago Times* (3 July 2014), http://santiagotimes.cl/police-launch-investigation-chilean-norwegian-jihadist-syria/.

Moore, J., 'Gaza crisis: Isis pledge to join the Palestinian fight against "barbaric Jews"', *International Business Times* (31 July 2014), www.ibtimes.co.uk/gaza-crisis-isis-pledge-join-palestinian-fight-against-barbaric-jews-1459190.

Mosul Eye, https://mosuleye.wordpress.com.

———, www.facebook.com/Mosul-Eye-552514844870022/?fref=ts.

Natali, D., 'The Islamic State's Baathist roots', *Al-Monitor* (24 April 2015), www.al-monitor.com/pulse/originals/2015/04/baathists-behind-the-islamic-state.html#.

Neumann, Peter R., 'Foreign fighter total in Syria/Iraq now exceeds 20,000; surpasses Afghanistan conflict in the 1980s', *International Centre for the Study of Radicalisation and Political Violence* (ICSR) (26 January 2015), http://icsr.info/2015/01/foreign-fighter-total-syriairaq-now-exceeds-20000-surpasses-afghanistan-conflict-1980s/.

New York Times, 'Excerpts from Khomeini Speeches' (4 August 1987), www.nytimes.com/1987/08/04/world/excerpts-from-khomeini-speeches.html.

Al-Obaidi, Amir, 'Surrendering to sectarianism: Iraq's Sunnis change their names', *Al-Araby* (8 May 2015), www.alaraby.co.uk/english/features/2015/5/8/surrendering-to-sectarianism-iraqs-sunnis-change-their-names.

Parker, N., 'Divided Iraq has two spy agencies', *Los Angeles Times* (15 April 2007), http://articles.latimes.com/2007/apr/15/world/fg-intel15.

Parker, N. and Al-Khalidi, S., 'Special Report: the doubt at the heart of Iraq's Sunni revolution' (4 August 2014), www.reuters.com/article/2014/08/04/us-iraq-security-alisuleiman-specialrepo-idUSKBN0G40OP20140804#VYx8KRGOttjQPHXe.97.

Pincus, Walter, 'US military urging Iraq to rein in guard force', *Washington Post* (25 December 2006), www.washingtonpost.com/wp-dyn/content/article/2006/12/24/AR2006122400551.html.

Rasheed, Ahmed and Stephen Kalin, 'Iraq blames Iran after thousands of pilgrims storm border crossing', *Reuters* (30 November 2015), www.reuters.com/article/us-iraq-iran-pilgrims-idUSKBN0TJ2RQ20151130.

Rasheed, Ahmed and Ned Parker, 'Shi'ite militias expand influence, redraw map in central Iraq', *Reuters* (31 December 2014), www.reuters.com/article/2014/12/31/us-mideast-crisis-iraq-idUSKBN0K909K20141231.

Al-Rasheed, Madawi, 'The shared history of Saudi Arabia and Isis' (20 November 2014), www.hurstpublishers.com/the-shared-history-of-saudi-arabia-and-isis/.

Reuters, 'Israel Warns Hizbullah War Would Invite Destruction' (10 March 2008), www.ynetnews.com/articles/0,7340,L-3604893,00.html.

———, 'Al Qaeda claims responsibility for Iraq's Tikrit attack' (2 September 2011), www.reuters.com/article/2011/04/02/us-iraq-violence-qaeda-idUSTRE7310R520110402.

———, 'Baath leader urges Sunnis to protest Iraqi premier' (5 January 2013), www.nytimes.com/2013/01/06/world/middleeast/baath-party-leader-encourages-sunni-protests-in-iraq.html?_r=0.

————, 'French weapons arrive in Lebanon in $3 billion Saudi-funded deal' (20 April 2015), www.reuters.com/article/2015/04/20/us-mideast-crisis-lebanon-army-idUSKBN0NB0GI20150420.

Rosenberg, Matt and Schmitt, Eric, 'In ISIS Strategy, U.S. Weighs Risk to Civilians', *New York Times* (19 December 2015), www.nytimes.com/2015/12/20/us/politics/in-isis-strategy-us-weighs-risk-to-civilians.html?_r=0.

Rumman, M., 'The politics of Sunni armed groups in Iraq', *The Carnegie Endowment for International Peace* (18 August 2008), http://carnegie endowment.org/sada/?fa=20836.

Russia Today, 'Evidence reveals Turkish regime affair with ISIS as global threat – Iraqi militia to RT' (25 December 2015), www.rt.com/news/327052-iraqi-militia-isis-turkey/.

Al-Salhy, S., 'How Iraq's "ghost soldiers" helped ISIL: Discovering 50,000 ghost soldiers in the army forced Iraq to rebuild their troops to face ISIL', *Al Jazeera* (11 December 2014), www.aljazeera.com/news/middleeast/2014/12/how-iraq-ghost-soldiers-helped-isil-2014121072749979252.html.

Al-Salhy, S. and Tim Arango, 'Iraq militants, pushing south, aim at capital', *New York Times* (11 November 2014), www.nytimes.com/2014/06/12/world/middleeast/iraq.html?_r=1.

Salih, M.A., 'With the Islamic State gone from Sinjar, Kurdish groups battle for control', *Al-Monitor* (10 December 2015), www.al-monitor.com/pulse/originals/2015/12/iraq-kurdistan-sinjar-liberated-isis-hegemony.html#ixzz3yRNmvwGi.

Saouli, A., (2014), 'Syria's Predicament: State (de-) Formation and International Rivalries' (Online): Konrad Adenauer Stiftung, www.iai.it/pdf/Sharaka/Sharaka_RP_10.pdf.

'Saudi refutes UK media claims of "ISIS support"', *Al Arabiya* (9 July 2014), http://english.alarabiya.net/en/News/world/2014/07/09/Saudi-Arabia-refutes-UK-media-allegations-of-supporting-ISIS-.html.

Schreck, A. and Q. Abdul-Zahra, 'Iraq: new protests break out in Sunni stronghold', *Associated Press* (26 December 2012), http://news.yahoo.com/iraq-protests-break-sunni-stronghold-184403534.html.

Shadid, A., 'In Iraq, chaos feared as U.S. closes prison, ex-inmates reanimate Sunni, Shiite militias', *Washington Post Foreign Service* (22 March 2009), www.washingtonpost.com/wp-dyn/content/article/2009/03/21/AR2009032102255_pf.html.

Shanker, Thom and Edward Wong, 'US troops in Iraq shifting to advisory roles', *New York Times* (5 December 2006), www.nytimes.com/2006/12/05/world/middleeast/05strategy.html?pagewanted=print&_r=0.

Al-Sharif, O., 'Jordan shaken by threats from ISIS, Iraq, Syria', *Al-Monitor* (25 June 2014), www.al-monitor.com/pulse/originals/2014/06/jordan-isis-anbar-iraq-salafi-jihadist-maan.html# ixzz36a4HAX2R.

Sherlock, Ruth and Malouf, Carol, 'Mosul governor calls for fragmentation of Iraq', *Telegraph* (12 June 2014), www.telegraph.co.uk/news/worldnews/middleeast/iraq/10895792/Mosul-governor-calls-for-fragmentation-of-Iraq.html.

———, 'Islamic Army of Iraq founder: Isis and Sunni Islamists will march on Baghdad', *Telegraph* (20 June 2014), www.telegraph.co.uk/news/worldnews/middleeast/iraq/10914567/Islamic-Army-of-Iraq-founder-Isis-and-Sunni-Islamists-will-march-on-Baghdad.html.

Sly, L., 'Iraq plans to cut Sunni fighters' salaries', *Chicago Tribune* (3 November 2008), http://articles.chicagotribune.com/2008-11-03/news/0811020469_1_awakening-leader-sunni-awakening-awakening-members.

———, 'Al-Qaeda disavows any ties with radical Islamist ISIS group in Syria, Iraq', *Washington Post* (3 February 2014), www.washingtonpost.com/world/middle_east/al-qaeda-disavows-any-ties-with-radical-islamist-isis-group-in-syria-iraq/2014/02/03/2c9afc3a-8cef-11e3-98ab-fe5228217bd1_story.html.

Smith, Robert, 'UK ambassador accuses Iran', *Gulf Digital News* (25 March 2013), www.gulf-daily-news.com/NewsDetails.aspx?storyid=350071.

Solomon, E., Robin Kwong and S. Bernard, 'Inside Isis Inc: The journey of a barrel of oil', *Financial Times* (11 December 2015), http://ig.ft.com/sites/2015/isis-oil/.

Sowell, Kirk, 'Maliki's Anbar blunder', *Foreign Policy* (15 January 2014), http://foreignpolicy.com/2014/01/15/malikis-anbar-blunder/?wp_login_redirect=0.

———, 'Iraq's Second Sunni Insurgency' (9 August 2014), www.hudson.org/research/10505-iraq-s-second-sunni-insurgency.

Stanford University 'Ansar al-Islam' (2 October 2015), http://web.stanford.edu/group/mappingmilitants/cgi-bin/groups/view/13#note39.

Stratfor, 'An uncertain future for Iraq's intelligence services' (11 January 2012), www.stratfor.com/sample/analysis/uncertain-future-iraqs-intelligence-services.

Suleiman, Abdallah, 'IS disciplines some emirs to avoid losing base', *Al-Monitor* (2 September 2014), www.al-monitor.com/pulse/security/2014/09/is-takfiri-caliphate.html#ixzz3xlwgdeNZ.

Tavernise, S. and A. Lehren, 'Detainees fared worse in Iraqi hands, logs say', *New York Times* (22 October 2010), www.nytimes.com/2010/10/23/world/middleeast/23detainees.html?_r=0.

Taylor, Guy, 'Nouri al-Maliki undermines U.S. interests in Iraq, plots return to power', *Washington Times* (15 June 2015), www.washingtontimes.com/news/2015/jun/15/nouri-al-maliki-undermines-us-interests-in-iraq-pl/?page=all.

'Text of Bush Speech' (1 May 2003), www.cbsnews.com/news/text-of-bush-speech-01-05-2003/.

Thompson, Andrew and Jeremi Surioct, 'How America helped ISIS', *New York Times* (2 October 2014), www.nytimes.com/2014/10/02/opinion/how-america-helped-isis.html?_r=0.

Thompson, Mark, 'Seeking a legacy, Bush cites security', *Time* (1 January 2009), http://content.time.com/time/nation/article/0,8599,1871060,00.html.

Voice of Iraq, '35 abducted from Ansar al-Islam and the Naqshbandi southwest of Kirkuk' (1 December 2015), www.sotaliraq.com/newsitem.php?id=308852#ixzz3xh7niWYs.

Wander, Andrew, 'Left to die in jail', *Al Jazeera* (24 October 2010), www.aljazeera.com/secretiraqfiles/2010/10/20101022163052530756.html.

Watt, Nicholas, 'Tony Blair makes qualified apology for Iraq war ahead of Chilcot report', *Guardian* (25 October 2015), www.theguardian.com/uk-news/2015/oct/25/tony-blair-sorry-iraq-war-mistakes-admits-conflict-role-in-rise-of-isis.

Weaver, Mary Anne, 'The short, violent life of Abu Musab al-Zarqawi', *The Atlantic* (July–August 2006), www.theatlantic.com/magazine/archive/2006/07/the-short-violent-life-of-abu-musab-al-zarqawi/304983/.

Weber, Max, 'Politik als Beruf', *Gesammelte Politische Schriften* (Muenchen, 1921), http://media.pfeiffer.edu/lridener/dss/Weber/polvoc.html.

Wing, Joel, 'Anbar before and after the Awakening Pt. IX: Sheikh Sabah Aziz of the Albu Mahal', (23 January 2014), http://musingsoniraq.blogspot.com/2014/01/anbar-before-and-after-awakening-pt-ix.html.

Wintour, Patrick and Ewen MacAskill, 'UK foreign secretary: US decision on Iraqi army led to rise of ISIS', *Guardian* (7 July 2016), www.theguardian.com/world/2016/jul/07/uk-foreign-secretary-us-decision-iraqi-army-rise-isis-philip-hammond.

Wong, Edward, 'U.S. faces latest trouble with Iraqi forces: loyalty', *New York Times* (6 March 2006), www.nytimes.com/2006/03/06/world/americas/06iht-military.html?pagewanted=all.

———, 'To stay alive, Iraqis change their names', *New York Times* (6 September 2006), www.nytimes.com/2006/09/06/world/middleeast/06identity.html?ref=familiesandfamilylife&_r=0.

Wood, Graeme, 'What ISIS really wants', *The Atlantic* (March 2015), www.theatlantic.com/magazine/archive/2015/03/what-isis-really-wants/384980/.
Wood, Michael, 'Abdul Majud al-Khoei', *Guardian* (12 April 2013), www.theguardian.com/news/2003/apr/12/guardianobituaries.iraq.

YouTube Videos

'ISIS – The End of Sykes–Picot', presented by spokesperson Abu Saffiya from Chile (29 June 2014), www.youtube.com/watch?v=YyM0_sv5h88.
'Statement No. 35 on the events in Hawija, Ramadi', YouTube, www.youtube.com/watch?v=NxXYi3GCjIA.

Index